THINKING
IN CONTEXT

THINKING
IN CONTEXT
TEACHING COGNITIVE PROCESSES ACROSS
THE ELEMENTARY SCHOOL CURRICULUM

ARTHUR A. HYDE
MARILYN BIZAR

National College of Education

Longman

New York & London

Thinking in Context: Teaching Cognitive Processes Across the Elementary School Curriculum

Longman, 10 Bank Street, White Plains, N.Y. 10606

Associated companies:
Longman Group Ltd., London
Longman Cheshire Pty., Melbourne
Longman Paul Pty., Auckland
Copp Clark Pitman, Toronto
Pitman Publishing Inc., New York

Pp. 76-78 : "Saved by the Bell," by Karin Ireland from TRIPLE ACTION STORIES, edited by Jeri Shapiro. © 1979 Scholastic Inc. Reprinted with permission of Scholastic Inc.

Pp. 84- 85 : "The Quest for Meaning from Expository Text: A Teacher-Guided Journey," by Annemarie Sullivan Palincsar from *Comprehension Instruction: Perspectives and Suggestions,* edited by Gerald G. Duffy, Laura R. Roehler and Jana Mason. © 1984 Longman Inc. Reprinted with permission of Longman Inc. and Annemarie Sullivan Palincsar.

Executive editor: Naomi Silverman
Development editor: Virginia L. Blanford
Production editor: Camilla T. K. Palmer
Text design: Susan J. Moore
Cover design: Jill Francis Wood
Director of Production: Eduardo Castillo

Library of Congress Cataloging-in-Publication Data

Hyde, Arthur A.

    Thinking in context.

    Bibliography: p.
    Includes index.
    1. Thought and thinking—Study and teaching
(Elementary)—United States.   2. Context area reading—
Study and teaching (Elementary)—United States.
3. Mathematics—Study and teaching (Elementary)—
United States.   4. Science—Study and teaching
(Elementary)—United States.   5. Social sciences—
Study and teaching (Elementary)—United States.
I. Bizar, Marilyn.   II. Title.
LB1590.3.H93   1989   372.19   88-9362
ISBN 0-8013-0065-7

   4 5 6 7 8 9 10 DO 959493

Acknowledgments

The authors wish to thank Naomi Silverman of Longman, Inc. for her suggestions and support in writing this book. We are grateful to Mary Vostal for preparing the graphics for all the figures. Our special thanks go to the numerous teachers who reviewed parts of the manuscript, especially to Pamela Regan Hyde whose insightful criticisms of each chapter produced a much clearer set of ideas.

Contents

Introduction

TEACHING THINKING IN SCHOOLS TODAY

The 1980s will probably be remembered in education as the time when schools rediscovered thinking. Teachers and administrators have been bombarded in the last few years by programs that train students to think. Apparently, students cannot think critically, reason logically, make inferences, organize ideas, or solve problems, so schools have adopted a variety of programs to teach thinking skills. Although many of the programs are aimed at secondary school students, some attempt to develop better thinking in elementary school students.

What do these programs that teach thinking contain? If a curriculum committee of teachers scrutinized these programs, it probably would be bewildered by the dazzling array of terminology in each program and the promises of intellectual competence to be attained. Students would learn to think productively, reflectively, laterally as well as vertically, both logically and analogically, inferentially, hypothetically, and so on. It would be a Herculean feat to define the terms used in a way that clarified what each author meant by each term (and how terms differed from one program to another).

To make matters even more complicated, to do a thorough and intellectually honest job, the curriculum committee would also have to answer (or at least consider) a set of rather thorny questions such as

- What do psychologists and educators mean by *thinking?*
- Are certain kinds of thinking more important than others? To whom?

1

- What *theories* are used to explain thinking, cognition, or intellectual processes? Are they similar or contradictory?
- How is thinking related to intelligence?
- What kinds of thinking characterize various age groups?
- How is thinking related to experience and development?
- How is thinking related to feelings and behavior?

These are not merely philosophical questions. Every program for thinking explicitly or implicitly has an answer for each of these questions. Anyone planning on adopting such a program without determining the validity of a program's assumptions about the issues raised in each of these questions is a naive consumer.

ANOTHER MAJOR ISSUE

If these issues weren't enough to send the committee off screaming, another truly central issue probably would. A number of psychologists and educators have concluded that thinking is intimately related to the *specific area of knowledge* in which a person is operating. How he thinks and what he thinks about are inseparable; how much he knows about an area will greatly influence how he is able to think about it. Thus, mathematical thinking probably differs in key ways from thinking about poetry. The knowledge one has about geometry or poetry will dramatically affect the kinds of thinking possible. (To avoid tripping over pronouns, we will use a genderless *he* when referring to an individual's thinking rather than *he or she,* or some other equally awkward expression.)

Pity the poor curriculum committee that now must ask how the various thinking programs relate to the different content areas of the school curriculum. It might assume that there are some general thinking skills that transcend areas of knowledge. Perhaps the general thinking programs will enable students to think better in the school subjects. On the other hand, it might decide that the district should carefully examine the kinds of thinking that texts and materials in each subject encourage. It might even conclude that teachers must attend to both general thinking skills and those specific to each content area.

Where do all these questions leave the individual teacher in the elementary school classroom—the person teaching reading, writing, spelling, handwriting, mathematics, social studies, and science to twenty-five or thirty children? Will the district adopt a thinking curriculum to be taught every Thursday from 11 to 12 o'clock? Will there be district guidelines for specific thinking skills to be mastered in each subject at each grade level? Will teachers be required to incorporate teaching for thinking skills into every lesson they design?

Is the concern for thinking in the schools merely a fad that will fade like previous school fads? Why all the current concern? There are several factors in psychology and education that are occurring simultaneously. We are not suggesting an order of importance by the following list:

1. Behavioral psychology's influence on education is being replaced by cognitive approaches to psychology. Cognitivists have had profound effects on educators in reading, writing, and mathematics. The "basic skills" are now being seen primarily as cognitive operations, important thinking processes that require much more thought than mere memory.
2. A concern for cognitive development in children, derived from developmental psychology, has affected the school curriculum for several decades. Its influence on teaching and curriculum has increased because of the burgeoning early-childhood-education movement.
3. Concerns for teaching for thinking are not new; they have been in and out of fashion repeatedly under a variety of labels such as inquiry, inductive teaching, discovery, and learning styles.

WHAT DOES THIS BOOK OFFER?

Like other educators, we have some definite opinions about the questions and issues we just raised. Based on our teaching of children and working in classrooms with teachers, we have concluded that yet another addition to the school curricula would be ill conceived. Furthermore, although there do seem to be some general intellectual processes that transcend subject areas, they can be addressed through particular contexts of knowledge. We strongly favor elementary school teachers using the existing curriculum to encourage and develop a variety of intellectual processes, some of which are specific to areas of knowledge and some of which are general.

Since we give our point of view on the important questions and issues concerning students' thinking, we do present some theoretical ideas in this book. We have tried, however, to write primarily a book of *strategies,* with illustrations, for teachers to use in developing activities for children. There are separate chapters covering the four major subject areas: literacy (reading, writing, language arts), mathematics, social studies, and science. Some strategies and activities, however, purposely relate to more than one area. You should experiment with these suggestions, adapting and modifying them to fit the needs of your students. They can be incorporated into the curriculum where possible, or they can be used to extend and enrich the curriculum at other times.

Basically, we suggest that you rethink what students are asked to do in school. All the strategies and activities have been developed in classrooms and have been used by children in many different schools. We hope they will act is catalysts in helping you create your own activities that encourage thinking by students.

A WORD OF CAUTION

This book is intended to be read in sequential order. As you come to understand our approach, you will be able to create your own activities by following the progression of ideas presented. Although you may find interesting ideas to try out by skipping around, the real value of the book lies in encouraging you to use your creativity in developing vital and exciting activities to do with children.

You could read the introductory sections of each chapter and then skim the rest of it to see what activity is suggested, but without understanding *why* we address thinking in a particular area, it would not be as productive, since that would be taking the activity out of its context.

We could not possibly address all that teachers could do to help children think more effectively in every subject area; each chapter offers only some essential ideas, approaches, and strategies, with illustrative activities. We strongly urge that you delve into some of the suggested resources, which will afford a more comprehensive and thorough discussion of these ideas.

PART ONE

Cognitive Processes
and Curricular Content

1

The Decontextualization of Thinking

TAKING THINKING OUT OF MEANINGFUL CONTEXTS

Today, we often hear educators calling for the direct teaching of thinking skills. It is important for us to think about the term *skills,* which traditionally referred to manual activities and behaviors. In the last two decades, however, educators have conceived of reading, writing, and mathematics in the elementary schools as the "basic skills." Now, some would have schools add "thinking" to the list of basic skills.

We are diametrically opposed to this notion. The reduction of reading, writing, and mathematics to overt behaviors that can be considered skills is itself a tragically mistaken notion. It is a holdover from the misguided application of behavioral psychology to education. This conception has trivialized children's work in reading, writing, and mathematics into ever smaller, distinct skills and subskills. The trend toward specifying discrete behaviors to be mastered individually has resulted in many teachers unwittingly destroying the *meaningfulness* for children of performing these activities.

These are strong words, but consider how decoding predominates in most curricula for the teaching of reading. What proportion of time are children reading passages about ideas? How often are they being read to by the teacher? Consider what constitutes the teaching of writing. Children are usually told to write on a specific theme selected by the teacher. Papers are then corrected in red pen for grammar, spelling, and punctuation. The product of writing is judged by very specific, discrete criteria, but how is the act of writing taught?

In mathematics, an enormous amount of time is spent on learning the math facts. In many schools, the results of arithmetic operations on pairs of the first 10 integers must be memorized and repeated on a timed test before children are allowed to do any other form of mathematics. Throughout elementary school, children spend most of their math time learning about arithmetic operations in more complicated forms.

In contrast with these common practices and conceptions, in the past ten years many psychologists and educators have come to think of what children do in each of these three areas as being primarily *cognitive*. In reading, educators are emphasizing the direct teaching of comprehension, helping children to understand the meaning of the ideas expressed in the text. For an excellent overview, see *Becoming a Nation of Readers* (Anderson et al., 1985). Reading is not merely decoding words; it is understanding the meaning of passages, sentences, and ideas. The context in which a word or an idea is expressed is absolutely crucial to its meaning. On the simplest level, whether *l-e-a-d* means a metal or the act of directing someone depends entirely on the sentence in which it is used. On a more abstract level, take the sentence

- The notes were sour because the seam was split.

What could this sentence mean? Do notes ever taste sour, like lemons? If one could imagine a seam splitting (in a dress or a pair of pants), what could it have to do with sour notes? However, if this sentence occurred within a paragraph describing the music of bagpipes, a context would be established in which the sentence would be meaningful (assuming that one knew what a bagpipe was).

In writing, educators are now encouraging specific processes to help students express their ideas in writing. Prewriting activities stimulate students' thinking and/or discussion about ideas or contexts. Activities for drafting, conferring with others on drafts, and revising drafts are used. Teachers provide opportunities for students to write for personally significant purposes. The mechanics of writing are taught in the context of students' own writing rather than through separate exercises and drills. An excellent book by Donald H. Graves, *Writing: Teachers and Children at Work (1983),* describes such an approach.

In mathematics, there has been a shift away from memorization of math facts to helping students "think" mathematically. See *Addition and Subtraction* by Thomas P. Carpenter et al. (1982) or *The Psychology of Mathematics Instruction* by Resnick and Ford (1981). Students are encouraged to use estimation, which virtually requires understanding the situation, task, or context involved. The arithmetic operations are considered to have both conceptual and procedural aspects; a child should be helped to understand what is happening in the multiplication of 3 times 2, as well as how to get the right answer. Perhaps, most significantly, educators are seeing that a major task of teaching mathematics involves *problem solving*. Students have to understand the problem or task at hand, determine how to attack it, work through a process to get an answer (or possible answers), and be able to evaluate its (their) reasonableness.

In each of these areas, the preoccupation with teaching distinct skills and sub-skills has been replaced with a concern for the child's thinking—the intellectual processes and the particular ideas, conceptions, and meaning of the material addressed. We can also make the same claim for social studies and the sciences in the elementary school. In successive chapters of this book, we will attempt to show how educators in each of these subject areas are now truly "teaching for thinking." Of course, no single book can exhaustively show the work of dozens of educators in these areas. Our hope is to provide a good overview and show the basic commonalities that we see. These commonalities can help teachers realize the essentially cognitive nature of the task of teaching any of these areas.

FACTS AND CONCEPTS

We have been talking about thinking as intellectual processes, but what is being thought about during the thinking? Each of the subject areas has ideas of varying abstraction for students to understand. These ideas are considered the knowledge within the field, and this knowledge is an important context for the thinking that humans do. Generally speaking, knowledge is an area is organized or structured by experts in ways that make sense to them. This knowledge deals with relatively concrete facts and somewhat abstract concepts (as well as more abstract principles and theories).

It is important for teachers to consider the difference between facts and concepts as they think about how students conceive of the ideas being taught and how these ideas are organized in their minds. We will return to these concerns in the next chapter, but for our discussion here, we can say that facts are statements such as

- Mixing equal amounts of red and yellow paint will result in orange.
- John Hancock singed the Declaration of Independence.
- One plus three is four.
- *Our Town* was written by Thornton Wilder.

It sometimes helps to identify concepts by their labels, usually abstract nouns like

honesty	beauty	truth
democracy	revolution	commerce
photosynthesis	phylum	mantle
metaphor	simile	personification
multiplication	sct	hyperbola

But what is a concept, and what good is it anyway? One way to think of a concept is as an abstraction; it pulls together a lot of facts. It organizes them and perhaps even makes sense of them. For instance, the construction of the scientific taxonomy (category system) for creatures on our planet uses concepts such as phylum, class, order, family, and species to organize our thinking about the millions of creatures we have encountered. Concepts can be used to group certain facts together (in this case, physical characteristics of creatures) and make useful distinctions.

In much the same way, concepts like monarchy, democracy, anarchy, and many "isms" (like socialism, communism, fascism, totalitarianism) help us think about the multitude of events of human history. Concepts can reveal patterns of similarities and differences that may not only organize but also explain. One should not forget, however, that like any abstract idea that a human can understand, a concept is *constructed* by humans. Concepts can organize and explain because we believe that they can.

When teaching concepts, it is very important for students to understand the rich meaning behind the label and not just memorize its dictionary (or textbook) definition. For instance, the concept of "revolution" has a variety of definitions. Even if a child can distinguish among these various meanings of the word, to what extent does he truly understand the concept that is being taught? If we defined revolution as "an uprising against government or authority," the student would also have to deal with the concepts of uprising, government, and authority. Having the child memorize a definition is clearly not to be mistaken for understanding the concept.

Another key aspect of understanding a concept is being able to see what is and what is not an example of it. This may seem easy when dealing with very familiar concepts like "dog" and "cat," but it is much trickier with less familiar concepts like "marsupial" or "differentiation" (biological). Experience with rich contexts and a multiplicity of examples is a vital part of understanding concepts.

For instance, what distinctions should one make among the concepts of revolution, rebellion, mutiny, and civil war? If one could conceive of differences at an abstract conceptual level, what distinguishes the events in the American colonies in 1776, in France in 1789, and in Russia in 1917 as compared to the Sepoy Mutiny in India in 1857, the Boxer Rebellion in China in 1899, or the secession of the Confederate states from the Union in 1860?

We will readily admit that there are different types of concepts. For instance, there are *qualitative* differences between the concepts in mathematics and those in social studies. Rather than elaborate these differences here, it may be more useful to examine the concepts of various subject areas in each of the succeeding chapters. For now, let us simply note that concepts are abstract ideas that humans construct. But even the term *abstract* can vary according to how much a person knows about an area, his own level of development, his age, and so forth.

For instance, what seems concrete to most 10-year-olds may be enormously abstract for 3-year-olds—such as colors. What is "red" and how do you distinguish between red and orange (let alone red-orange)? And what about magenta? Kindergarten teachers often refer to a child as "knowing her colors." Truly, the colors are "hers" when she has come to understand the concept of red (and other common colors). She has made "redness" her own; she has *constructed* her own understanding of the concept. A major part of this understanding is being able to recognize things in her world as either being examples of redness or not.

This understanding may not be perfect; she may still get confused with fuscia. But concept learning is not the pedantic, all-or-none understanding of the logician.

We don't "either know it or we don't." We make successive approximations; we get closer to the essential, common understandings of our culture or to the knowledge structure of experts. We accomplish this increased understanding by constructing our own meanings.

EXPLANATIONS AND EXAMPLES

How did the child come to these understandings? What was the process used? While cognitive psychologists puzzle over these questions, educators can tell you what did *not* help: Explanations by the child's physicist uncle about wavelengths of light probably were irrelevant. Of course, that would be an absurdly abstract explanation to give a kindergartner. But what explanation was given at all? Perhaps not any.

The child probably experienced a multiyear process of people (adults or older siblings) talking with her about hundreds of specific examples of colors. Some psychologists suggest that at some time a prototype of the color red developed in her mind. She constructed from the many examples in her experience an image of the basic prototype. Thereafter, the prototype may be refined to include various shades and hues. Difficulties in discrimination would still persist as examples encountered differed markedly from the prototype (like fuscia) or when the example might seem too close to either of two prototypes (like red-orange).

Two additional notions should be apparent at this point: (1) concepts are not just for older students and (2) teachers and adults ought to exercise thoughtfulness in providing explanations, along with examples. The 4-5- and 6-year-olds entering schools and classrooms are literally bombarded with concepts to be learned. The older people around them continually use concept labels that make sense to the speaker but do not necessarily conform to the experienced reality of the child.

The kindergarten teacher probably introduces more concepts than all the other elementary teachers combined. Consider the list: colors, numerals, letters, thousands of prototypical objects that may not have been encountered in the home—blackboards, globes, felt, paste, manila folders. Then consider some remarkably abstract concepts that are crucial for a successful classroom: sharing, respect for others, tardiness, honesty, lying, cooperation, and the like. What goes through the mind of a 5-year-old when he hears these terms?

Shall the teacher recite what the dictionary says the terms mean? Of course not. The teacher skillfully combines explanations and examples, seizing on every naturally occurring, real-life event as an opportunity for a concrete example to be discussed in a way that makes sense to the children. The teacher talks about the examples in language that, from her experience with these particular children (and others of that age, perhaps), she believes will make a *connection*. She wants to build on the ways they currently think about the idea and to enrich their thinking about it. Therefore, the concept exists within a context—what the children know already, how they are thinking about something, and common ways that they have to talk about the idea (the current example as well as the many previous examples). A crucial aspect of teaching is using one's awareness and knowledge of all these ideas and creating ways to talk about them.

Psychologists and philosophers have terms (concept labels) to describe the processes we have been discussing as explanation and examples: deduction and induction. What are these concepts? All of us probably memorized at some time in school the definition that deduction is going from the general to the particular; induction is going from the particular to the general. But what does that mean? Not understanding that sentence meant that the essentially deductive explanation of the two concepts was insufficient.

In fact, we are convinced that most people, in most areas of life, do not learn very well if the teaching is largely deductive. Lectures, explanations, definitions, general descriptions, and overviews rarely give people the raw material to construct meaning. Perhaps a few who are gifted in an area have a natural affinity and can learn without examples. On the other hand, perhaps their interest has led to exploring a wealth of examples outside of school. Most of us need examples, and lots of them. These are the particulars from which we build our understanding of concepts through a somewhat inductive process.

It is rare, however, for students in school to encounter situations that are either purely deductive or purely inductive. Most teachers provide a balance of explanations about a concept (general ideas about how this concept differs from that, and so on) and many examples to clarify, illustrate, make distinctions, and so forth. Twenty years ago some curricula emphasized discovery learning, which appeared to be primarily inductive. They used numerous experiments with particulars through which students could discover relationships, rules, concepts, and the like. For a variety of reasons, these curricula were not universally successful.

It is clear to us that both deductive and inductive processes are useful and necessary in the classroom to foster thinking about concepts. However, we see tremendous pressures on teachers to hurry through content on a fixed timetable, which invites deductive explanations with minimal examples. This pressure for "covering" material is perhaps the single biggest hindrance to thinking in schools. Inductive wrestling with examples takes time, more time than simple explanations from the teacher that can be memorized. Wrestling with the examples is absolutely crucial for conceptual understanding. Without it, thinking is short-circuited, meaningfulness is lost, and concepts are barely understood, in any sense of the word.

Perhaps someone will protest, "But don't most children learn the material reasonably well at the current pace of coverage?" The issue is not how much material they are exposed to: it is *how* they deal with what they are exposed to. Strategies that promote more real thinking (instead of memorizing prepackaged ideas), that call for wrestling with examples along with careful explanation, will result in deeper understanding of more material. We suggest two reasons why this may be so.

First, richer, deeper understanding of concepts will greatly facilitate the learning of facts as well as other related concepts. Truly understanding a few initial concepts early in the year will greatly enhance the learning of other material later in the year. Some psychologists think of this phenomenon as a scaffolding of ideas (like erecting a scaffold alongside a building that you are going to paint). Properly constructed, the parts of the scaffold are highly interconnected to allow one to go back and forth between sections. But the scaffold also allows one to go up and down (in abstraction) freely.

It is worthwhile building conceptual scaffolds early in the year to be used throughout the year because of a key property of concepts: They organize reality to let one see things one might not have seen without the concept. Teachers can build on such understanding and can help students create their own scaffolds. A concept that is clearly understood in September can be used by the teacher throughout the year. When introducing other related ideas, a well-understood concept can take on the role of a *concrete example.*

Take the concept "onomatopoeia." If you have never heard this term, it is probably meaningless. But his concept unites words like *buzz, clang, ping, flop, moo, mew, woof,* and *ding-dong.* Some people have never realized that all these words (and many others) represent a sound by imitating it. They might go through their whole lives never thinking about this idea. They might never consider that there are words like these that were made up, perhaps recently, and not handed down from Greek, Latin, or Sanskrit, yet they would frequently use these words. Understanding this concept provides insight, gives meaning, and enriches intellectually. It can also be used to help understand other figures of speech (an interesting concept in itself, of which onomatopoeia is an example).

MOTIVATION AND ATTITUDES

There is a second compelling reason why wrestling with examples and thinking in rich contests will ultimately make for more and better learning: enhanced motivation and attitudes in students. It may be an overstatement to say that much of a child's schooling consists of memorizing words, terms, facts, and ideas that have only marginal meaning and are retained only as long as they are likely to be needed for tests. But what percentage of all the ideas encountered tin school becomes a vital part of our adult thinking?

Consider the possibility of students really caring about what they learned, idealistic as this may seem. Yet the opposite is often the case. Much of the time, teaching seems like dragging the children through the curriculum. If they were excited, if they did care, so much more could be accomplished.

Unfortunately, we more commonly find strong negative emotions toward various school subjects—anxiety, fear, and avoidance. Adults, who are no longer compelled to do academic work they find unpleasant, will freely state their panic at having to speak in public, write a letter, or compute the surface area of a room. They will purposely, and often quite consciously, avoid reading certain kinds of books, writing a letter of inquiry for a job, watching "Nova" on television, and so forth. These are merely the more extreme reactions among a host of lesser bad feelings.

From their experiences as students (usually in elementary school), most people decide that there are certain areas of the curriculum, or topics within an area, that they are simply incapable of learning. It seems that once that decision has been made, a person spends the rest of his life trying to avoid the subject and concealing these felt inadequacies from others (especially teachers).

It is a major task in our teaching for thinking to provide experiences for students that not only engage them intellectually but also sustain their emotional involvement. They must understand and believe that they can understand. They must feel that they will find *meaningfulness* in what we ask them to do. This does not mean simplifying the curriculum or making everything so easy that they don't make mistakes.

We have found that students care more when they are encouraged to think, when they are challenged to an intellectual wrestling match. We don't mean challenged by ideas that are so abstract that students are not intellectually ready for them; that kind of challenge invites frustration. We mean challenging them to understand through contexts that are meaningful, where ideas come with examples and explanations, where problems and situations are perplexing and solutions are not apparent, where the intellectual processes are not simple and obvious, where answers cannot readily be memorized. All these processes should occur within a classroom climate that encourages perseverance, allows time to think and work things out, and does not quickly judge and penalize mistakes. That is what this book is all about.

2

Intellectual Processes in the Curriculum

At the beginning of this book, we talked about the bewildering number of terms used to describe or explain the thinking that people do. Since it is important to be able to talk sensibly about thinking, how can we cut through the barrage of terms? What do people mean when they refer to such things as *analysis, synthesis, hypothesizing, drawing inferences, making analogies, classifying,* and so forth?

Since the purpose of this book is the help teachers foster thinking in their students, we are less concerned about the excruciating distinctions that psychologists who are doing research on cognition might make than we are with understanding some key issues related to teaching for thinking. While psychologists continue to debate and study, educators must make some decisions about what we should be doing with children to promote thinking.

As we mentioned earlier, some very complex issues about the nature of thinking are not yet resolved. Each program for teaching thinking, in essence, has a "theoretical model" that defines the basic intellectual processes the program seeks to promote. We have carefully reviewed the many programs and have concluded that they are each valuable but incomplete. Each seems to stake out only a section of the territory on what might be considered key intellectual processes. In promoting his program, each author exaggerates the importance of the *kind of thinking* encouraged by his program, as if that is all there is or should be to thinking.

A few programs attempt to be more complete or comprehensive, to encompass the many varied kinds of thinking. However, these seem to be like a smorgasboard of processes, without a clearly defined theoretical model that shows teachers how they fit together. How do the various valuable intellectual processes of the program relate to one another? How can teachers build on some to foster others?

We believe that teachers want to understand how techniques they are using with their students fit together. It is not enough simply to do some activities with children and hope for the best. Teachers desire to know why something works, how one kind of thinking can lead to another, and so forth.

We would be unforgivably presumptuous if we claimed to have figured out the best, most comprehensive model for teaching thinking. We haven't. What we have done is really two things: First, we have spent a lot of time trying to understand the similarities and differences in the kinds of thinking in various subject areas. Second, we have tried to determine from the cognitive psychology research and various thinking programs the range of thinking processes that probably should be included. We realize that conceptions in both these areas will change over the next 5 to 10 years. That is as it should be.

In the subsequent chapters, we will take the reader through our ideas about teaching for thinking in the major content fields. Before doing this, we want to present a way we have devised to pull together the intellectual processes. It is a model of teaching for thinking that involves six key aspects:

- Schema
- Focus
- Pattern
- Extension
- Projection
- Metacognition

The model is designed to help teachers think about the key issues. We feel it captures the most important distinctions that teachers should make when teaching for thinking in their students. Table 2.1 gives an overview of our conception.

SCHEMA

A major dilemma all teachers face is how to get their students to use what they already know. Psychologists talk about the importance of "accessing prior knowledge." Although some consider this issue to be a memory problem, others have focused on how a person organizes knowledge or information that he has. Psychologists, as well as educators in each of the content fields, have a variety of ways of thinking and talking about how information is organized, structured, or "stored" as well as how it might be accessed, retrieved, or made available for use. Some speak of knowledge about an idea being arranged in a schema (the plural of *schema* is *schemata*). Although many people use the term *schema,* they do not all consider it to mean exactly the same thing. For instance, some use *schema* to mean specific knowledge and how it is structured, whereas others mean both the way the

TABLE 2.1 AN OVERVIEW OF THESE INTELLECTUAL PROCESSES.

SCHEMA— Using prior knowledge, relating ideas to experience, integrating the old and the new
  • Relating information to oneself
  • Using tacit knowledge
  • Looking for assumptions
  • Interpreting
  • Finding analogies, metaphors, and similes
  • Criticizing and evaluating

FOCUS— Breaking things down, analyzing, encoding, representing, deciding what is relevant and what are the key units to focus on
  • Identifying key aspects, attributes, features, characteristics
  • Observing events, phenomena, creatures, things
  • Comparing and contrasting
  • Collecting, recording, and representing

PATTERN— Combining, putting together, synthesizing, seeing patterns, forming concepts, conceiving of the whole entity
  • Organizing information
  • Classifying and categorizing
  • Summarizing
  • Inferring and concluding
  • Predicting and hypothesizing

EXTENSION— Using what is known to understand and act upon increasingly complex problems and situations
  • Decision making
  • Problem solving
  • Conducting investigations and inquiries

PROJECTION— Diverging from the known to create new and different understandings or forms
  • Imagining
  • Expressing
  • Creating
  • Inventing
  • Designing

METACOGNITION— Thinking about one's own thinking; using executive/control processes
  • Planning or strategizing
  • Monitoring or checking
  • Regulating
  • Questioning
  • Reflecting
  • Reviewing

---

information is organized and how it is habitually used (likely actions, such as a script an actor would follow). In fact, some use the term *script*.

For teachers, there are two ways in which the idea of schema is useful: planning for teaching and the actual teaching of children. We must be continuously looking for signals from students about how they are *conceiving* the ideas we are teaching; that is, what do the ideas mean to them? How are the ideas represented in their minds. How are various ideas organized? We watch for misunderstandings and misconceptions, as well as for statements that give us insight into what they know and how they have put it together. These insights are crucial to planning what to teach and how to teach it. We probably get more of this information from our continual interaction with the students in discussions, through questioning, and so forth than we do from testing.

This awareness informs not only our planning for teaching but also our immediate, on-the-spot responses, questions, examples, and explanations right in the middle of the lesson or activity. This kind of spontaneous interaction is the vital, energizing, life-blood of teaching. There is an exciting, *creative* aspect to planning an activity, to imagining something that might work and putting together materials and ideas. There is also the creative act of modifying, adapting, or rearranging an activity as the students *become engaged* in the processes.

Our bias against prepackaged curricula is clear. While any teacher needs good materials and texts for students, any curriculum that requires teachers to follow slavishly a prearranged set of lessons, day after day, is robbing the teacher and the students of the most vital part of their lives together—their personal interaction. The notion of a "teacher-proof" curriculum (that is, a curriculum so carefully, clearly, and completely laid out that the most ignorant, incompetent teacher could "deliver it" to students) is absolutely abhorrent to us. Our warning at the beginning of this book was quite genuine. We do not offer a prepackaged set of lessons but rather something more like strategies for how teachers might do things with children. Modifications and adaptations are encouraged; the creative part is left for the teacher.

All these concerns about prior knowledge or schemata are at the heart of the issue of the extent to which thinking in one context is similar to thinking in another. What do students need to know in order to think in a sophisticated manner about these ideas? Do certain kinds of thinking depend on the amount and nature of the knowledge about a subject that one has already acquired and organized? To a certain extent, the answer is clearly yes. From our previous discussion about the concept of revolution, it is clear that the more experience one has had with the potential examples of revolutions (the particulars by which one can inductively understand the concept or clarify the explanation a teacher might give of it) the easier it would be to construct a valid meaning. For an excellent discussion of this idea, see the article by Robert Glaser (1984).

What about the intellectual processes involved in constructing the meaning of the information? What are the processes of structuring or restructuring the knowledge? We will soon look at some ideas people have about these processes. First, it is worth noting that whatever processes are involved, they are definitely related to the students' existing schemata. Teachers *must* deal with these schemata.

In recent years, a variety of approaches or techniques have been developed and used for helping students use their prior knowledge and for giving teachers a picture of students' schemata. One of our favorites (because of its versatility) is *semantic mapping*. Although it was developed for use in language arts or vocabulary lessons, it can be easily used in any subject area.

By the third or fourth grade in school, children have heard an extremely large number of words. They have some idea about what each means, even if their notions are dim or faulty. Perhaps they have frequently heard a word in a particular context but have never asked what the speaker meant. Also, a word, term, or concept label may be quite well known to some students in a class and virtually unheard of and unknown to others. Teachers have learned not to assume they know their students' prior knowledge on any concept or topic.

Imagine that you were about to begin a social studies unit on deserts. A simple way to elicit the students' schemata (as a group) would be to construct a semantic map. You would ask the class what comes to mind with the word *desert,* writing the word in the center of the blackboard. The students suggest aloud things they know already about deserts, perhaps specific deserts they have been to, read about, seen on television, and so on. Write with connecting lines or arrows the key ideas and words the students say. Do *not* ask such questions as what lives in a desert? Instead, allow the students to stimulate each other's thinking, remembrance, and personal information.

Develop a preliminary list or map on the blackboard until a reasonable number of ideas are listed (or until the children get silly or run out of thoughts). Do not correct the ideas as they are generated. In fact, do not say much at all; merely record. Making judgments about the students' ideas will definitely stifle their expression.

Two good results occur through this process. First, you'll get a picture of what the students know already and how they think about the concept, term, or idea. There may be some excellent aspects of the concept that a few children already know in some form that can be built on. This map or list will also show any important aspects of the idea that are not mentioned. It will also indicate any erroneous notions that some (or all) have. For instance, perhaps some children regularly vacation at Palm Springs, California. Their idea of a desert is a country club with a lot of sand. When such strange conceptions surface early in a lesson or unit, you should consider how to deal with them. You can directly address misconceptions when discussing the semantic map. You also can develop some activity that addresses them later in the unit.

A second desirable result from this mapping is *wrestling* with what was put up on the board, the basic ideas the students expressed. Do some ideas seem to go together? Do some ideas seem different or contradictory? Two broad discussion questions like these call for intellectual processes that we will deal with in the next section (we'd probably call them *comparing* and *contrasting).* The point here is that discussing what the children already know or think about an idea also provides rich information about their schemata and affords the opportunity to stimulate their awareness of what they already know. In the jargon of cognition, this is called *activating schemata.*

In this process of actively recalling what is already known, you can direct the process to the relevant schemata. Any process like semantic mapping may activate erroneous information or aspects of the concept that ae irrelevant for your subsequent purposes in the curriculum. Notice that to a student, all aspects of his schema are relevant, and you also need to be aware of what information is there. However, any curriculum asks you to make some decisions about which avenues to pursue, which to emphasize, and how much time to spend on related ideas.

For instance, perhaps the movie *The Black Stallion Returns* is a significant part of students' schemata of what a desert is like. For some, the ability of camels to walk long distances without water is a salient aspect of their schema. For others, the kinds of horses ridden by desert tribesmen stands out. The movie provides some very exciting images of these aspects of desert life. How much time should students spend discussing transportation in the desert or animals or tribes or whatever? No textbook or curriculum should entirely make that decision for the teacher. In subsequent sections we will address what kinds of thinking students might do with such ideas.

As this example suggests, semantic mapping can be used to initiate students' thinking about what they already know so that the teacher can make *connections* between the new ideas that will be addressed and the existing knowledge. This is one of the key issues in this section. New thinking and knowledge will build on what is already there. Prior knowledge will be expanded, enriched, broadened, and deepened, or they will be modified, changed, rearranged, and adapted.

Any new information heard, read, or otherwise experienced cannot be understood without an interpretive framework. Children use their schemata to construct their interpretations of experiences. New information may be assimilated into existing schemata in ways that gradually extend and refine them. Also, some cognitive changes are more pronounced, requiring significant modifications in schemata, including discarding native or erroneous concepts, theories, representations, and the like in favor of the more sophisticated schemata of adults or experts. Some believe that these larger shifts in perspective or conceptual framework occur only when children pass through specific developmental stages. Others feel that when children are confronted with inconsistencies in their existing schemata, through examples, experiences, and activities, along with good adult explanations, they can make these shifts. See Susan Carey (1986) for a discussion of these ideas.

All people are remarkably resistant to new information that requires major cognitive reorganization. New ideas, inconsistencies, and so forth can be distorted to conform with existing schemata and assimilated without major change. For example, a student who has created a political schema from her parents' notions of liberal Democrats versus conservative Republicans will have great difficulty assimilating Lowell Wiecker or George Wallace. Not being in a position to rethink the two-party system and the political philosophies of liberalism and conservativism, she will probably ignore the new information. Even if provided with extensive information about the parties and these philosophies, she will have strong initial resistance to rethinking or conceptual reorganization, which the teacher must overcome.

In this book, we present activities designed to get beyond such resistance and help students *make major cognitive shifts*. Each of the following sections in this chapter addresses a somewhat different kind of thinking. Note here how important it is to get students to be more aware of what they already know, to become conscious of how they have put things together, to realize what they take for granted based on their prior experiences. We could label the intellectual processes involved in such activities as

- Relating information to oneself
- Using tacit knowledge

- Looking for assumptions
- Interpreting
- Finding analogies, metaphors, and similes
- Criticizing and evaluating

Some writers ask teachers to learn key distinctions among these intellectual processes. We do not believe that fine distinctions are crucial. Rather, each of these processes (and others) asks teachers to foster awareness in their students' thinking concerning what they know or think they know.

As we have already discussed, schemata are personal; students are always relating information to their own personal sense of what they know. We all use daily our tacit knowledge (the ideas and facts that no one taught us directly, that we just picked up through experience) even though it is rarely thought about and evaluated consciously. For instance, no high school counselor needs to tell a freshman, new to the high school, where he should sit (or not sit) in the lunchroom. The freshman knows from the first walk through the room. Not all tacit knowledge is necessarily social awareness or "street smarts." This example just carries the flavor of what is known, but not taught, that informs our actions.

Similarly, students must become aware of their assumptions. Humans continually make assumptions about an enormous variety of things in their lives and their world. We assume that we will live through the day. We assume that everyone in the lane of oncoming traffic will not cross over into our lane. We assume that the person wearing a gold band on the third finger of the left hand is married. We assume that the letter *I* will precede the letter *E* unless it is preceded by the letter *C*. We assume that we should stay within the lines when using crayons in a coloring book.

Many assumptions are necessary and useful social conventions that rarely need to be examined. However, we all, adults and children, make assumptions and take things for granted that occassionally get in our way. For instance, try the following problem.

Late Saturday night a friend told you that the pet store had just received a shipment of kangaroos and dingoes from Australia. He wanted to know how many of each had arrived. The store was closed, but he peeked through the glass door—at the bottom, below the shade. He was able to see 24 feet. How many dingoes and kangaroos were there?

Although this may sound like an absurd problem, don't dismiss it lightly. Try to work it out.

Notice that immediately, you must make several assumptions, such as, there is at least one kangaroo and one dingo. Also, kangaroos walk on two feet. But what about dingoes? They are wild dogs that walk on all four feet (and don't bark—an ideal pet). Did all 24 feet that were seen belong to these two kinds of creatures? Assume that they did. Now try the problem.

Did you come up with the right answer? Did you assume that there was one right answer? In fact, there are several possibilities. Any of the following pairs is possible:

Kangaroos	Dingoes
10	1
8	2
6	3
4	4
2	5

Each of these combinations would produce a total of 24 feet, given our assumptions.

Despite the virtual exclusion of multiple-answer problems from mathematics textbooks, life is full of situations in which several answers are possible. Furthermore, the intellectual process of carefully thinking through what assumptions one is making about a problem, situation, or question is vital in life and well worth teaching in school.

Interpretation is ascribing meaning to something encountered. Like the other intellectual processes in this section, interpreting requires relating the new to what is known or believed—one's schemata. Some educators use the term *inferring* or *inferencing* in much the same way, such as inferring meaning from text in the process of reading. To avoid confusion, we will only use the term *inference* to refer to a somewhat more complicated process described in the section on forming meaningful patterns. Certainly one's schemata are involved in all the cognitive processes described here.

Analogies, metaphors, and similes are excellent devices for relating new ideas to existing knowledge. Of course, each depends on the existence of a good representation of the idea or concept for the known half of the comparison. In this discussion on schema, we are less concerned with using these devices as vehicles of language than as ways to relate new ideas to what is already known.

For instance, in some important respects, Simon Bolivar was analogous to George Washington as a revolutionary patriot, victorious military leader, and first president of his country. Substantial knowledge of the life and career of Washington can be used by the teacher to help students understand not only Bolivar but also the events in the history of South America in the early nineteenth century.

As before, the intellectual processes involved in using analogies, metaphors, and similes have aspects beyond the idea of schemata. We introduce the ideas here to signal how they depend on prior knowledge.

The process of interpreting, using analogies, and the like may be quite different in different contexts. Are the mathematical analogies expressing part-to-whole relationships (e.g., fractions) really the same as those in nature (e.g., snakes of the reptile family), in writing (e.g., sentences of a paragraph), or in government (e.g., states in a country)?

Can these thinking processes help students make connections *across contexts?* Perhaps. Although we are careful not to suggest that intellectual processes are readily transferable from one context to another (thus our concern with teaching for thinking in each subject area), it does seem that there are occasions when a student will create a surprisingly cogent understanding in one area by using an analogy from another: "Oh yeah! I know what you mean by negative numbers, Mrs. Jones. They're like the wind-chill factor. It makes the temperature go below zero."

Similarly, there are occasions when teachers can promote a real breakthrough in understanding through cross-context analogies, metaphors, or similes. For instance, the biological process of peristalsis (the movement of waste through the intestines) depends on the *wavelike* contractions of muscles that push the matter along. In fact, many organs and processes of mammals' bodies are extremely hard to comprehend without analogical or metaphorical devices.

To go one step further, perhaps the phenomenon of insight or intuition is actually some kind of cross-contextual, analogical, or metaphorical process. Insight or intuition appears to be a rather sudden coming together of understanding, a leap beyond usual inductive examples or more deductive explanations. It appears to be a form of *synergy,* a concept expressing a process by which separate pieces, when combined, have a significantly greater effect or meaning than they could when taken individually. One barbiturate pill has a certain tranquilizing effect, as do several ounces of alcohol. Yet taken simultaneously, their combined effects are synergistic, not simply what would be expected from adding the effects of each; their summative effects are greatly expanded.

It is possible that students can be helped to make insightful leaps from one context to another. Some believe that such leaps are at the heart of creativity. They cite the brilliant breakthroughs of scientists, such as the one who discovered the structure of benzene through the insight that the carbon and hydrogen atoms were linked like snakes coiled back on themselves, biting their tails. We will address intellectual processes related to creativity in the section on *projection*.

We believe that teachers should foster the intellectual processes of criticizing and evaluating. These are often thought of as very sophisticated thinking processes, only for the most able or advanced students. Instead, we would like the teacher to view them as rather basic, personal kinds of thinking in which a student considers the value or goodness of something newly encountered relative to his existing knowledge, beliefs, feelings, and so forth. In a sense then, criticizing and evaluating are value judgments based on one's schemata. We realize that a major movement in education has emerged around the term *critical thinking*. We will address this idea in the next section, on *focus*.

As students become more experienced with ideas and concepts, they can become more aware of the evaluative criteria they are using; they can be helped to establish more sophisticated and extensive criteria, based on substantive knowledge of a subject. Nonetheless, even young children engage in this intellectual process.

Finally, when a student "evaluates" something, it is highly unlikely that this judgment is entirely intellectual. We would probably say the same thing about adults. As we stressed in the previous chapter, the separation of feelings from intellectualizations is neither possible nor desirable. One way to ensure that we do not overlook these connections is to suggest that intertwined with a person's schemata are one's attitudes. Imagine that for each schema there exists an interwoven feeling.

Traditionally, the concept of attitude is conceived to include three facets—the cognitive, the affective, and the behavioral. Attitudes concern feelings about actions and what we know or believe. Likewise, what we do (behaviors, actions) and what happens affects how we think and feel—about ideas, people, things, and ourselves.

These intellectual contexts and processes we've been discussing probably involve not only the students' personally constructed schemata but also their strongly held feelings. In the previous chapter we discussed the fears and avoidances that students (and adults) have toward various subjects in school. Note here that experiences students have had in the past and are having currently as they create and modify schemata are simultaneously creating or modifying attitudes toward

- The specific topic, concept, or idea being addressed
- The broader context of the content, subject, or field
- The kind of thinking required in the activity
- The kind of interactions among classmates and their ideas
- One's capability of understanding this idea and the general area

As teachers, we need to be sensitive to any expressions of feelings from students in these areas. These expressions signal possibilities for powerful motivation for intellectual engagement (interest, excitement, puzzlement, job) or potential obstacles to thinking (boredom, frustration, anxiety)

The topics of schemata and schema theory are frequently discussed along with the concept of "metacognition"—a kind of thinking that transcends one's usual cognition, being very aware of one's own thinking processes. We will discuss this special kind of thinking after dealing with several other important aspects of teaching for thinking.

FOCUS

When people (students) encounter a situation, problem, task, or communication of some kind, they do not merely sit back and passively "receive" information. Rather they actively attack the situation with their minds to try to make sense of what is there, to make the information meaningful. This "meaning" is created and constructed by the individual in relation to her existing schemata. In some way, the new must relate to the old.

But how does a person even "perceive" the new? What does she look at? What does she see? What does she focus on when thrust into a situation or when hearing a message? Consider figure 2.1.

What was the *first* part of the figure on which you focused your attention? What did you do next? How did you reconcile the inconsistencies in what you saw? If you had seen this exact figure previously, what did you first think? Had you seen any similar figures previously? How did that affect what you focused on first?

Although these questions are essentially metacognitive in nature (asking you to reflect on your own thinking), in all situations, familiar or novel, humans can rap-

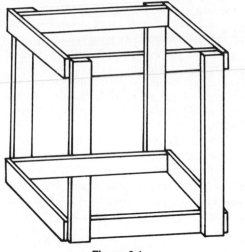

Figure 2.1

idly shift their focus among various aspects. Let's take a somewhat more complex task. It is called Eleusis, a game of pure induction.

The following is a *series* of cards from a standard fifty-two-card deck. What card or cards could come next in the series?

3 of hearts, 6 of clubs, 9 of diamonds, queen of spades

As in any essentially inductive task, having enough information through a variety of examples is crucial. But even at this early stage, you have probably noticed some aspects of this four-card series. What have you focused on so far? Based on your previous experience (formed into a schema), you have probably thought that the standard deck has cards with numbers, pictures, and/or letters (A, K, Q, J). Also there are four suits. We take the term *suits* for granted, whereas a 4-year-old without a schema for playing cards might laugh at our use of this term if it conjured up images of apparel.

Perhaps you focused on the suits and noticed that each of the four suits are represented in the series. Perhaps you focused on the value of the cards and noticed that the numbers progressed 3, 6, 9, queen. Perhaps you noticed both features.

One remarkable attribute of human thinking is that when we attack a task and attempt to make it meaningful, we *almost simultaneously* focus on aspects and construct patterns. We try to make sense of the smaller pieces that we focus on by relating them to what we already know about the world—our schemata. But with amazing speed, we also try out various meaningful patterns from our schemata that might pull the pieces together into meaningful wholes. We will discuss more about patterns in the next section.

When you focused on the value of the cards and noted 3, 6, 9, queen, your substantial experience with our number system might have seen a potential pattern of counting by threes. But what about the queen? What schema could account for that card? Familiarity with a variety of cards games might have suggested that within the thirteen cards in each suit the ace counts as 1, the numbered cards 2 through 10 as their stated value, the jack as 11, the queen as 12, and the king as 13. You might have thought that the cards represented a numerical sequence.

Your mind may have rapidly analyzed the four examples in the series, focusing on one or more features and interpreting possible meanings for individual pieces (based on prior knowledge), and begun to construct possible patterns that could account for the rule governing the series.

What could come next in the series? Does the pattern depend on the numbers, the suits, or both? If merely the suits, any heart could go next. If merely the numerical pattern of counting by threes, any 2 could go next. This may seem very strange unless your schema allows for "wrap-around" sequences. The cards might go numerically from A, 2, 3 through 10, J, Q, K and back to A, 2, and so on. Counting by threes would skip two cards each time: 3, 6, 9, Q, 2, 5, 8, J, A, 4, 7, 10, K, 3, 6. A strange series, indeed.

If the pattern depends on both numbers and suits, only one card could go next in the series: the 2 of hearts.

In the standard version of Eleusis, one person decides on a pattern. He writes down a rule for the pattern on a slip of paper and conceals it from the other players. Players are dealt cards and must create the initial series of permissible examples through trial and error. The one who chose the pattern simply indicates by yes or no whether the guess is permissible at this time.

Patterns must always create a sequence that prohibits certain cards at a given point in a sequence but allows them later. For instance, "play cards in the sequence heart, club, diamond, spade, and repeat" is allowed in Eleusis. However, "play hearts in numerical order" is not allowed because some cards (in fact, three-fourths of the cards) can never by played in the series.

Cards that fit the sequence are placed on a table (or in the chalkboard tray) in their order so all can see as each player makes a correct guess. The simple version of the game declares a winner when someone has discarded all of her cards into the sequence. Many variations of the game are possible (e.g., to win one must not only discard all cards in one's hand but also correctly write the rule for the pattern on paper).

Let's get back to the series we started with:

3 of hearts, 6 of clubs, 9 of diamonds, and Q of spades

What if someone attempted to play the Q of diamonds and was told yes by the rule maker? What does that do to your meaning?

Let's abbreviate the series as 3H, 6C, 9D, QS, QD. . . .

Since this card does not seem to fit the patterns we've discussed from the previous analyses, we need to *refocus* or *reanalyze* the information. In order to help, let's look at more examples.

The series continues:

3H, 6C, 9D, QS, QD, 2C, 10H, 5C, KH, JS, 4D, 7S, 8D . . .

Now there are quite a lot of data to analyze. But how does your mind "like" the way we have represented the information in the series? Do you feel comfortable with KH representing the king of hearts? Would you "feel" better if the series was shown as

> 3 of hearts, 6 of clubs, 9 of diamonds, queen of spades, queen of diamonds, 2 of clubs, 10 of hearts, 5 of clubs, king of hearts, jack of spades, 4 of diamonds, 7 of spades, 8 of diamonds . . .

How about this way:

3 of hearts	10 of hearts
6 of clubs	5 of clubs
9 of diamonds	king of hearts
queen of spades	jack of spades
queen of	4 of diamonds
diamonds	7 of spades
2 of clubs	8 of diamonds

The ways in which we represent information—what we select to focus on and how we encode it—are quite crucial to our understanding. They can dramatically facilitate or hinder how we decide what is relevant or irrelevant and to what extent the information is judged similar to existing schemata.

In this case, we have deliberately inhibited your understanding of the only relevant aspect of the cards for this series. That is, we represented the examples in ways that minimized your opportunities for focusing on the relevant aspect. We also represented the examples through their names of labels rather than having a pictoral representation such as

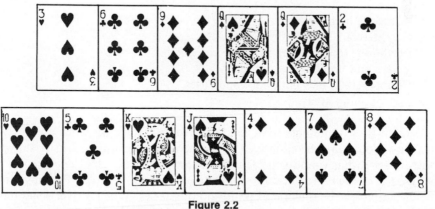

Figure 2.2

What did you focus on now? Did certain features of the visual images jump out at you?

Some people focus on the number cards versus the face cards and note the pattern of three numbers then two faces and so on. They would expect the next card in the series to be a face card. Others notice that the first pair of face cards is female and the next pair is male. Some people try to analyze the three number cards between these pairs.

But we have kept you in suspense too long. As adults, you have used the incredibly complex and sophisticated schemata that you have built from many, many experiences. If we had shown the actual cards to a kindergartner (with far less experience than you), the most obvious feature of the cards (which we did not use in our representations for you) would have jumped out at them: the colors. The rule is rather simple: Alternate red and black cards.

Please don't feel tricked. We only made the task sufficiently difficult to challenge your superior level of thinking. All the necessary information to derive this pattern inductively was represented in the examples. However, some representations are more readily analyzed than others.

For a detailed description of Eleusis and a truly ingenious scoring system, see *The Second Scientific American Book of Mathematical Puzzles and Diversions* by Martin Gardner (1961), pp. 165–73.

Representations of information can be quite varied. Consider the incredible differences between words and pictures, language labels and visual images, horizontal and vertical lists, and words and abbreviations. For some people certain representations are quite adequate, whereas these representations are hopelessly inadequate for other people less familiar with the particular context (or with such representations). For instance, players of contract bridge may have been quick to see a pattern in the preceding series even with a highly abbreviated representation that used numbers and the four symbols familiar to them.

Think about the special kind of representations contained in various maps:

- Interstate highways
- City streets
- Elevations (color-coded into five categories)
- Rivers and bodies of water
- County, state, and national boundaries
- Metropolitan areas

Each of these represents some kind of "reality," most of which are fairly concrete. How would they be conceived of by the average third-grader? If shown one of these maps, what would she focus on? How would the child *analyze* the map? What aspects of the representation would be obvious to the child? Perhaps the most difficult map might be the one of political boundaries. When a river separates two states (or countries), the boundary makes some sense. But what does the dotted line on the map *mean?* Some children imagine that there are painted lines out there showing where Massachusetts ends and Rhode Island begins.

To summarize: The idea of focusing is remarkably related to both schemata and creating patterns. Under this broad heading of *focus* we can imagine several somewhat different intellectual processes:

- Analyzing
- Breaking down things into pieces
- Identifying key aspects, attributes, features, characteristics
- Observing events, phenomena, creatures, things
- Comparing and contrasting
- Collecting, recording, or representing

As before, we are not asking teachers to make unnecessarily fine distinctions amount these intellectual processes. Our point is that although these processes may vary in nature or in difficulty (depending on the complexity of the task, one's knowledge and experience with the context, etc.), each requires the student to focus in some way.

Most of the current so-called critical thinking curricula around today rely heavily on some type of analysis of various information and ignore other aspects of thinking. Some emphasize visual perception, others the recognition of simple patterns. Although these operations are important, we believe that they are components of much more complex processes. We will discuss several examples of a broader sense of critical thinking in the chapter on social studies.

We would like to raise a serious issue that we alluded to earlier: To what extent or in what ways does performing one of these intellectual processes in one context prepare a student for the process in another context? For instance, do first-grader's experiences in comparing and contrasting U.S. coins help them compare and contrast leaves from various kinds of trees? Or does fifth-graders' experience in analyzing the Bill of Rights facilitate their analysis of other written documents (such as *Poor Richard's Almanac,* a poem by Tennyson, a speech by the president, or a description of a wolf pack's hunting behavior)?

Many of the thinking programs unwittingly assume that training in analyzing (e.g., comparing and contrasting) in one context will automatically help a student analyze all kinds of things. It is not so simple. Different types of analyses depend primarily on the kinds of things one is analyzing. Focusing on the various inscriptions, images, sizes, colors, metals, and so forth of coins can elicit substantial understanding of relevant information and initiate the valuable habit of attending to details. However, it is questionable how much of the practice in focusing on coins would transfer to focusing on leaves. How many students would readily begin to think carefully about relevant features, distinctive differences, and the like? Prior experiences with these two contexts would exert a very powerful pull on a student's attention, largely determining what she would focus on.

The most forthright of the programs that advocate a fairly generalized training in analysis urge the teacher to pay particular attention to helping the students realize that they are making an analysis. These programs encourage the students to be aware of what they are doing. Furthermore, the teacher must overtly give the students experience in other contexts and make it explicit that they are doing the same basic kind of thinking in this additional context.

Thus, the first-grade teacher would help the children think through the similarities and differences among the coins. The class would discuss what they had seen, draw pictures, and so on. Then the teacher would initiate a similar activity with leaves; but not only do the children compare and contrast the leaves but also the teacher directly asks how this activity is similar to what was done with the coins. The teacher might bolster the students' awareness by particularly pointing out the similarities. Then the teacher would do the same kind of activity with another kind of object, such as hand gear (gloves, mittens, etc.) or stuffed animals or pictures of pets and so forth.

If those who favor the teaching of general thinking skills are correct, eventually, if given enough practice in a variety of areas, students will be able to transfer the intellectual process, performing capably in a wide range of contexts. For us this idea is only partially accurate, for two reasons.

First, this kind of transfer seems to occur only when the teacher really does what was stated: provides many contexts and explicitly shows the similarity in what was done in each. This is essentially a metacognitive strategy—getting students to think about their own thinking. However, our work with children and teachers indicates that direct metacognitive strategies are much more successful with children in upper primary grades or middle school than with those in early primary grades. Peterson and Swing (1983) discuss this and related ideas in an article cited at the end of this book.

We believe that the younger children profit more from many varied contexts than from explicit metacognition. The range of experiences, each of which is rich and experiential, provides the raw material for building up knowledge and schemata that can be drawn on later. It is certainly valuable to make explicit connections for children, especially the older ones, as we will discuss in the section on metacognition.

Second, consider a concern that arises from the analysis of various written documents. Notice how there would be a definite interaction between the kind of analysis and the kind of document. The particular way in which the document would be analyzed would depend on both what the students were asked to do and the nature of the information, ideas, words, terms, concepts, language style, and so forth. Consider the difference between analyzing the Bill of Rights for its attention to specific aspects in the lives of eighteenth-century people or for its specification of federal power. Consider analyzing "The Charge of the Light Brigade" for its metaphors ("the valley of death,") or for its details of a military strategy.

In these cases we can see that analyses are quite different in nature. Doing them requires not only practice in breaking down things and focusing on specific pieces or features but also some understanding, schemata, or knowledge of the ideas one is asked to consider. Analyzing poetry is not necessarily the same process as analyzing a nation's constitution, although both are written documents. Different types of analysis are greatly influenced by the knowledge the student has of the content being addressed. To be even more dramatic: Compare statistical analysis to document analysis.

We are not suggesting that various types of analysis are not worthwhile, only that we cannot assume that transfer readily occurs across contexts. See the article by Perkins and Salomon (1987) for a discussion of the problems of transfer. Teachers must pay particular attention to the kinds of *focusing* they require of students in each context. They should certainly provide many varied opportunities for analyzing, comparing, contrasting, observing, and collecting information. However, they should specifically show students the similarities (and the differences) in these different contexts. Teachers must not take for granted that because students were able to perform a certain intellectual process in one context they can do so in another. The great danger is that the teacher will skip an activity that would give good experience in another context, thus short-changing students from getting vital experience with the process and with another somewhat different context.

PATTERN

The human mind is really quite amazing. Virtually simultaneously with focusing on specific pieces, we start putting pieces into *patterns that are meaningful to us*. A pattern is our way of making sense out of a very complex world or a complicated mass of information. We all continually *create* patterns from everything around us, synthesizing what we selectively focus on or perceive. These patterns are meaningful wholes. Pulling ideas, data, or information together is crucial to our daily lives. If we didn't do this, we would be swamped with scattered and random information in such volume and complexity that it would paralyze us.

When you are being bombarded with information, you will try to organize it into patterns that are based on your own experience or schemata. Recall the example from the series of cards. Trying to figure out what comes next in the series meant that you had to create a pattern. But what possible patterns did you conceive of? Any possible pattern you thought of was based in some way on your own past experiences.

Consider what happened in your mind when you thought that you knew what the rule or patterns for the series was. You could compare the next example in the series to the hypothesis you had in mind. Notice how this is a definite shift in your thinking: from focusing on bits of information to making a guess, hunch, or hypothesis that can be tested through more examples. This kind of thinking—observing phenomena or collecting data, trying to see patterns, and then generating hypotheses that you can test—is an important part of inquiry, which we will discuss in the chapters on science and social studies.

Let's look at a different way to form patterns, categorizing.

Following is a list of creatures in alphabetical order. The task is to arrange them into meaningful categories. Simply put things together that you feel ought to go together *based on a good reason*. You should be able to explain the reasons for your groupings. To assist the students with sorting, make sets of index cards that each have the name of one creature.

abalone	amoeba	anaconda
anemone	angel fish	barnacle
beaver	black widow spider	blue whale

butterfly	carpenter ant	catfish
centipede	clam	crocodile
eagle	earthworm	fluke
frog	gila monster	honeybee
hummingbird	hydra	iguana
kangaroo	king crab	Kodiak bear
krill	lobster	millipede
moose	ostrich	oyster
panda	penguin	rattlesnake
salamander	scallop	shrimp
snail	sponge	starfish
tarantula	tiger	toad
wasp	yak	zebra

If you have done the task (or at least really thought about what categories you would use), try to come up with a completely different set of categories or a different category system.

This activity is best done with a small group of three or four students working together with one set of cards. They stimulate each other's thinking. Also, it is rare that one person knows what all these creatures are. Asking for additional ways to categorize pushes students who quickly create one simple system. It also allows other (perhaps more thoughtful students) to feel less rushed.

Students may come up with some pretty strange ways to group these creatures, such as by the number of syllables or by names that start with vowels. That is acceptable for a first try, but then students should be gently urged to think about the creatures' characteristics, features, habits, and so forth.

This activity obviously draws on students' previous knowledge. There will undoubtedly be some creatures that none of the students will know. Having a category called ''We don't know what this is!'' is quite reasonable. You probably had a set of creatures yourself that you weren't sure of.

The point of this initial activity is not to see who can re-create the standard scientific taxonomy (even though the teacher certainly can get some good diagnostic information about what the students seem to know). The point is to allow for the type of thinking that creates meaningful patterns and then to follow up by examining the *concepts* that are at the base of each pattern. For instance, some students will undoubtedly arrange the list into air, water, and land creatures (a kind of ''where they live'' system). We may think this simplistic, but it was the major system used for a long time by the classical Greeks and is a very good, commonsense look at some obvious phenomena. These three categories can generate some excellent questions related to key concepts. For example,

> Do you mean where they actually live? (Birds don't really live in the air). What you're getting at is more what they are capable of doing. Birds are capable of flying. But what is ''flying''? Do flying squirrels fly? Examining the concept of flying or flight for creatures or humans (hang-gliders?) can be very worthwhile.

This simple three-category system also has some inconsistencies because some creatures are equally at home in the water or only land (such as frogs) or enjoy both water and land (such as seals). What about birds that don't fly (such as penguins)? You can have the students carefully think through a set of questions that forces them to go back and forth between focusing on characteristics and possible categories (or patterns).

What about those students who know a good deal about the standard taxonomy? They might start out suggesting categories like "amphibians." That is just fine. There is plenty of work here to do with any group of student in *clearly establishing the key criteria for the concept.* Exactly what determines whether or not a creature is an amphibian or any of the other classes of zoology: amphibia, annelida (worms), arachnida, aves (birds), coelentrata, crustacea, echinodermata, insecta, mammalia, mollusca, myriopoda, pisces (fish), prochordata, protozoa, reptilia, and spongidae (sponges)? Making clear distinctions among creatures in terms of these categories is often quite difficult. For instance, try this set of follow-up questions:

- To what category would a creature belong that lays eggs with a leathery outside covering?
- To what category would a creature belong that lives in a burrow in the bank of a river?
- To what category would a creature belong that has a venom-filled spur on its hind leg?
- To what category would a creature belong that has webbed feet and a bill-like snout?

Notice how these questions are going in the opposite direction from the first task. Rather than characterizing by name (and anything else one might know about them), this task requires thinking through whether or not the characteristic described fits into the pattern of each of the categories (or concepts).

A variation on this activity is to have the students create creatures—to make up their own outlandish organisms. If each student made up two or three, you'd have quite a menagerie! You could write down basic descriptions and reproduce them for the class. Next, have them imagine being the first explorers on a distant planet and finding these beasts. The students then have to "taxonomize" them into a reasonable set of classes.

Of course, besides the concept of class, the scientific taxonomy also has the concepts of phylum, orders, families, genera, and species. A rather dazzling array of over a million and a half species have been organized. The concepts of our category systems are crucial in making sense of this enormous complexity of organisms.

Were you curious about the answers to the four questions? The four characteristics are lay leathery eggs, burrows in a bank, has a venom-filled spur, has webbed feet and billed snout. There is only one category. The four characteristics all pertain to the same creature. Now to what class does it belong? We'll tell you at the end of the section.

Another key aspect of discerning patterns is drawing inferences. Inferential thinking involves putting together individual bits of information to derive a greater meaning than what one might expect form merely focusing on the bits themselves. When reading a passage, we infer a great deal; that is, we derive much more meaning than a literal interpretation of the words. This kind of thinking is the basis for much of our communication as a species; irony, connotations, allusions, satire, and puns require that we pull together a special meaning that is more than the simple information presented. For instance, the series of children's books focusing on the character Amelia Redelia depends heavily on the misunderstanding of phrases (e.g., planting bulbs—flowers or light bulbs?).

Summarizing is an excellent activity because it requires students to pull together the most important features of something into a coherent pattern. For instance, students could provide a caption for a cartoon or a title for a story that conveys the major point or message. For a broad task, they would summarize the changing of seasons according to the most important features. Or they could summarize a newspaper article or the plot of a movie. If you want a truly weird task, ask your students to give you a summary of *Pee Wee's Big Adventure*.

Another kind of inferential thinking is drawing a conclusion, in which we also take pieces of information and synthesize them into a meaningful idea that is greater than the separate pieces. For instance, dropping objects off a tower and noting that they all take about the same time to fall, regardless of differences in weight, might lead to a variety of conclusions about our world (or the concept of gravity).

Inferences and conclusions, like other entities we are calling patterns, depend heavily on our schemata. If a student has erroneous ideas, misconceptions, or an "immature" schema regarding the material you are teaching, he will probably not infer or conclude from data what you, the teacher, expect. It seems that students (and adults) are frequently highly selective in what they focus on in order to *confirm their existing, ill-conceived schemata*. An inference that seems obvious to us simply won't occur to someone who doesn't have the requisite knowledge or accurate schemata. Consider the following:

A car is heading directly toward a very steep cliff at 50 miles per hour. Which drawing in Figure 2.3 accurately shows the path of its fall?

What schema will your students draw on in answering this question? If they have watched a lot of Saturday morning cartoons, they might pick drawing A, in which the car goes straight out and them straight down. Unfortunately, Wily Coyote (or his animator) doesn't know much about our world. Drawing B is also incorrect. Once the car leaves the cliff, gravity begins to pull it toward the rocks below; it does not continue straight out at all, nor would it go straight down. Drawing C correctly

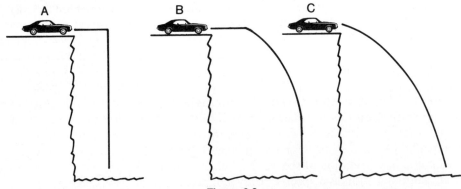

Figure 2.3

shows how the car's forward momentum while still on the cliff and gravity combine to ensure a lovely parabolic curve. The shape of the curve will vary according to the takeoff speed of the car.

You could have older students actually draw the path of descent for themselves. Then put them in groups to discuss their answers and come up with a group decision on the actual path. Discussing theoretical explanations or trying small experiments could be encouraged.

In many ways, real learning takes place only when an existing schema is either modified to handle richer, more complex ideas or replaced with a more powerful conception or way of thinking about the content. There is a wonderful, dynamic relationship among what a student focuses on, what pieces are put together, what patterns she sees, and what schema exists. Notice how seemingly simple information can be synthesized and resynthesized quickly in the following activity.

Here is a list of fifteen characteristics that describe three common objects. There are five characteristics for each object, but these fifteen are scrambled. What are the objects?

   1. Some are rare and expensive; others are discarded.
   2. It can be dissolved.
   3. It has various numbers on it.
   4. It is rubbed on the skin.
   5. Early versions took years to produce.
   6. It may be powered by electricity, batteries, or mechanics.
   7. Some are worn as jewelry.
   8. It is made primarily of sodium tallowate.
   9. Its main parts are usually held together with glue.
   10. Early versions used sand and sun.
   11. Its main parts may vary in thickness.
   12. It gets smaller with use.
   13. It is more used in industrial than primitive societies.
   14. It is solid, but it can also be liquid or powder.
   15. It comes in many different sizes and colors.

This is not an easy task, yet we've found that fifth-graders working in groups can do it. We put these fifteen pieces of information on separate cards and let the students shuffle them around until they find five that really seem to fit together (synthesis). We usually let them think for a while before adding another key criterion for their patterns; all three objects could fit into a briefcase, which we have in the classroom. With that datum in mind, what are the objects?

Of course, this is much too complex for younger children. However, they can begin to synthesize information, carefully considering two characteristics at once. What has legs? Students will suggest some possibilities. What has leaves? Some more possibilities. What has legs and also has leaves? Students will have a good idea if their schema for table includes the kind that slides open to allow another piece to be added to its top.

Older children can readily synthesize five pieces of information for the same object. However, they often want to base their guess on a synthesis of only two or three. They resist carefully comparing their guess to all available data (all five characteristics). You should ask, Does your guess fit all five? What else might also fit these five?

Here are five characteristics that fit the same object.

1. It has movable parts.
2. It is designed to provide intellectual enjoyment.
3. It is made of plastic.
4. It is the first in a line of similar objects.
5. It can be taken apart with a screwdriver.

In this case, as in all others, we have purposely chosen characteristics so that no one alone will obviously suggest the object. For each characteristic many different objects are possible. What comes to mind will depend on what schemata you activate for various words. What does "intellectual enjoyment" suggest? Not the same things for different people. Only when the five clues are taken together will the object be imagined. We will tell you below.

This type of synthesizing activity can be used with a wide variety of contexts: famous people, historical events, creatures, locations (cities, states, countries, continents), or even concepts. When used in the context of a curriculum, the activity will have more to draw on than this isolated example of common objects. You can help students by giving them feedback on their guesses. When they have synthesized one correctly (even if it was based on only four actual characteristics and one from a different set), we tell them yes. Often the one erroneous clue has a bit of ambiguity. We then put the correct fifth card together with its other four in front of them. This replacement allows the student to continue with only ten cards to determine the remaining two objects.

The first three objects mixed together at the beginning of this activity are a book, a bar of soap, and a clock. They are based on the following clues: (1, 5, 9, 11, 15); (2, 4, 8, 12, 14); and (3, 6, 7, 10, 13). The last object, with just five clues, is a Rubik's Cube.

Changing existing schemata usually requires more than merely presenting or explaining a new way to think about something. New ideas need grappling hooks in order to take hold of the existing structures. Even the most brilliant lecture will be only partially understood (let alone remembered) if it does not make connections with the ideas that are already there in the minds of the audience.

What grappling hooks can a teacher use? We have found that you can go a long way with activities that have an initial novelty, an unusual premise that perplexes, puzzles, and challenges. Sometimes the novel, strange, and unfamiliar go beyond merely grabbing students' attention. They can *confront* existing schema with inconsistencies that cannot be readily ignored. Many science demonstrations offer such possibilities. For instance, consider the following demonstration.

Get two beakers of slightly different sizes so that the base of the larger can completely cover the mouth of the smaller. Place four or five mothballs (naphthalene) in the smaller beaker and place it on a ring stand; slowly heat this beaker with an alcohol burner below the stand. Fill the larger beaker half full with cold water and stack it on top of the mouth of the smaller beaker. Leave the burner on until all the mothballs are melted. Then blow out the burner and wait for 10 to 15 minutes. Lift the larger beaker and examine its bottom; crystals will have formed. Ask the students to describe what they observed int his demonstration. Ask them to explain what happened. What purpose did the cold water serve in the top beaker? When the mothballs are heated, they change from a solid to a liquid (and even directly to a gas). Going directly from solid to gas or vice versa is called *sublimation*. In this activity, naphthalene crystals will form on the bottom of the beaker because the cold water causes sublimation of the gas.

This little demonstration will provoke a fair amount of puzzlement that can lead to inquiry on crystals. There are many simple ways for students to create crystals by heating highly saturated solutions of salt, sugar, alum, or copper sulfate and then letting them cool slowly.

By the way, what is the strange creature with the venom-filled spur, leathery eggs, and so on? Were you able to synthesize the characteristics? It is the duck-billed platypus, a marsupial mammal that confused scientists for years.

EXTENSION

In this section we want to go beyond the basic intellectual processes of focus and pattern to more complicated kinds of thinking. We call these kinds of thinking *extension* because they extend and build on the analyzing, comparing, contrasting, classifying, inferring, organizing, and so on that we introduced earlier. In more complex thinking, students can handle a variety of tasks that require them to apply directly what they know or can do—to use their knowledge, to generalize, make decisions, and solve problems.

Also, students can be helped to extend their thinking across contexts and subject areas. The elementary school curriculum is remarkably diverse, interactive, and complicated. For instance, when fourth-graders are engaged in studying science, they are using a wide variety of skills, thinking processes, and schemata. They must be able to comprehend ideas they read in the textbook. They will probably encounter graphs, charts, measurements, and other material requiring mathematical knowledge. Although the later chapters of this book mainly focus on single subjects, we are well aware of the potential for interrelating aspects of the curriculum. In this section we will look at extending the thinking processes themselves.

Experience and Intelligence

As children get older, they become more capable of doing increasingly complex intellectual tasks. Psychologists have not really figured out how all the various factors are related. Clearly, just raw experience with more and different kinds of things, people, and ideas plays some role, but it is not enough by itself. Some kind of "mediation" by more knowledgeable adults and other children is important—giving feedback, suggestions, explaining, and so forth. Those who follow Piaget's theories believe that there are definite stages of thinking that each child must go through; the child simply cannot do certain types of thinking unless he has gone through prior stages. Others believe that the notion of invariant stages is too rigid and that children are able to do more complex thinking earlier than we give them credit for; see the book by Margaret Donaldson (1979), for example.

Along with various conceptions and theories about intellectual development, there is a wide variety of notions about "intelligence." Some psychologists see it as innate, its limit set biologically at birth. Some see it as a specific kind of reasoning ability, others as multifaceted. For an excellent overview of current theories about intelligence, see the book edited by Sternberg and Detterman (1986). We will mention only a few here.

In the theory proposed by Rueven Feuerstein (1979), intelligence is an ability to learn from experience with mediation. If I ask a child to try a certain task and see that he cannot do it, I then teach him how to do it. If he then shows that he has learned it, he has demonstrated that he is more intelligent than another child of similar age and background who did not learn it from my teaching. Of course, this is an oversimplification and the nature of the task is critical. But notice how different this idea of intelligence is from that in the familiar IQ test, in which the task is something that I expect most children of the same age to be able to do.

Two other current theories contrast sharply with the idea of a single, general intelligence. One theory, suggested by Robert Sternberg (1986), looks at several different components of intelligence: control processes that examine the nature of the task, performance processes for working on the task, and processes for acquiring new knowledge. These components interact dramatically with a person's social and cultural context and with the way that person handles new experiences. The other theory espouses seven quite different kinds of intelligence, only some of which would fit under most people's conception of the term (linguistic, logical-mathematical, spatial, musical, bodily-kinesthetic, and personal—inward and outward). See Howard Gardner's *Frames of Mind* (1983).

This book could not possibly do justice to these many different theories and points of view. However, it is our belief that psychology and education are at an important juncture, and we must discard some of our dysfunctional beliefs about how children learn and develop. For instance, it is clear that children can and do learn a tremendous amount form one another. Discussing ideas, defending points of view, arguing over facts, and so forth are marvelous (and perhaps quite necessary) intellectual and interpersonal experiences. The intellectual processes we have been describing (and others to follow) do not have to be seen purely as those of an individual alone, thinking. Instead, we would like you to think of them as processes that can be shared. In fact, the sharing of one's thinking may be particularly valuable and necessary for the development of certain key intellectual processes, as we shall see shortly.

Student Collaboration

If sharing of one's intellectual processes with others is valuable, how can the teacher help this to occur? Consider the two most prevalent acts in teaching: (1) presenting, explaining, and lecturing, and (2) leading a class discussion with questioning. In the first, students are not encouraged to express their thinking: in the second, several of the twenty-five students express their thinking while the others listen.

Today we are seeing in classrooms a dramatic resurgence of another way to stimulate and share thinking: students working cooperatively in small groups of two, three, four, or five on many different kinds of tasks. In writing, they may be using "peer conferences" to help one another revise their stories. In social studies, they may be conducting an investigation of some community problem. In reading or language arts, they may be sharing their different interpretations of a story. In mathematics, they may be collaborating on solving a word problem. In science, they may be designing an experiment. In each situation, the students are working on some task that is cognitively appropriate (neither way over their heads nor beneath them). Also, the task is an integral part of the curriculum; it is not for fun, play, or the traditional enrichment as a supplement. The small-group work is not a break from "real" learning. The task has been selected or designed either by the teacher or by the students to be a challenging part of the curriculum.

Collaborative student groups generally provoke discussion about the grouping of students by ability. It is rather common practice in elementary schools to group students by their ability in reading and math. What we have in mind is quite different. Many educators have realized the value of more flexible groupings of students, arranging them into temporary work groups for 20 minutes for a brief activity or longer for more extensive activities. Also, in math and reading, we see more frequent use of flexible task groups, a small group of students who have a common need, such as working on a specific skill. Intensive work for a few lessons for a few days might be all that is necessary, rather than staying together for a marking period (or a year) as a homogeneous group.

One model for fostering collaborative small groups of students has been developed by David W. Johnson and Roger T. Johnson (1987) and Johnson, Johnson, and Holubec (1986). Students work in cooperative learning groups in which the goals of the tasks are structured to foster positive *interdependence:* Each member of the group has to be concerned about the work of all members. The groups are heterogeneous in ability and personal characteristics, and all members share responsibility for group functioning, leadership, and performance as well as the achievement of the individual members. The teacher helps the groups learn how to function well: developing good working relations among members, developing social skills (leadership, communication, building trust, conflict resolution, finding consensus), and structuring procedures to discuss how well they are collaborating.

As worthwhile as social and cooperative skills may be in their own right, our purpose in discussing collaborative work groups is to show their value for provoking intellectual discussion. Wrestling with ideas is perhaps best done with others. Seriously considering an idea, explaining an inference, defending an opinion, carefully thinking through implications, and the like are stimulated by interaction.

Teachers can make the curriculum come alive and draw on students' interest and motivation by developing ways for them to engage in

- Decision making
- Problem solving
- Conducting investigations and inquiries

These terms cover a lot of territory. Like others we have used, they may mean quite different things to different people. Before discussing them, let us offer a sample activity.

In this activity the student should come to understand the community in which they live *by using key concepts* that they have begun to study. Community studies can make these concepts come alive and be concrete referents in the children's lives.

You may choose from the curriculum an initial list of concepts, topics, and themes that lead to key aspects of social studies. For instance, studying different civilizations may require an understanding of such concepts as government, architecture, technology, and so forth. Studying states in the United States can profit from understanding branches of government, transportation systems, municipal services, and taxation.

Using an initial list and additional topics or concepts suggested by the students, arrange the children into small work groups of three to five to focus on one of the topics. The group will gather information about its topic in order to put together some kind of presentation of its findings for the other groups.

Depending on the grade, ages, and abilities of the students, you may provide varying amounts of structure and resources. For instance, younger children may need you to provide some initial questions to ask, things to find out, sources for more information, or places to visit with their parents. For older students, a major aspect of their learning and thinking can involve formulating and deciding these activities.

For instance, with a group of fifth-graders who are investigating municipal services, deciding what is or what is not to be included is a major and important subtask. Establishing their own thoughtful criteria for what is included should not be short-circuited by the teacher. Brainstorming ideas for how to get information, where to go, to whom to talk, and so forth is extremely worthwhile.

You should set a time limit on this activity that is reasonable for the students' interest and attention span since the task is somewhat open-ended and could extend for a long time.

The next phase of the activity is extremely important. When the groups report to one another, we encourage a particular process of *debriefing* that encourages maximum involvement from all groups. When one group presents, the other groups must listen (or take notes, if appropriate) because every group will then meet for a period of time to generate a list of propositions about the topic. A proposition is a declarative statement formulating a conclusion such as "If businesses moved away from our town and the buildings were empty, we would lose tax money." Obviously, these ideas (propositions, conclusions, inferences) may vary greatly in abstraction. Some may be quite factual, others more conceptual.

Each group should discuss what they heard (or saw) from the presenting group and *by consensus* decide on the five (or more, if you want) important propositions. Consensus means discussing and refining ideas (or their wording) until everyone in the group can agree, not simply voting, which usually suppresses ideas and opinions of a few. These statements should be written down, if appropriate for that grade.

Each group reads its propositions, and you can then lead the class in a discussion of them. At this point, the group who investigated the topic plays a major role in reacting to the ideas of the other groups. You can have this group generate its own list, if desired. However, we have had success with having this group list the surprising, unexpected, or particularly unusual ideas they learned from the investigation. If this group is asked to do the same kind of list as the others, there is a tendency for students to view them as the experts and to defer to them, rather than really thinking about the ideas.

Your task in the group discussion is to help the students move beyond the simple, factual level. Propositions, like concepts, should help organize facts. For older students, the teacher can make distinctions between the more concrete and factual statements on students' lists and the more abstract and conceptual. Both can be praised or acknowledged while helping the students recognize the differences and striving for more conceptual propositions. Thus, you can help the students to *restate or reconstruct* their propositions. Various propositions can be integrated and merged.

For instance, the previous proposition on businesses moving away could be combined with "Schools depend on property taxes for most of their money" for a more general and abstract statement about how the tax base of community supports municipal services. Note that such a proposition synthesizes ideas from two different themes or groups. It is exactly this kind of synthesis that you are trying to attain in the discussion, which can draw the students back to the larger contexts of the curriculum. What are the major themes or concepts from the curriculum that you can help the students understand more fully by this activity? You have to judge how much to intervene with shaping the ideas of the discussion. We feel that intervention should be as minimal as possible to allow the students the time and freedom to think. Tolerating silence and allowing reasonable tangents are better than premature interruption that signals that they can stop thinking (because you will now tell them).

The presentation, followed by the small-group listing and ensuing discussion, can be time consuming but valuable. Usually only one of these can be done in a day, and thus, it may take a week or so for all the groups to present. Each successive group presentation and listing will yield more complex discussions, so that after the last group presents, a powerful synthesizing can and should occur.

To have the students pull together their ideas, as a last step, you may ask each group to develop some propositions that truly synthesize or at least combine various themes. They should be trying to conceive of the most significant or important things that they have learned from this activity. Again, they should develop this list from consensus. Such group collaboration on this culminating activity is necessary because of the breadth of what was addressed across the various groups and the time that has elapsed during the presentations. Although the debriefing discussions tend to be cumulative, building on and integrating each other, groups remember more than individuals in this activity.

From this example, you can see that our idea of extension goes quite beyond a simple application; it is meant to be substantial. This activity melds together the various terms of extension: decision making, problem solving, inquiring, investigating, and so on. It starts with a task or set of questions that you hope will intrigue students. It spins off from what they have been studying but doesn't merely call for summarizing what they have already learned. They must build on it and use it in some way.

Of course, extensions don't have to be done in groups. They can be done by individual students stretching themselves beyond a simplistic, knee-jerk application or decision. The key is that they require real *thought,* the kind of intellectual wrestling that we have been talking about. Through extensions the students become actively involved in the complexities of life and learning.

Another way to illustrate our concern here is to consider the idea of a problem. The field of problem solving is extremely diverse. People have very different definitions of what constitutes a problem. For us, a problem is a question or task that has neither a simple answer nor an obvious way to solve it. It should be a task or question that perplexes and intrigues, creating a desire to explore or attack. We are especially fond of problems that have clearly identifiable components of real life or are related to existing schemata of the students. However, we know that some exciting problems can draw on unusual and imaginative (unreal, or at least novel) situations. Consider the following different kinds of problems.

---

1. Get two cans of soups that are the same size and weight. One should be very thick (like tomato) and the other more watery (like vegetable). Find or make a long and not very steep incline—about 12 feet long at a 20 degree angle. If you roll the two cans down in a fair race, will they arrive at the same time or will one arrive sooner?

The students should explain and justify their answers and then roll the cans. Even if the vegetable soup starts to pull away after a few feet, the tomato will overtake it and clearly win the race to the bottom of the incline. Now ask the students *why?*

2. Five families are going to car-pool to and from school next year. From looking at the calendar, each of the five days in the week are equally represented over the 185 days of school. For various reasons (which you can supply), some days are good and some are bad for each family. But each family wants to have the same day all year long (so they won't get confused or forget). The Browns can not drive on Monday, Wednesday, or Friday. The Schmidts can drive Wednesday or Thursday. Monday or Tuesday are possible for the Randalls. Mr. Gross can to it on either Tuesday or Friday. Wednesday or Friday is fine with the Opolous family. Figure out the schedule.

3. Consider the Hanging Gardens of Babylon, one of the Seven Wonders of the ancient world. These were terraced gardens of incredible beauty. Babylon itself was magnificent. Its 196 square miles included beautiful architecture, palaces, temples, and towers, enclosed by walls 200 feet high and 187 feet thick at the base. The city was considered impregnable.

Today we can find the remains of many ancient cities; some have even continued to exist, but not Babylon. Nothing remains but some heaps of rubbish. The Great Wall of China, not nearly as large or as strong or as recent as the immense walls of Babylon, still stands; yet there are not even remnants of the walls of Babylon. The rich, fertile land that once supported thousands of people is now utterly desolate.

What happened to Babylon that it should virtually disappear from the face of the earth?

Can you see some similarities in these examples? Although there are some definite differences, they give an idea of the kinds of questions or problems that start children thinking. Some teachers (for instance, in social studies) think of these as "inquiries" or "investigations." Science teachers may think of them as demonstrations that lead to "experiments." Math teachers would pose problems for solving. In later chapters, we will explain and give examples of problem solving and inquiry in each of the content areas of the curriculum.

Notice that each example requires definite thought; none can be simply solved or answered. Each requires a plan of attack or problem-solving strategy to be developed. There may be more than one right answer. For us, the *intellectual processes* involved in working on these tasks is what is important. Therefore, it is crucial that the students become interested in and want to work on tasks like these, which are messy, complicated, and time consuming.

When setting up problem solving or inquiry, there are several key dimensions to keep in mind. For each dimension there are a set of issues to consider or decisions for you to make.

1. The students' foundation: What are their skills, schemata, previous activities? What am I (and they) going to build on conceptually?
2. The introduction to the activity: How am I going to set it up? What is the purpose? How is the task going to appeal intellectually to the students? How much do I structure the task for them?
3. The workforce: Will students work as individuals, in small groups, or as a whole class?
4. Key questions and conclusions: Do I formulate the key questions or let the students generate their own? Do I want to encourage a variety of conclusions or one primary one? What form should the conclusions take? How much justification is necessary?
5. The nature of the data and its collection: How much do I organize the data for the students (summary vs. raw data)? Should they collect the raw data themselves? Should I give them the data all at once or in some sequence? How much information should I give in response to their questions? How abstract (vs. concrete or manipulative) should the data be?
6. The time dimension: How much time should I allow for each part in class or at home? Should the work be done in one session or spread over days (weeks)? Where can I compress or stretch the activity while it is happening?

Most of the ideas mentioned in these dimensions are self-explanatory. However, we will describe how some might be dealt with by using the preceding activities and examples.

Note how the community studies activity made some definite decisions about each of these dimensions. (Your may want to reread the activity.) It was supposed to build directly on topics or concepts that already had been worked on to some extent. It allowed the teacher to vary the specificity of the questions and the resources according to the age of the children. It required students to collect their own data, but the teacher was responsible for moving students' ideas to increasingly abstract conceptions. It encouraged out-of-class data collection and took place over perhaps two weeks or more.

In the example of the soup cans, what do the students know about objects that roll? What concepts are part of their world? Friction? Acceleration? Gravity? How would you get them started on this task? Would you supply a variety of things that roll? Would you have them bring things in? Do you want to suggest possible factors that might influence how fast an object rolls? Would you suggest certain experiments they might conduct? How much do they understand about holding some factors constant while varying others? Do you want to help them structure some experimental trials? Should the whole class decide on a particular set of experiments to perform or should small groups of two, three, or four individuals? Should all experiments be done in class with a standard incline? And so on.

In the problem of the car pool, how would your students *conceive* of what is going on? That is, what is their conception of a car pool? Are there other terms or concepts that might be confusing or for which they did not have an adequate schema? Would you have them discuss the problem to make sure everyone understood what was being asked? Would you have them work in small groups? If so, would the groups discuss what they thought the problem called for? In this example, all the data are given. But what assumptions ought to be made? How students formulate strategies and analyze the data will depend on their understanding and assumptions. Is there one right answer? How does this problem fit in with the curriculum? What prior work has been done with problem-solving strategies?

In the example of Babylon's demise, how does the history of this civilization fit into the curriculum? What are the students' conceptions and beliefs about this region and its peoples (Assyrians, Sumerians, Chaldeans, Hittites, Hebrews, Egyptians, Persians—and later, the Greeks and Romans)? How do they conceive of the time frame of thousands of years? In this example, perhaps the key aspects of structuring deal with multiple causes and varieties of evidence. There is no one simple answer, and they must consider several sources for data. Then they must consider how we evaluate the data. How do people of the 1980s learn about events and people thousands of years before us? Finally, in this example, you have to consider what kinds of resources and data to provide.

Extensions do not have to be as complex as these examples. Of course, the point is to help students use and apply their intellectual capabilities to analyze, compare, contrast, and synthesize with their existing schema to successively more complicated problems, questions, and situations. Therefore, teachers of different grades in a school should discuss how they are structuring inquiry to encourage a progression through the grades. Likewise, within a school year a teacher should increase the complexity of the tasks asked of students. Finally, our experience has shown that students become increasingly able not only to structure the tasks and collect their own data but also to design their own inquiries. We have seen many students, especially in the upper primary grades, deciding for themselves the inquiries that they believe are worthwhile to conduct. This kind of thinking and learning is the essence of education. We include this notion of design in the next section.

PROJECTION

In this section we describe several complex intellectual processes that are similar to those we described as extension, but with a major difference. Projection involves kinds of thinking that *diverge* from the direction application of what has been learned into new and creative expressions and understandings. In projection, students are encouraged to engage in

- Imagining
- Expressing
- Creating
- Inventing
- Designing

In each subject area there should be opportunities for students to think and explore new (and perhaps unusual) conceptions, metaphors, analogies, perspectives, ideas, problems, and situations. They should be encouraged to create their own representations or models and express their ideas and understanding in a variety of ways. Since cognition itself is largely a process of *constructing* meaning and understanding in personal ways, it is very important for teachers to encourage students' discussing, writing, and sharing their own conceptions. As we stated earlier, students confronting one another's beliefs and conceptions are dramatically powerful in facilitating changes in schemata.

Students should be encouraged to designed their own inquiries, formulate their own questions, and create their own criteria for decisions. This may sound like a tall order for younger children and potentially chaotic for older ones. However, if this kind of intellectual process is valuable, we should be working toward it continually. Teachers at each grade level should be discussing with one another how to help students think indpendently of the teacher, assume more responsibility for their own learning, become more self-directed, and become more able to decide what project to do and go on to do it.

Before going any further with these grand ideas, let us illustrate our sense of projection with an activity.

Arrange the students into small groups of three, four, or five. Each group has the same basic assignment: to develop a set of propositions about their world in the future. You can direct their work by having them propose what schools will be like, or home life, sports, buildings, communication, and so forth. Similarly, you can ask them to consider a particular time period, such as the year 2000.

Propositions are the kinds of statements we discussed earlier. For instance, a group of students may state that "In the year 2000, the center of each home in the United States will be a multimedia entertainment room." Each group must develop a list of propositions (five or ten). They do not have to write a paper. Instead, they must be able to explain clearly each proposition to the other groups and the teacher in discussion or presentation; they would elaborate, clarify, and describe how they came up with this idea. They would also have to be able to defend the proposition, showing their thinking and evidence. Thus, student interaction across groups would be fostered.

To ensure that all members of the group contribute to the thinking and thoroughly understand each proposition, it should be made explicit that anyone in the group may be called on to explain or defend any proposition from that group. Thus, the group is discouraged from farming out topics or having resident experts. One person may do the background research, but all members must be knowledgeable concerning the proposition. Each proposition represents an actual consensus of the entire group since anyone may be called on to answer questions about it.

Where do the ideas originate for the propositions? The teacher can pose the task in a variety of ways to build on the ideas and material that the students have been using. For instance, if their social studies material has been dealing with the states or the countries of North America, you may want to suggest that they generate propositions about transportation or types of housing in different climates. If you've been studying about hospitals or health education, you might suggest propositions on medicine or health care. Just about any theme from literature can be spun off into imaginable futures—family life, peer relations, friendships. By building on the ideas and materials they have been using, you are getting them to think about these concepts in a different and perhaps powerful way.

You may also want to point them toward a variety of resources outside of the classroom or school. Certainly there are many ideas and predictions for the future in books, magazines, and newspapers; so libraries of all kinds (school, public, home) may be valuable. You may give them articles to read in which people from "think tanks" have made suggestions.

Since each group is working independently, each may come up with quite different propositions. There is no right answer. It is the process of generating ideas and examining resources by the group members that is important. Some groups may need help in deciding on a plan of action. Some may need help in collaborating with one another.

The initial work on this project should be done in class under your supervision. However, some groups may want to meet after school or on weekends. This is acceptable if they are ready to work without the kind of assistance that makes sure they understand what the task is, have some ideas for the resources needed, and have decided what each member will do (sharing the workload).

Since the overall task has no one right answer, students could work on it indefinitely. Interest wanes quickly with younger children, and a week (five in-class sessions and a weekend, if they want it) is about right for third- or fourth-graders.

When the groups meet to report on propositions (debriefing), it is usually best to have copies of each group's propositions available for all to read. Groups (or a spokesperson) can initially present and explain a proposition. From then on, you and any other student may ask questions of the group about this proposition. You may want to group together similar (or contradictory) propositions from different groups to facilitate the discussion.

The climate for this discussion is important. After cooperative work within each group, there may be a tendency for competitiveness between groups. By "defending" propositions, we do not mean for you or the students to "attack." Rather, simply to tell what the students think the future will be like is insufficient; they must also clearly show their thinking, how they came to that (these) conclusion(s) and the basis for their assertion. Although there may be no one right answer, there are some propositions that may be based on more substance, more suggestive evidence, than others; also some may be more carefully considered, more discussed, and more researched than others.

One way for teachers to initiate a good discussion and careful consideration of each presented proposition is to tell students that the purpose of the debriefing is to come up with some large propositions that the whole class can agree to. This idea pushes all the students into a kind of cooperative synthesis of the propositions. Usually several themes emerge, such as "high tech" versus "high touch" (interpersonal relations)—people still need people, even with great gadgets.

We encourage a second debriefing about the process by which each group worked on the task. The students should think about and discuss how they got ideas, found resources, worked together, and made decisions. This kind of debriefing solidifies the learning about the content and about the processes of thinking and collaborating.

This project melds together the various aspects of extension and projection: Students are applying their knowledge, making decisions, and inquiring, but they are also designing their own investigation of the ideas, creatively imagining possibilities, and so forth. The activity starts with a task or question that you hope will intrigue students. It spins off from what they have been studying but doesn't merely call for summarizing what they have already learned. They must build on it and apply it in a creative way. They can draw on a breadth of experiences that each group member has had (e.g., EPCOT, movies, science fiction).

Perhaps the most difficult part of the task is deciding exactly what they should do, how they should approach the task, and what the teacher wants. A host of decisions must be made and real-life problems addressed. Since they will have to gather some background materials or find evidence to support their own ideas, they have to decide who will do what. When they begin in earnest to develop propositions and examine materials, major decisions will have to be made by consensus. A thorough hashing over of ideas and how propositions will be stated will have to occur.

The kinds of thinking we consider under the heading of projection should include both creative *processes* and *products*. This means encouraging students to see things in imaginative and unusual ways, using novel approaches, trying the unorthodox and developing innovative conceptions, creating unique expressions, and inventing original concoctions. These intellectual processes have been studied by educators and psychologists who call them by various names, such as divergent production (Guilford, 1977), lateral thinking (DeBono,1970), and creative problem solving (Parnes, 1972). As before, fine distinctions among these terms are not our major concern. There are also a number of *general* methods and techniques that have been put together for fostering this kind of thinking. There are relatively simple devices like brainstorming, in which a group generates as many ideas as possible about the topic or task without evaluating them. Outlandish ideas and an atmosphere of levity are encouraged for volume and creativity. Serious consideration and refinement of ideas can come later. Brainstorming probably can be done more effectively in groups of five or six than with the whole class.

There are more elaborate procedures to help people think in atypical ways, such as *synectics,* which uses emotional and nonrational thought processes to stimulate creativity, insight, and problem solving. Its activities use metaphors, analogies, and oxymorons ("iron butterfly" or creative destruction"—phrases with words that seem to contradict one another) to create something new and make the familiar strange. It has been used by industry to solve problems imaginatively and create inventions and products. See William Gordon's *Synectics (1961).* Teachers have used it to stimulate creativity in prewriting activities. (See the chapter in Joyce and Weils, 1985, on synectics.) In addition, examine the box at the bottom of the page.

Studies of various kinds of creativity (artistic, scientific, etc.) suggest that there has to be a thorough grouding in the raw material that you want to be creative with. People need immersion with the material to be prepared for creative thinking about it, Next, people must have time—some refer to this as *incubation.* You need to be able to think about it in many ways—to mull it over, to let it all sink in, to ruminate (as cows chew their curd). Some even suggest that after intense preparation, you must get away from it all, relax, and let your unconscious mind take over. (See James Adams' *Conceptual Blockbusting, 1979.*)

Schools rarely allow anyone, student or teacher, time to incubate ideas. Somehow schools have equated intelligence with speed—especially the speed of recalling

---

For instance, if the class were about to write a story about their playground, first ask, "In what ways is the playground like a circus?" Write on the board key phrases that they suggest: "The teacher in charge of recess is like a ringmaster." You only need about ten or so good suggestions for this request and each of the others that follow. Every class member doesn't have to make a suggestion.

Second, ask them to give a weather report about the playground. Again write down key phrases: "Tornado warnings are in effect!" Third, ask them to describe a machine that makes weather. What kind of machines could create the weather conditions listed? How would they work? Fourth, ask them to imagine being that machine. What it would feel like? Again, write down their ideas.

Fifth, ask them to pick two words from their ideas that "argue with each other." This is a key step, creating a compressed conflict that leads to oxymorons. Two nouns (or noun phrases) can be combined by making one an adjective. *Explosion* versus *tranquility* can become *explosive tranquility* or *tranquil explosiveness.* What images are suggested by this phrase? The incredible potential energy about to be released as storm clouds begin to form?

Sixth, ask them to pick a few of the most unusual phrases that argue with each other (note the dynamism of the expression). Have them suggest some animals that come to mind and explain why.

Now they are ready to write a draft of their stories about the playground. Ask them to think about how they can use all this information to help say something interesting about what life on the playground is like. After the 15 or 20 minutes of generating some pretty wild expressions and images, they will be less likely to use trite, hackneyed expressions. This activity provokes more vivid images and colorful expressions than the dry run. You are priming the pump. Sorry! How about *dynamiting the well?*

factual information. Of course, they had a lot of help from behavioral psychologists. But the lives of acknowledged geniuses clearly demonstrate that the significant problems they have solved or insights they have made were not speedily done.

We believe that schools should be engaging the students in activities instead of lessons. Activities may span days or weeks and contain many parts (perhaps we could call them subactivities). Lessons are begun and ended on the same day, usually within the same hour. But lessons with prearranged steps rarely allow for spontaneous follow-up of creative responses or ideas from students. Furthermore, longer-term activities can allow time for formulating ideas, for thinking carefully and thoughtfully. Realizations and understandings come after processing, thinking through, going over, refining, playing with ideas, discussing, sharing, elaborating, and so forth. These processes can occur within oneself or with others.

Psychologists are still debating exactly what happens in this process of incubation. But is appears that all this mulling over, when the proper preliminary work has been done, can result in *insight*. Of course, psychologists also are still debating what insight is. In a current view espoused by Sternberg (1986), insight involves three separate, interrelated psychological processes: selective encoding (distinguishing between relevant and irrelevant information), selective combination (synthesizing what may appear to be unrelated pieces of information), and selective comparison (relating new information to prior information). Sternberg acknowledges that these are the basic cognitive processes (we called them focus, pattern, and schema) applied in a "nonobvious" or seemingly "inappropriate" way.

Consider the insight in the following example. An adult is trying to cut a candy bar in half for two screaming children. He may perceive the task as essentially mathematical—carefully measuring the candy to get precisely two equal pieces. However, one could see the task as primarily psychological—getting each of the children to be happy with his or her piece after the cut. Thus, the adult could explain to them that one child will cut the candy in half and the other will choose his piece first. The child cutting the candy will be compelled to do it fairly to the eye because the other will surely take an obviously bigger piece. A coin could be flipped to see who makes the cut.

It is our belief that the kinds of creative thinking envisioned under this heading can take place in all subject areas. It may be obvious that writing can be creative or that storytelling, acting, improvisation, and role playing call for creative expression. But consider the possibilities of using projection in social studies: doing dramatic renderings of events, creating photographic or pictorial presentations or collages, conducting mock trials and simulations, or developing and giving a talk by someone from a historical period (not only a famous person but also a regular, common person). How about telling a story from an unusual point of view—what was it like to be a Tory during the American Revolution? What about having students create their own political slogans or cartoons?

In science (as well as in social studies) students can conduct their own investigations that they design themselves. We don't just mean laboratory experiments that you and the book already know the answer to. The Science Olympiad has many wonderful events in which students in multiage work groups have to devise some ways to accomplish intriguing feats, such as encasing a raw egg in some material that will prevent it from breaking when dropped from great heights. Also consider the possibilities for representing phenomena (biological processes, chemical reactions, etc.) in original ways through drawings, cartoons, sketches, and images.

And now mathematics: How in the world can we have students be creative in mathematics? Two basic ways relate to either the thinking process or the product. First, the standard math curriculum of the past has been highly focused on math facts. The only problems to be solved were one-step story problems ("Pencils cost 25 cents apiece; how much will 6 pencils cost?"). Today, it is clear that the tide has turned to math problems that involve much more complex thinking. Problems may have multiple right answers and cannot be solved by applying an algorithm. Teachers (and some publishers) have developed problems that may be attacked by a variety of problem-solving strategies. After helping the students understand the aspects of problem solving, the teacher can encourage creative solutions through uncovering exotic assumptions and using personally meaningful (but not obvious) strategies.

A second kind of creativity in mathematics involves computer applications. Using the LOGO computer language, students have made simple applications of mathematics to screen graphics and created their own often very complex pictures. These pictures are graphical representations of the mathematical tools that were built into the language. However, what the students can create is often absolutely *unique and unanticipated* by the teacher. Students are often quite amazed and excited to think that they could create something unique. A major issue for the teacher is to help the students understand the mathematical concepts and principles that underlie their pictures.

In each of these areas, the role of the teacher is very different from the traditional omniscient provider of information and the right answer. Rather than dispensing information, the teacher facilitates the active formulation of students' own meanings and the creation of their own worlds to explore. We have all been assailed by the child who asks a bizarre question at the wrong time or by the classroom genius who has a better way to describe what we are trying to show the class. These wild ideas and crazy questions can be extremely valuable to the child who utters them as well as to the entire class. Occasionally (or frequently) the wild idea is a truly marvelous way to help the others think about the topic under discussion; it makes a *connection* with their schemata that you had been searching for ("Oh yeah! Recursion is like when you are holding a picture of yourself holding a picture of yourself holding a . . .").

The teacher must establish a climate for creativity. Students have to believe that their own precious ideas are going to be appreciated and respected; that when they speak in the class, they will be listened to, their ideas considered.

All the forms of projection we have mentioned flourish when they are nourished by a friendly, open, and supportive atmosphere. Intensive pressure, criticism, and competition definitely inhibit the flow of ideas, creating narrow and rigid thoughts. Obviously, the teacher must balance openness and order, joviality and seriousness. The noise level may increase, but that may be good indication of active intellectual involvement in the task: organized noise, playful concentration, attentive excitement.

METACOGNITION

In this section we want to discuss some rather dramatic conclusions that cognitive psychologists have drawn about how people become more able to think and learn effectively. Metacognition (literally, *over* or overseeing cognition) refers to our ability to understand and manipulate our own cognitive processes. It involves thinking about our own thinking and purposely making changes in how we think. We have introduced some of the ideas about metacognition in previous sections of this chapter. Here we will directly discuss some of the key aspects of teaching to develop metacognitive abilities in students.

The concept of metacognition has actually been around for many decades (perhaps centuries) although the term was coined rather recently. Certainly, we all know that we can be aware of our own thoughts. We can be conscious of how we tend to think about something, that is, the way in which we habitually think, the usual way we approach a problem.

When a teacher helps students engage in *metacognitive processes* they become more successful learners and more able to take responsibility for the kinds of intellectual processes we have been discussing in this chapter. Metacognitive processes are those in which the individual carefully considers for herself what she is doing and thinking through

- Self-planning or -strategizing
- Self-monitoring or -checking
- Self-regulating
- Self-questioning
- Self-reflecting
- Self-reviewing

The prefix of *self-* is important because we want each student to become increasingly able to engage in these processes willingly, capably, and consciously. In fact, a major part of teaching for thinking is enabling the students to take more responsibility for their own thinking.

As in so many aspects of schooling, teachers have to help children become more aware and more capable, initially providing examples, explanations, assistance support, and suggestions. Over time, with practice and experience, the children acquire the abilities to do more with less guidance from the teacher. The same basic process happens in thinking in metacognition.

Recall the way we described debriefing in previous sections. After an activity (e.g., the futures project), the teacher leads the students in debriefing the content (the propositions and concepts) as well as the processes (the way the group generated ideas, discussed possibilities, and reached decisions). Getting them to reflect directly on how they did what they did makes them more aware of both the interpersonal interactions and the cognitive processes used.

Thus, metacognition is helping students *reflect* on their own thinking. It can be done one to one or in a group. You should carefully think about how to create metacognitive experiences as a part of virtually every activity with children. Seek opportunities for provoking reflection on what they are doing. Just as considering schemata should always be part of your teaching, the potential for metacognition is always present.

Strangely, you do not have to hit the children over the head with metacognitive strategies; instead just build them into content-related activities. For instance, when students are reading stories or passages (or in fact, any potentially meaningful text), you can gently pose questions about the material, asking them to summarize what was just read or what happened or predict what will happen next. In the planning of writing, you can ask students questions to stimulate their thinking about different ideas, angles, or perspectives. We will have more to say about these in the next chapter. Note here that the teacher can model for the students what they should begin to do for themselves: ask themselves key questions and stop and think at key moments about what they are doing.

In mathematical problem solving, students should learn to think through a problem before trying to solve it. This self-checking for initial understanding is crucial. You should model this process with the students to show how to do it and why it is so important. Also, show students a wide variety of *strategies* for solving problems. However, it is extremely important for the students to understand a strategy and believe that it is valuable to use. Consider the problem in the box at the bottom of the page.

It is very helpful to the cognitive processes in any task for students to stop and ask themselves a variety of questions: "Do I understand what is going on?" "Am I on the right track?" "Should I take some notes on this part?" These questions illustrate some of the *self-regulating* that we want to become habitual. Students should monitor their progress and understanding, whether it is reading a passage, writing a story, and working on a problem. When finished, students should look back on their work, review what was done, see if it was what they wanted, and so forth.

It is important that teachers help students develop their metacognitive abilities because such abilities can greatly facilitate the cognitive processes we've been dis-

---

You and your dog are visiting your friend's farm. Since it is unfamiliar to your dog, you want him tied on a lead while outside. Your friend gives you a 20-foot rope and mentions that it could be tied to one of the hooks on the walls of his barn (a 20-foot-by-30-foot rectangle). One hook is on the corner of the barn, the other in the middle of the long side. Which hook should you use to give your dog more running room (the larger area to explore).

Can you do this problem without drawing a picture of it? Perhaps, but few people can. However, with a picture (assuming it is accurate), it is fairly obvious which hook should be used. Drawing a picture is a major problem-solving strategy that students can readily use and *see the need for.* In a later chapter we will illustrate some other mathematical problem-solving strategies.

cussing. Furthermore, it appears that a person's cognitive abilities can be limited dramatically when metacognitive ability is not well developed. Think about the highly impulsive students you know who will rush into a task without thinking it through beforehand, racing to finish and unconcerned with the quality of the work.

Psychologists believe that metacognition develops primarily through social interaction with adults and other children who mediate a child's experience, giving him feedback and suggestions. Awareness of the need for self-regulation (and other aspects of metacognition) come through these interpersonal transactions. Obviously, highly specific one-to-one mediation (e.g., parent to child or tutoring) is most beneficial. Classrooms rarely offer such focused opportunities.

Therefore, educators have found that the kinds of collaborative interchanges among students working in small groups as we've discussed previously can be very beneficial in promoting metacognition. Of course, the students have to engage in appropriate behavior to stimulate metacognitive experiences for each other (e.g., vocalizing plans and strategies or asking task-based questions). What the teacher has modeled for the class, the students can do for themselves in a group (with some help and practice). Perhaps the modeling by the teacher is best translated to the individual child through some kind of small-group modeling by peers.

For instance, in the technique or reciprocal teaching, the teacher models by asking a variety of questions concerning comprehension as a story or a text passage is read. With some practice, students become dialogue leaders in their own small groups, asking these questions of one another. Before too long, they have moved from an initial parroting of the teacher's questions to internalizing the questioning process, not only in dialogue with one another but also within their own minds as they read. We'll talk more about this technique in the next chapter.

Another aspect of metacognition that makes it so important is its relation to the affective dimension we discussed earlier. We know that all of us have powerful attitudes and feelings about ourselves and areas of knowledge. Children develop strong perceptions and beliefs about their own competence in these areas. In the extreme, there are children who have decided that they will never succeed in any aspect of school; others believe that they cannot write or do math. When such a child makes a mistake, he will attribute his error to his inability, a confirmation of his incompetence, and he will tend to give up. In contrast, a child who believes in her own competence will deal with a mistake as a temporary obstacle, a challenge to be overcome by *changing strategies:* She'll slow down, think about what she did wrong, rethink assumptions, and so forth.

How do we help all children acquire confidence in their thinking in different areas? How do we get them to believe they can succeed so that they persevere? Several general things may be done. First, we know that constant critical evaluation and negative feedback can be more demoralizing than enlightening. Unfortunately, our school districts have become obsessed with grading, marking, scoring, testing, and timing every piece of work a child does. Why should a child bother to think about whether he has done the task in a reasonable way? His work will come back soon enough with a grade and copious red pencil marks.

Of course, feedback is essential. The question is, How do we give a child information about how well she is doing without driving her to the conclusion that she is just incompetent in this (or several areas)? Several possibilities exist. Formal testing could be dramatically curtailed. Magazine tests of discrete subskills in reading are significantly less important than reading aloud and discussing one's understanding of a passage. Teaching writing in several stages rather than two (rough draft and final copy) would allow constructive feedback at many steps along the way, cutting down on evaluative judgments. Setting up larger activities with multiple facets and opportunities for feedback is also helpful. And, heresy of heresies, how about *not grading* some assignments? Give constructive feedback without grades, and call it practice.

Second, the teacher can provide opportunities for more feedback from peers in the kinds of small-group activities we've discussed. If properly developed, group assistance can be more helpful than teacher feedback. This means you will have to spend some time helping students develop ways of giving positive yet honest and helpful feedback to one another. In writing consider peer editing, in which groups of three students help each other.

After the teacher has spent a fair amount of time with the class on group skills such as listening to one another and giving constructive criticism, small groups can meet to discuss the writing assignment. Subsequent meetings would focus on helping each other edit drafts. Group members become a clear audience for the writing in that the ideas the writer seeks to express can be responded to and discussed. The writer gets much more feedback about his ideas and their expression than from a teacher's written response. As you can see, we are stressing the thought and expression rather than the mechanics, grammar, and punctuation. These can always be addressed through revision and editing.

Third, helping elementary school students to develop metacognitively can instill the willingness to think through, switch tactics, find erroneous assumptions, and so forth. These processes will go a long way in facilitating an attitude toward oneself and subjects that obstacles can be overcome.

The development of habitual metacognitive thinking takes time. Some psychologists believe that it cannot be fully established until children are 11 or 12. At this age, their abilities for self-reflection seem more substantial than when younger. However, modeling by the teacher and encouragement in small groups, through reciprocal teaching and the like, should go on throughout the elementary school to build the metacognitive experiences that will lead to metacognitive knowledge.

Psychologists and educators will continue to research and debate the intricacies of metacognition for years to come. Some believe that metacognition is the key to generalized transfer of thinking across knowledge domains. Others believe that students can develop metacognitively in one domain through a successful strategy (like reciprocal teaching in reading) but that the metacognitive habit will not carry over into other domains. So our position is this: Stimulate metacognition purposely in a variety of ways, in every area, and in as many activities as possible. Then help the students see the commonalities in what they have been doing; help them build the bridges.

SUMMARY

In the previous six sections, we have sketched six key aspects of thinking that need to be considered. It would be a serious error to assume that they are somehow discrete and separate. Rather, they are highly interrelated and overlapping. They exist in a *dynamic* relationship to one another. In any activity, you can probably see each of these six factors operating. Look at Figure 2.4.

This diagram is meant to convey the continual flow of the six aspects of thinking. In every activity, students' schemata are at work, and you should attend to them in some way. Similarly, you can stimulate or model metacognitive thinking in any activity. We believe that people will continually, spontaneously choose foci and consider patterns; these are key parts of actively constructing meaningfulness. You can provide for wide variations in the information, ideas, and encounters that students have in your classroom. You can emphasize extending and going beyond simple forms of meaning into more complex understandings and encourage creative projection. These two more complex kinds of thinking would not be possible without the other four operating simultaneously.

You can also use a variety of questions to provoke good thinking. Questions should stimulate thought and not merely evaluate what students know. Questions calling for recall of facts are not very stimulating. Neither are those that can be answered with yes or no. However, questions that ask students to draw on their experiences are excellent for activating schemata ("Do you remember ever having to . . . ?" "Could you put that idea in your own words?" "What does that drawing mean to you?"). Similarly valuable are questions that provoke breaking down and pulling together ideas ("What similarities do you see?" "What differences?" "How are all these things alike?" "Why do you think these examples go together?")

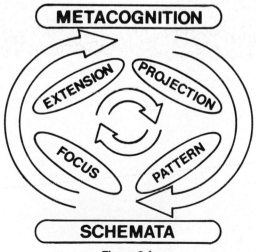

Figure 2.4

Questions can get students to move beyond basic analysis and synthesis to more complicated ideas ("Why did you conclude that . . . ?" "How can you be sure that . . . ? "Can you think of a new way to . . . ?" "What if . . . ?"). Finally, we can help students become more aware of their own thinking by asking reflective questions ("How did you begin to work on this task?" "What did you do next?" "How did you know you were having difficulty?" "What went wrong?" "How is this way of doing the task similar to the way you did yesterday's task?")

In the chapters that follow, we will attempt to build on the general ideas from this chapter about thinking and teaching for thinking. The next four chapters will each address a major area of the elementary school curriculum and show how activities can be created to foster these six kinds of thinking. Because of their highly interrelated nature, we will not try to separate them artificially as we did in this chapter. Here we wanted you to have a feeling for some important distinctions and issues. In the chapters that follow, we will present what might be done and describe what kinds of thinking would be fostered.

As before, we urge you to go through the book and this activities in sequence. We have written each chapter to build directly on the previous ones. For instance, there are some key ideas in the next chapter on literacy that will make our introductory discussion in this chapter on schema and metacognition even clearer. Certain strategies in reading and writing will be the basis for suggestions in later chapters.

PART TWO

The Basic Skills Are
Cognitive Processes

3

The Literacy Connection

In the previous chapters we examined the six aspects of thinking as we see them. In this chapter on literacy we are going to take a more holistic view of thinking as we reconsider our instructional practices. Our premise is that sound strategies for teaching reading, writing, and language are those that give students opportunities for wrestling with ideas and concepts. Reading is thinking and will be discussed in this chapter as such.

READING IS A HOLISTIC PROCESS

Over the past 10 years, cognitive psychologists have studied the complex cognitive process of reading in order to learn more about the workings of the mind. We have come a long way from the reductionist point of view that sees reading as the sum total of the discrete skills that we have children practice in the name of teaching reading. Reading is a holistic process whereby the various subskills, such as finding the main idea, identifying the topic sentence, and locating details, must be integrated to form a smooth, coherent whole. In many classrooms reading instruction consists of the teaching and practice of these subskills without pulling them together into the actual process of reading. In other words, often students are practicing skills on worksheets without the opportunity to apply these skills to contextual reading.

The teaching of reading can be compared to teaching a child to ride a bicycle. We don't break the bicycle-riding process down into each discrete skill. Emerging bike riders are not told to practice pushing down on their right leg while lifting up their left leg. Instead we place the child on the bike, hold on, and run alongside him. It is the same with reading. We need to put students into books and support them in the process. If the child learning to ride the bicycle rides into a tree when he needs to stop, we take him off the bike and give him more explicit instruction in how to use his brakes. Our skill teaching is far more relevant when the child has "the need to know." Likewise in reading, the *teachable moment* for much of the skill instruction that the child needs comes when some aspect of the reading process has broken down. Because we have a more holistic view of the reading process, we know that practice in the subskills without relevant application in reading the whole text will not result in comprehension.

To get meaning from text, the reader must be challenged by information and ideas. If we want students to be thinkers, we must structure our instruction away from mindless practice and toward active participation in the search for meaning. The instructional implications of the holistic view of reading are many. First, children need to be given time in each and every schoolday to read. We need to have classroom libraries and to be sure that each classroom is an atmosphere that encourages reading. Time spent in silent sustained reading each day is time that pays off in understanding and achievement.

Second, children all through the grades need to be read aloud to. Children need to be invited into the process of reading and to hear the sounds of language. Teachers who read to students and give them the opportunity to discuss and wrestle with ideas are providing a model of the kinds of thinking that they must do when they are reading on their own. As early as preschool and kindergarten, children can have the opportunities to have discussions around text. Students can be predicting, inferring, and confronting ideas from books that are read aloud to them. However, it is not just primary students who need to be read to. Students throughout the grades should also be read to. Novels above the instructional reading level of the class that are read aloud and discussed can help to motivate and challenge thinking. It is also important to read from expository, or informational, text as students need to know about the worlds that can open up to them through reading.

Much of the reading instruction we see today in the schools has not yet responded to what we know about the holistic nature of the reading process. Workbooks and skillsheets play much too great a role. According to *Becoming a Nation of Readers* (Anderson et al., 1985) students spend 75 percent of their reading time on individual seat-work activities. The activities often found in workbooks that accompany basal texts offer little or no practice in the total process of thinking and constructing meaning from text. In these activities, children are not asked to reason, make inferences, draw conclusions, or wrestle with ideas and concepts. Practice and drill of skills that have little value in learning to read take thinking and motivation out of the process.

Teachers typically use these skillsheets as a method of classroom management. When the Redbirds are reading with the teacher, what are the Bluebirds doing? We as teachers must critically evaluate the seat work that students do in light of what we know about the holistic nature of reading. Theory must inform our decision-making process, and we must look for more intelligent ways for students to spend the time in which they are not actively engaged with the teacher. We must critically evaluate publishers' workbook pages and skillsheets and eliminate those that provide infrequent opportunities for thinking. Students need to use this "off time" in meaningful reading and writing activities that encourage active thinking about text.

READING IS AN INTERACTIVE PROCESS

In the previous chapters we have discussed schema as one of the aspects of thinking. In the area of reading, schema theory has helped to provide a basis for understanding how the reading process works (Anderson, 1977). We have come to think of reading as an interactive process, in which the reader must interact with the author for meaning to occur. What the reader brings to the process (his schema), in terms of prior knowledge of content, structure, and vocabulary, determines how well he will be able to interact with the author in order to derive a rich meaning from the text. We have all had the experience of reading something about which we had little or no background knowledge. We soon realized that although we understood most of the words and the syntactic structure was regular, we could not make sense of what we were reading. We did not have the prior knowledge of the content that we needed to construct a rich meaning.

For example, read this paragraph attributed to Rob Tierney (Tierney and Pearson, 1981):

> The Batsmen were merciless against the Bowlers. The Bowlers placed their men in slips and covers. But to no avail. The Batsmen hit one four after another along with an occasional six. Not once did a ball look like it would hit their stumps or be caught.

Even if you do not know what is happening in this paragraph and you have not constructed a rich meaning of the text, you probably have some schema that will help you get some idea of what the paragraph is about. Your schema for competition probably helps you see that it is about some kind of game or contest. Someone is being merciless. There seem to be two teams, the Batsmen and the Bowlers. Your schema for game or sport may help interpret the vocabulary: *hit, ball, caught*. However without the prior knowledge you need, you cannot form an image from this passage and construct a rich meaning. You can, however, answer questions about the passage.

- Who was merciless?
- What did the Batsmen place their men in?
- What did the Batsmen hit?

Children can answer literal questions without really being able to construct a full meaning of what they read. This passage is about a game of cricket, and those of you who are familiar with the sport were able to construct the meaning. If this paragraph had been about baseball, we probably would have been more likely to create a visual image of the text and to construct a meaning. Fluent readers bring their schema of content, structure, syntax, and vocabulary to their reading. If we do not have the necessary schema, we are unable to comprehend what we read.

If our schema, or prior knowledge, is such an important factor in determining comprehension, what can be done instructionally to ensure that students both have and use the necessary schema for reading text? We find that many children who have the schemata they need do not necessarily use them if the teacher doesn't access them through questioning. We also find that the group knows more than the individual about a particular topic. Therefore, as teachers, we must do those things that will activate, access, and build on the prior knowledge of the group. We have already discussed semantic mapping as one way to access schema.

Another way would be simply to brainstorm with the group to elicit what the members know about a particular topic to read about. If the selection to be read is about black widow spiders, the teacher asks the students to raise their hands and tell the group any information they know about these creatures, information the teacher writes on the board. What one child knows often triggers knowledge in another child. This simple brainstorming procedure helps to activate the schema of the group, and it also helps to build schema for those who don't have much prior knowledge of spiders. The group is told to read the selection to confirm or disconfirm their existing knowledge. Reading not only helps us add information to the schema we have but also enables us to change misconceptions that we bring to the process.

Fluent reading is an active search for meaning based on what we bring to the process and what is written on the page. If students are to be thoughtful readers we must help them begin their thinking process before they enter the text. By activating their schema, students are preparing their processing system for what is coming. The students are now able to attach new information to known information. They are ready for the active search for meaning.

READING IS A CONSTRUCTIVE PROCESS

We have come to think of reading as the construction of meaning from text (Langer, 1982; Spiro, Bruce, and Brewer, 1980). As the fluent reader interacts with the text, meaning is being constructed in his mind. The meaning does not lie on the page but instead is in the mind of the reader. That is, the reader uses what is in his head and what is on the page and constructs a meaning that is the interaction of both forces. Thus, fluent reading is a constant process of making inferences, "filling in the blanks" in the text. As readers we are constantly making inferences as we read. This simple paragraph illustrates our point.

> The man went to the window and asked what time the feature began. The cashier answered him. He handed her $10 and rushed into the dark room with his companion.

In reading this passage, we infer that the man has asked his question of a cashier in a movie theater. We infer that each ticket costs $5. We infer that the movie has either just begun or is about to start. We have a schema for going to the movies, and we use this schema to make the low-level inferences that are necessary for understanding this passage. As we read and infer, we are building meaning based on what is in our heads and what is on the page. Thus inferences, some much more complex than others, are constantly being made. We must be aware of the constructive nature of the reading process so that we can help students have the necessary tools to participate in this meaning building process.

Because reading is constructive, we can assume different interpretations of text based on what the reader brings to the process. Instructional practices that don't take the interactive, constructive nature of the reading process into account don't allow for the range of thinking that can occur around text. As teachers, we cannot expect the one "right" answer. We must structure our lessons to encourage and validate different interpretations of text.

READING IS A STRATEGIC PROCESS

We also know that fluent reading is a strategic process. Fluent readers use different strategies based on the difficulty of the material and their purpose for reading. Fluent readers always read for some reason. We read to entertain ourselves, to keep up with current events, to learn how to use our new washing machine, or to enhance our professional lives. Having these purposes leads us to read in different ways. Being strategic in our reading ensures that we do the necessary kind of thinking based on the nature of the task. We want students to read for purposes that they understand and find important. We want them to adjust their strategies accordingly. Students need to monitor their ongoing comprehension activities to see that their purposes are being met. Effective readers are aware of what they are doing and thinking about as they read. (Brown, 1982). Instructionally, we want to make students metacognitively aware so that they can monitor their comprehension and know what to do if they have lost it. In other words, students need to be thinking about their thinking.

INSTRUCTION FOR THINKING

In reading, the teaching of the cognitive process must be embedded in the instructional process. Reading is thinking and making inferences. For comprehension to occur, readers must put it together and synthesize and reconstruct what they have read. In much of the current reading instruction that we see in schools, teachers are evaluating comprehension rather than teaching it. The typical basal reading lesson in many teacher's manuals tells the teacher to set a purpose for reading. "Tell the students to read the story to find all they can about bears" or "Tell the students to read the story to find out what happened to Johnny when he got lost in the woods." The crucial prereading stage is very often just one sentence of "purpose setting." Then the class is instructed to read the story silently. After reading there are questions. Basal publishers have certainly learned to ask good questions. There are literal, inferential, and critical-creative questions, and many basals even label the questions as such.

However, this typical lesson does not encourage the type of thinking that we are discussing in this book. The purpose-setting statement does not take into account that we want students to be able to set their own purposes for reading and to adjust their strategies accordingly. The typical lesson does not encourage active reading and thinking. As teachers we wonder why some of our students are not good at answering the inferential questions at the end of the selection. How can we expect students to think effectively after reading if they were not actively involved in thinking and constructing during reading?

The strategies that we are about to suggest encourage thinking before, during, and after reading. With the understanding we have gained about the importance of using what students bring to the process from prior knowledge, we have come to realize that what we do before students read is crucial in activating thinking. Dolores Durkin (1978–9) has observed comprehension instruction in classrooms throughout the country. She has reported that although prereading instruction is the most important part of the guided reading lesson, it is by far the most neglected part. Basal manuals have contributed to this neglect by simply giving a purpose-setting statement, which may or may not be relevant to the story. In one second-grade basal there is a lovely story about a bear noisily entering a quiet forest and disturbing the peace in order to get his food. The manual tells the students to read the story to find out all the facts that they can about animals. This story is much better read and enjoyed for a more affective purpose than for the bland one stated in the manual.

What students do *during* their reading is also frequently neglected in typical basal reading instruction, especially in the intermediate and upper grades. Students are instructed to read the complete story. Instructionally, however, it is important for us to break up the reading process in order to teach students strategies that they will use on their own. Students need to become metacognitively aware, to know if they are comprehending what they are reading and to know what to do about it if they are not. We know that older and fluent readers demand clarity of their reading, and have strategies to use if their comprehension breaks down. Younger and less fluent readers frequently do not use these "fix-up" strategies. In fact many of them are so used to not comprehending that they are not even aware that they have ceased to understand what they are reading. We must instruct students in how to employ metacognitive strategies during reading.

After reading, we must focus our instruction on encouraging students to reconstruct what they have read. If we are predicting, making inferences, and constructing while reading, we must be able to recall, reconstruct, and synthesize after reading. When students answer questions after reading, they are frequently pulling apart and analyzing what they have read. We also want to give students the opportunity to write in response to their reading so that they have a format for synthesizing their thinking.

Our instruction should focus on activities and strategies that encourage students to reconstruct the coherent whole. They must learn ways to link new information with known information and to make important connections in what they are reading. Too often what students learn in school seems to exist in the vacuum of that day's, or that unit's, instruction. After reading, students must be taught how to use what they have learned to help them to learn more.

Writing activities that come out of reading enable students to think and to synthesize. We have all used writing as a way of crystallizing our own thinking, and students need to use writing in this way. We are not suggesting that we should no longer ask students to answer questions. Evaluation is an important aspect of our teaching. However, before we ask the questions and evaluate the product of their thinking, we must concentrate on teaching them the process.

The remainder of this chapter will be divided into two sections. The first section will deal with strategies for thinking in narrative text and the second section with strategies for thinking in expository text. Reading stories and reading to learn are two different types of reading, have different purposes, and require different strategies. As teachers, we have done a good job of teaching students to read fiction. The basal texts are about 80 percent fiction, and as Hillerich (1986) points out, basal instruction accounts for 75 percent of the reading instruction in this country.

Reading and thinking about expository material require a particular type of instructional practice. It has become almost a cliché to say that every teacher, no matter what subject he teaches, should be a teacher of reading. However, this demand cannot be stressed too strongly. If we are to maximize our content area instruction (i.e., math, science, and social studies), where the conceptual load is high and the materials are not always well organized, we must aim our teaching at the process of reading to learn as well as at the content to be covered. For example, when students are studying the Civil War in social studies, we want to make sure that they learn about the war (the content) but also learn a *process* for comprehending the information that they can use in other contexts. If we are to help students become good thinkers and use their cognitive skills when confronted with different types of text, we must teach certain techniques before, during, and after reading.

We are not able to give you *the* formula for instruction. Just as reading is thinking, teaching is thinking and decision making. The strategies and activities that you employ are all affected by the ability and background of your group, the difficulty of the material, and your particular style of teaching. There is more than one way to get students to think actively about what they read. We will offer suggestions to make students active thinkers, and learners, before, during, and after reading.

Good thinking requires active participation in the learning process, and learning requires taking risks. It is our job to establish an atmosphere in our classrooms so that risk taking is the order of the day. We must encourage and positively respond to good thinking and not just "right" answers. We must encourage students to have different interpretations of text if they have evidence to support their interpretations. Good thinking takes time, and we must allow students the time they need to draw conclusions, refine hypotheses, and interpret and synthesize ideas.

NARRATIVE TEXT

Narrative text, or fiction, follows a predictable structure. A story has characters and a setting. The characters usually have some type of problem, and the story tells how the problem is resolved. Students need to understand the structure of narrative text and use it to help them read.

Prereading

Prereading is the most important part of the reading lesson. In the prereading part of the lesson, several crucial aspects of the reading process occur. First it is in this phase of reading that we activate schemata of content and structure. We set the stage for learning. Second, it is in this phase that a purpose is set for reading. Here we must give guidance for students to become interested in the process and set their own purposes. Third, the prereading stage serves to bring together the disparate parts of the class. By establishing a context and a purpose for reading, assessing background knowledge, and exploring vocabulary, we are "priming the pump" and helping to pull the group together. Some of our poorest readers are good thinkers. It is in this phase of instruction that we activate their thinking and help them to deal with difficult text.

The first strategy we are going talk about is the Directed Reading-Thinking Activity, DR-TA, which was developed by Russell Stauffer (1969). It is a guided reading strategy that follows a three-step procedure for reading fiction: predict, read, and prove. The students are given an initial stimulus, perhaps a picture from the story and/or the title, and are asked to make predictions about what the story will be about. The story is then broken up into meaningful sections, and the class is told to read silently to the first stopping point to check the accuracy of their predictions. The students are then asked to prove their predictions by finding evidence in the story to support them. This strategy helps students establish their own purpose for reading, that is, their prediction. They become active readers as they read to confirm or disconfirm their predictions, and in this way, enter the text actively thinking.

The heart of the DR-TA strategy is prediction, which

- Helps to set purposes
- Heightens interest and motivation
- Activates thinking and is a critical thinking skill
- Makes students active readers
- Is part of the fluent reading process

The prereading or prediction phase can be handled in various ways. To begin the lesson, the teacher might say the following:

- Today I am looking for good thinking and not "right" answers.
- Think like detectives and use clues from the story to try to predict what will happen.
- Be prepared to support your predictions by using evidence from the story.

In working with the DR-TA strategy, we have made several adaptations. The initial stimulus for thinking can be the title and/or picture, as previously stated. A powerful adaptation is to use some prechosen vocabulary words from the story as the initial stimulus. The teacher must choose words that give important information to the reader. For example, in the seventh-grade Houghton Mifflin story "The Messenger to Maftam" (*encore* basal reader, 1978), these words might serve as a stimulus for prediction:

Bahene	circumstances
Mamadi	virtue
Gulf of Guinea	arrogance
falsehood	lesson

The teacher tells the students that the first two words are names. All the words are then discussed: "What is a falsehood?" "What is a virtue?" "Give me some examples of virtues." "Is arrogance a virtue?" Next the teacher might say, "Look at the title and vocabulary words and think about four things:"

1. Who do you think the story will be about?
2. Where do you think the story takes place?
3. What do you think the problem is in the story?
4. What kind of story do you think it is?

Try to answer these questions yourself by using the title and vocabulary words. Here is a sample predictive discussion.

TEACHER: Who do you think the story may be about?

STUDENT 1: The story is about Bahene and Mamadi.

STUDENT 2: Perhaps one of them is a messenger.

TEACHER: Good thinking; you are using the clues in the title. Where do you think the story takes place?

STUDENT 3: It takes place near the Gulf of Guinea.

TEACHER: Where is that?

STUDENT 4: We said that the Gulf of Guinea is in West Africa, so the story must take place in Africa.

TEACHER: Good. Now this question really requires good thinking. What do you think is the problem in the story? What may happen?

STUDENT 5: Perhaps one of the characters tells a falsehood and learns a lesson about lying.

STUDENT 6: I think that one of the characters is arrogant and one is virtuous, and the arrogant person learns a lesson about virtue.

TEACHER: Both were good predictions. You are both using what you know about stories having conflicts. Any other predictions? What may happen in the story?

STUDENT 7: I think one of the characters will be sent to deliver a message, and there will be circumstances that force him to tell a lie.

TEACHER: Good thinking. Any other predictions?

STUDENT 8: The messenger will tell a lie and somebody will get hurt, and he will learn a lesson about lying.

TEACHER: All good predictions. From all the clues, what kind of a story do you think this is?

STUDENT 9: I think it is a folktale, because it takes place in Africa. Also one of the words from the story is *lesson*. Folktales are stories that teach lessons.

TEACHER: Good thinking. Now read the first two pages of the story to check your predictions.

In this discussion, several things occurred before the students read the text. First, the students set their own purposes by making predictions. Thus, they will become active readers to see if their predictions are confirmed or disconfirmed. By reading actively, they will be thinking and constructing meaning. By using vocabulary words from the story and discussing them in a meaningful, predictive way, the students are manipulating words and concepts even before they read. A context has been set for learning. The class has predicted that the story takes place in Africa and is a folktale. Their schema for West African folktale has been activated by the predictive discussion.

This discussion concerned a story from the seventh-grade basal *Encore*. The basal text is a good anthology of stories but how the teacher uses these stories is what makes the basal into an asset or a liability. For example, the preceding discussion was student-centered. Here is what the manual listed as the prereading, purpose-setting discussion.

Tell students that they are going to read an interesting, humorous West African folktale. Ask them them whether they remember what a folktale is ("an anonymous timeless story that has been passed on orally from generation to generation by the common people of a region"). Have students read to learn the clever way Mamadi uses double talk to make sure that he does not tell a falsehood.

The message, delivered with so many qualifications and exceptions, really amounted to no message at all (Durr, Pescosolido and Poetter, 1978).

The manual tells the students the whole story and the type of story. In contrast, through the predictive discussion the students are able to infer the type of story and set their own purposes. By allowing students to make predictions and inferences, we are using our prereading time for good thinking.

Choosing vocabulary words to activate student thinking is the job of the teacher. The words must enable the students to make predictions about the characters, the setting, and the plot, elements because they make up the structure of narrative text. Understanding that stories have characters, a setting, a problem, and a resolution is important to the meaning-getting process. Therefore, words must be chosen carefully to give students enough information to begin to think about these textual elements.

Another prereading strategy to activate student thinking is the "vocab-o-gram" developed by Camille Blachowicz (1986). Here a chart is used to organize the vocabulary according to the structure of narrative text. Again the students will have a preliminary discussion of the words to activate there schemata. Next is the prediction phase, in which students will classify the vocabulary according to the way they believe the author will use the words in the selection.

Predict how the author will use these words in the story to tell about:

The setting	The characters	The goal or problem
The actions	The resolution	Other things

The predictive discussion of the words can be held with the whole group or in small groups. The discussion activates the groups' thinking and also allows the teacher to gauge the state of their knowledge. Here again the students are thinking before they enter the text. By classifying the words according to the structure of the narrative, we are activating their schemata of both content and structure. The students begin to link word meaning to prior knowledge and to textual structure. They are beginning to make the necessary connections from the new to the known.

To summarize, if reading is to be a thinking experience, prereading is a crucial time for activating thinking and setting purposes. Activities and strategies that force the students to begin thinking before they enter the text should be stressed.

During Reading

The prereading phase serves to activate thinking, and the during-reading phase should refine, clarify, refocus, and synthesize thinking. We need to take time during reading to teach strategies for thinking. When children read in school, they need to be guided in developing metacognitive awareness in the hope that this awareness will become an integral part of their reading behavior.

It is important for the reader to have a sense of her own schema. She should be aware of how much or how little she brings to the process. The type of reading strategy she uses often depends on this knowledge. The reader must be aware of the task and what is expected. The reader must closely self-monitor her thinking in order to know if her comprehension has broken down. She must know and be able to use "fix-up" strategies to correct the situation.

The M.E.R.I.T. Chapter 2 Project (1986) from the School District of Philadelphia refers to fluent reading as C-L-I-C-K-I-N-G A-L-O-N-G. When the student does not understand something while reading, he has hit a C-L-U-N-K. If the student is thinking about his reading and demanding clarity as he reads, he will realize that he has a problem. The important thing is to know what to do about it. The M.E.R.I.T. project lists seven "fix-up," or metacognitive, strategies that students should be aware of:

1. Slow Down! Information in a textbook may be difficult to understand. We have different reading rates for reading textbooks and for reading stories.
2. Continue reading to see if the author explains the Clunk. The Clunk could be a word or an idea. Look for context clues.

3. Reread—Sometimes a segment of text makes more sense the second or third time you read it.
4. Use maps, charts, graphs or any other aids the author may give you.
5. Use the glossary in the textbook or your dictionary.
6. Ask another student, if permitted. Sometimes talking it through, straightens it out.
7. Ask your teacher to help you "fix-up" the Clunk.

The benefits of this kind of explicit student instruction are many:

- We are letting students into the rules of the game. Mature and fluent readers naturally use these strategies. Younger and less fluent readers need to know that if they take responsibility for their processing of text, they can correct comprehension that has broken down.
- Using the language of Clicking and Clunking gives students an easy way to talk and think about what they are doing while reading.
- Metacognitive strategies must be used whenever students read. Raising these strategies to the level of students' awareness helps them to feel in control of their reading. If we are to shift the responsibility for understanding to the students, they need tools to guide them when they are in trouble.

Therefore, we suggest that *metacognition* should not be just a word that teachers toss around. It is a word and a concept that should be shared with the learners. A pamphlet from the M.E.R.I.T., project concludes, "Knowing about metacognition will not help you to be a better reader. Using metacognition will help you to be a better reader."

As part of our instruction for metacognitive awareness during the reading of narrative text, we must help students confirm and refine predictions, clarify ideas, attend to key vocabulary, evaluate ideas, and construct meaning from text. To achieve these goals, it is necessary to interrupt students' reading by telling them to read to a specific stopping point, as in the DR-TA strategy. At his point, we need to ask three questions that force the students to focus their thinking and construct meaning.

- How accurate were our initial predictions? (What has happened so far?)
- What do you think will happen next?
- What evidence in the story makes you think so?

The first question focuses on the student's purpose for reading, that of checking her prediction. It also touches on the metacognitive issue of being aware of comprehension: Are you Clicking along, or have you hit a Clunk?

The second question asks students to *refine* their predictions. If we are reading actively, we are able to make clearer predictions and construct meaning based on each new segment of text.

The third question helps to keep the student's thinking process *story-based*. We are asking students to make complex inferences based on what they know and on what is in the text. Our goal is for them to use clues from the story to guide their thinking. Their predictions should become more refined and story-based with each new segment of text.

Our job as teachers is to stop the story at important points so that students have enough evidence to make good predictions. To do so, we have to know the material intimately. Only if we know the story well and understand its issues can we make intelligent decisions about how to teach it. Again, we are not looking for correct answers. We are guiding the process of good thinking. Thinking takes time, and in classrooms, time is a scarce commodity. If our goal is to encourage thinking, we must take the time to stop the story at relevant points in order to have predictive discussions around text.

Inherent in those DR-TA process is the management problem of students with different reading rates. One teacher we know gives the students three by five cards. The students place a card at the point in the text where they are to stop reading. As they finish reading the section, they write on that card a new prediction and evidence from the story to support it.

Our goal in interrupting the reading of the story is to teach students a process that helps them to be active, thinking readers. We want them to commit to predictions in order to set their own purposes for reading the next section of text. Some teachers, after eliciting three or four good predictions, will take a vote: "How many of you agree with Mary's prediction? How many of you agree with the prediction made by Todd and Susan?" In this way, teachers enable everyone in the group to commit to a prediction without taking time for everyone to speak. Students find this strategy highly motivating, and their motivation helps to drive the active thinking process.

After Reading

Our goals after reading a narrative selection, are to reconstruct meaning for the whole passage, confirm predictions, generate new questions, synthesize ideas, and make connections. Writing that comes out of reading is an intelligent way to achieve these goals. Reading and writing are reciprocal processes. Writing should be used on a regular basis to apply and synthesize thinking.

Reading and writing both are constructive processes and involve the use of language to communicate ideas. Readers and writers are both building meaning; readers build meaning from already-existing text, and writers build meaning by creating text. Moreover, both readers and writers bring their background knowledge to bear as they build meaning. In other words, both reading and writing are active thinking processes, and teachers who use writing as a regular part of their instructional program need to build relationships between them.

One writing strategy that asks students to think critically about what they have read is summary writing, a specific skill that asks students to reconstruct what they have read in a concise form. Summary writing is not a retelling of the story and does not call for the inclusion of details.

Summary Writing

The goal of this strategy is to summarize a narrative story in four sentences.

- First sentence: Characters
- Second sentence: Setting
- Third sentence: Problem
- Fourth sentence: Resolution

Step 1. After all the students have read the story, the teacher models the summary writing procedure with the group.
  - A. The teacher explains the summary model and writes it on the board.
  - B. The teacher explains that because the summary will be only four sentences long, each sentence should contain the most important information.
  - C. The teacher asks students for a complete sentence that tells about the main characters: for example, "This story is about a boy named Jack and a giant."
  - D. The teacher asks the group to elaborate and refine the sentence: for example, "This story is about a boy named Jack, who grew a beanstalk, and a mean giant who lived at the top of the beanstalk."
  - E. The teacher follows the same process with the other three sentences.
  - F. The teacher models this process following the reading of two or three other stories.

Step 2. A. After a story is read, the teacher breaks the class into groups of four to five students.
  - B. The students collaborate and write their own group summaries.
  - C. Each summary is shared with the whole class.
  - D. The class repeats this process in groups several times.

Step 3. The students write their own summaries using the four-sentence model.

This strategy is an effective use of writing that comes out of reading. If a student is able to summarize a story in four sentences, we can assume that he has been able to reconstruct thoughtfully what he has read. The small-group work is a crucial part of the procedure. Talking to others about one's thinking helps to refine and crystallize it. When listening to groups performing this task, we hear them having intelligent discussions about text: "I think the problem has two parts; Bahene wants to force Mamadi into telling a lie, so he sets out to trick him." "We need to be more specific about the setting. It took place in the village of Ogo, near the Gulf of Guinea." Again, thinking takes time, and we have to give students the time to think and discuss their thinking.

Another method is to have students write endings to stories. As part of the predictive reading-thinking process, the students stop reading before the ending of the story and write the endings they have predicted. Many times the students' predicted endings are more interesting that the real ones.

For example, in a mystery story from a basal reader, two children, John and Ely, who live in an old, creaky house hear noises on the attic stairs at night. Ely convinces John to go up to the attic to investigate. They find an open window and a pair of shoes wrapped in a newspaper only a week old. The students, using the clues in the story, often have wonderful predictions about who may be using the attic. (The actual ending of the story is anticlimatic: The intruder turns out to be Uncle Charles, who is out of work and looking for a job.) Children who have followed the predictive thinking process before and during reading are eager to write their own endings, which can be written before or after completing the story. It is interesting to compare students' endings to the real ones, as it gives them a sense of authorship.

Another possibility is for students to write in the same genre of the stories they have read. We want students to use their knowledge of genre and the structure of narrative to help them read and write. If students read on folktale, they should read more folktales. If they are exposed to one science fiction story, they should read others. We want them to use what they have learned about mysteries to help them read other mysteries. This is where a teacher's resourcefulness comes in because most basals are not structured in this way. There may be one folktale in the fifth-grade basal and one or two in the sixth-grade basal. We as teachers need to pull stories from other sources.

Folktales, for example, have regular patterns, and students can use their knowledge of these patterns to read other folktales. Folktales often teach lessons and have morals: right over might, slow and steady wins the game, brains over brawn, and so on. Folktales frequently have patterns of three: three wishes, three kings, three questions, three animals. It is this redundancy in the genre that helps students to feel in control of their reading and predicting.

After having read many stories from a particular genre, students should be given the opportunity to write in that genre. We learn how to write by reading. It is through wide reading that we become aware of the patterns and conventions of a certain genre.

Just as reading follows a process of purpose setting, monitoring, and reconstructing, writing also follows a process. According to Humes (1983), writing involves four subprocesses:

1. **Planning:** Before, during, and after writing, writers are planning and thinking about the ideas they want to express and ways to express them.
2. **Translating:** In this phase the writer puts thoughts down in written words.
3. **Reviewing:** This is the phase in which writers reread what they have written to check for ideas, syntax, and so on, to see if more planning is needed.
4. **Revising:** This is the ongoing phase of making changes in the text. These changes may occur at the idea level or at the word and punctuation level.

For instruction, we need to be aware of the writing process, just as we do the reading process. Students need the opportunity to go through the stages of the process. The planning stage in writing is as important as the prereading stage. For example, a strategy to help students plan their writing of a folktale would be to tell them to generate words that they might use in their writing. This brainstorming process helps them to activate schema for folktale and to think about what they will write.

Here is an example of a list of words that a fifth-grade class brainstormed prior to writing folktales:

wish	king	poor	prince
maiden	kingdom	honest	tale
turtle	village	peasant	tiger
ladder	race	frog	sun
son	father	India	Africa

Our old-fashioned writing activities, where we gave students a "creative" title and told them to write, did not take into account the planning stage. For example, we told students to write about what it will be like in the year 2000; the students were then expected to pick up their pens and begin to write. We need to activate schema and set purposes for both reading and writing.

Another activity is for students to map the story they have read. A story map is a graphic representation that demonstrates the student's understanding of a story's components and their interrelationships. Story-maps can be different and allow for different interpretations of text. There is no right or wrong way to draw a story map, although students should be able to explain it. They may use lines, circles, squares, or other shapes. Figure 3.1 shows two examples of story maps for the story "Jack and the Beanstalk."

Putting It Together in Narrative Text

To put it all together, there are certain things we should do before, during, and after reading a narrative story. Here is an example of a predictive reading lesson for a story from Scholastic Book Services called "Saved by the Bell," which is included at the end of this section.

Pre-reading

Show the students the title.
Ask them to think about the following:
    Who is the story about?
    Where does the story take place?
    What is the problem in the story?
Elicit their good thinking by having them make predictions.
Tell them to read the first page of the story to check their predictions.

During Reading

After reading the first page, ask the students:
    How accurate were your predictions?
    Who is the story about?

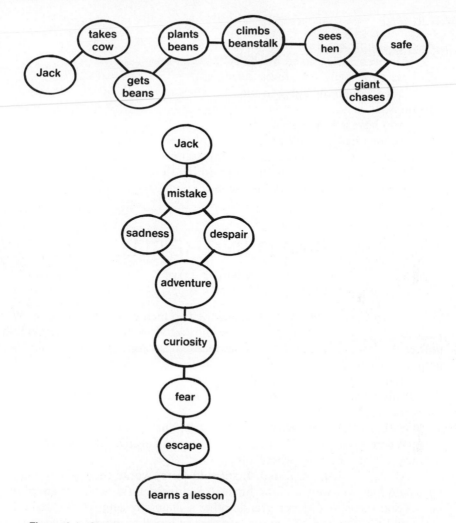

Figure 3.1. Students should be allowed to draw their maps individually or in groups. Time should be allowed for students to share their maps with the group.

Where does it take place?

What is the problem?

Discuss what has happened so far, and then ask:

What do you think will happen next?

What evidence in the story makes you think so?

Elicit several predictions and be sure to ask students to support their thinking with evidence.

Tell them to read the next page to check their predictions.

Repeat the predictive process.

Tell them to read to the end of the story.

After Reading

Ask them how accurate their predictions were.
How was Shelly saved by the bell?
Discuss how Shelly's deafness saved her.
Go back through the story to look for clues to her deafness.
Examples:
"You have a funny accent."
The men had to yank Shelly to the phone.
Shelly gave clues in the phone conversation.
Shelly felt vibrations of footsteps on the floor.
Have the students write the four sentence summary of the story.

SAVED BY THE BELL
by Karin Ireland

Shelly jumped, terrified, when she saw the two men come into the den. Who were they? What were they doing in her house? How had they gotten in? She pushed her long brown hair out of her face and sat staring at them. Her heart pounded furiously.

"You alone?" snarled the blond.

Shelly nodded yes to his question. She wished someone else were at home. Then she wouldn't be so scared.

"Well, don't worry. We won't harm you—just as long as you cooperate."

"Where's the money?" the other man asked angrily. He took a menacing step toward her. "I said, where's the money?"

"Money?" Shelly repeated. If she told them, would they take it and go? Or would they still want to look further? Suddenly, a flash of fear swept over her as she remembered her grandmother's diamond ring in the desk. Her mother had just gotten it from the safe-deposit box that morning. She couldn't let the burglars find it. It was worth thousands of dollars.

"Every family has some money hidden somewhere." the blonde said. "Where's yours?"

"Between some pages in the telephone book," Shelly said, pointing to the shelf by the phone.

"You have a funny accent," said the blond. "You European or something?"

Shelly looked down at the floor. She'd been asked that question a dozen times. When she looked up, the men were tearing apart the telephone book. It wouldn't be long before they found the money. Then what? How could she keep them from finding the ring?

Escape. That was it—escape, and get the neighbor to call the police—to get help.

The men were still busy with the telephone book. *Now,* Shelly told herself. *Now!* She lunged for the back door. It seemed to take forever to get it open. But at last, she flew down the back stairs and ran toward the gate.

Suddenly, she was jerked painfully to a stop. Someone had her by the hair. It was the blond. He had jumped over the railing to same time on the stairs. He grabbed her arm and swung her around to face him.

"Don't try that again, understand?" he snapped.

Shelly nodded meekly. Tears of fear and frustration ran down her face.

"You come back up here and sit," he ordered.

The man with the brown hair was standing at the door. He looked really angry now. He grabbed her arm and threw her into a chair. Then the men went back to the telephone book.

Shelly looked at her watch. It was getting late. She had to do something to get rid of them before anyone came home. If someone walked in the door, the men would panic. She couldn't be sure what they'd do out of fear.

Her thoughts were interrupted as the blond crossed the room and yanked her to her feet. Shelly looked up at him, startled.

"I said answer it," he growled.

"What?" Shelly answered, confused.

"The phone! Answer it, and don't get cute. Just get rid of whoever it is." He thrust the phone into her hand.

"Hello," Shelly said into the receiver. "I'm sorry I let the phone ring so long. I was listening to the radio. I was waiting to hear the name of the song they just played."

She looked nervously at the two men. *So far, so good,* she thought. "I hear someone at the front door now," she said into the phone. "I'll have to call you back. Bye." She slammed the phone down and held her breath.

[Finish reading the story to find out what happens.]

She looked back at the two men. They didn't seem suspicious or anything. They looked pleased. They had found the $100 bill that was tucked away in the phone book.

"You sure have some accent," the blond buy said, shaking his head.

"Do your folks have any jewelry?" the man with brown hair cut in.

"No," Shelly lied.

"What about a tape recorder or a camera? Go look."

The men followed Shelly into her brother's room. She reached into a drawer and pulled out a tape recorder. Before she could turn and hand it to them, she felt vibrations on the floor. She spun around just in time to see the two men being overpowered by police. The police slipped handcuffs around the men's wrists and pushed them to the door. Shelly stood dazed by all the action. Her knees felt weak with relief. One of the police officers came to stand in front of her.

"That was very clever of you," she said slowly. "It was your teacher on

the phone. He called to speak to your mother. He knew right away that something was wrong, and he called us.

"You read lips very well," the officer went on. "The men never did realize
you are deaf."

Instructional Issues in Narrative Text

Embedded in this discussion of narrative text are three instructional methods that
promote good thinking.

1. Shift responsibility for thinking and learning from the teacher to the student. We have always believed that we had to provide the knowledge and
   purpose for reading. Students bring much to the learning process, and we
   have to tap into what they bring.
2. We must explicitly instruct students in the use of different strategies for
   different purposes. We need to familiarize the students with the rules of the
   game.
3. The aim of our instruction is for students to internalize the process. Instruction that begins with teacher modeling, shifts to small-group work, and then
   asks for individual performance encourages thinking.

EXPOSITORY TEXT

Expository text is usually written to convey factual information and/or to explain
ideas. It has a different structure and is written for a different purpose than narrative text. In expository material, students need to use different strategies and read
for different purposes. Expository material has a different text structure and frequently has a high conceptual load. In this section, we will discuss strategies that
deal with the specific nature of expository material and the strategy of reading to
learn.

Prereading

Before reading expository text, we need to activate schema and set purposes. We
will discuss two important strategies that work well in reading nonfiction.

The K-W-L is a strategy for reading expository text that was developed by
Donna Ogle (1986). It is an adaptation of the DR-TA that meets the conceptual and
structural needs of expository material. K-W-L stands for

- K—What you Know
- W—What you Want to learn
- L—What you have Learned

This strategy is based on the understanding that it is easier to learn something if we first access schema (what you know) and set purposes (what you want to learn). Our prereading goal in this strategy is to activate knowledge of content, categories, structure, and vocabulary and to ask questions of text.

The first part of the strategy, what you know, activates schema in a simple brainstorming process. The second section, what you want to learn, requires the reader to examine her uncertainty and figure out what she does not know. The reader enters the text with questions which enable her to tie new information into already existing categories. The questions are self-generated, and thus the student is setting her own purposes for reading. This strategy is especially effective in the content areas, such as science and social studies, where the conceptual load is high and the materials are not always well organized. Here is a worksheet that students can use to follow the three steps in the process.

K-W-L STRATEGY SHEET

What We Know	What We Want To Find Out	What We Learn

To illustrate the strategy, we will discuss an article from a third-grade basal about catfish and how snoopy they are.

STEP 1. The teacher tells the group that they are going to read this article. The group is asked to brainstorm anything they know about catfish. The students raise their hands and tell what they know, and the teacher writes it all down on the board.

Here is a student-generated list of facts:

What We Know:

- They taste good.
- They have whiskers like cats.
- They are caught in ponds.
- They are cooked in frying pans.
- They have big heads.
- They are ugly.
- They are easy to catch.

Through this brainstorming process, several things occur. We elicit what students know, as students do not always use their knowledge unless we take the time to access it. Also the group knows more than the individual student. Information that one student presents often triggers knowledge in another student. It allows a student who may have specific knowledge about a certain subject to share it with the group. Some of our poor readers can be excellent thinkers when given a forum in which to do so.

STEP 2. The next step in the prereading discussion concerns what the students want to learn. Here the teacher poses this question: "In an article about catfish, what kinds of questions would you expect the author to answer about catfish?" Here we want to focus on the categories of knowledge that would probably be found in an article about catfish, or for that matter, any animal. The students present their questions, and the teacher writes them down on the board.

Here is a list of student-generated questions about catfish:

1. What do they look like? (appearance)
2. Why are they called snoopy?
3. How did they get the name catfish?
4. Where are they found? (habitat)
5. What do they eat?
6. How do they make babies? (reproduction)
7. Who are their enemies?
8. How do they protect themselves?

After generating the list of questions, students are told to read part of the text to find the answers. In this way, students are entering the text with their own questions and their own purposes. These content-based questions give structure to what they are reading and help them find information in different sections of the text. This process illustrates that in different types of expository text, we can anticipate certain categories of information.

For example, authors of articles about animals usually include the kinds of information the questions asked for. If we read one article about animals, we should read several. Students need to know that they can generalize these categories, and we have to bring the categories to their level of awareness. For example,

TEACHER: Today we are going to read an article about spiders. Remember the questions that we asked about catfish? This article about spiders will deal with many of those same categories.

Think about how this prereading strategy could be used in other kinds of expository text. For example, if you were about to read a biography of Eleanor Roosevelt, what categories of information would you expect the author to discuss?

1. What were her accomplishments?
2. Why was a biography written about her?
3. When did she live?
4. Where did she live?
5. What was her childhood like?
6. What kind of education did she have?
7. What was her family like?
8. Did she have children?

After reading this biography together, the students might be sent to the library to read biographies of their own choice. The same categories of information would most likely be dealt with in their biographies.

If you were beginning a unit in social studies about the Civil War, you would first ask the students what they know about this time in history. Next you would ask them to generate questions that the author was likely to answer in a chapter on the Civil War. Here is a possible list:

1. When did the war take place?
2. Where was it fought?
3. What were the issues?
4. Who won?
5. What was the aftermath?
6. What were the important battles?
7. Who were the important historical figures?

Again, students are setting their own purposes and laying the groundwork for their reading. It is important for them to know that while they are reading on their own, they need to take the time to ask questions of the text. Student-generated questions are more effective than those of the teacher. This process gives students a sense of control over their reading because they learn that they can expect an author to include certain categories of information.

This strategy is effective because it focuses both on the content to be learned and on the process of reading to learn. Students need to have opportunities to read expository material so that they can become familiar with efficient strategies for reading to learn. We need to give students theoretically sound methods for thinking about complex text.

Another prereading strategy for expository material is semantic mapping, which was introduced in Chapter 1. Semantic mapping is one of the most effective ways to obtain access to schemata, set purposes, and set the stage for learning. The semantic map is an arrangement of vocabulary, and hence the concepts that the words represent, around a topic. When we construct a semantic map, we are providing a vehicle for connecting new knowledge to known knowledge.

Here is an example of semantic mapping for the article on catfish.

STEP 1: Brainstorming—the teacher asks the students to think of words or phrases that come to mind when they think of catfish. Here is a list that a class of third-graders generated:

whiskers	found in ponds	easy to catch
ugly	big head	thick skin
taste good	cook in pan	catch with worms
catch with bugs		

STEP 2: Categories—the teacher and students construct a map by grouping the words into their categories. This sets the stage for learning. Figure 3.2 is a semantic map that was devised by the same third-grade class before reading the article.

STEP 3: Revision based on reading—after reading the selection the students revise the map in response to the text. Categories are added, and information is added to

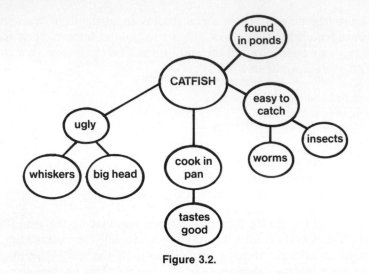

Figure 3.2.

already-existing categories. Figure 3.3 is an example of the map constructed by the class after they read the article.

The level of knowledge that the students bring and the complexity of the topic will determine the complexity of the semantic map. The map may be simple, as in the example, or much more elaborate on a more complex topic. Mapping should be modeled with the whole group several times.

Dolores Durkin (1978–9) cautions us not to be merely "assignment givers" or "mentioners." By modeling this strategy with the group, we are instructing in comprehension rather than merely assigning a task. After we have modeled the process several times, students can try the mapping strategy in small groups, and the maps can be shared with the whole class. In this way, we can reinforce the understanding that there is not just one "right" way to think about a topic. We allow for different interpretations. The group map is an important step before the students try the process on their own. Instruction that follows the process of the teacher modeling to the whole group, followed by small groups, and ending in individual performance is instruction that makes sense.

In summary, before reading expository text we need to activate schemata and enable students to enter the text with self-generated questions. If we think in terms of content categories, as in the K-W-L and in semantic mapping, we are activating students' thinking so that the will enter the text thinking.

During Reading

We must stop our reading of expository material to see what questions have been answered and what new questions have arisen as a result of our reading. We need to attend to key vocabulary, revise ideas, evaluate thinking, make necessary connections, and generate new questions. It is important to know that while reading answers questions, it also gives rise to more questions.

During the reading of expository text, students need to check their comprehen-

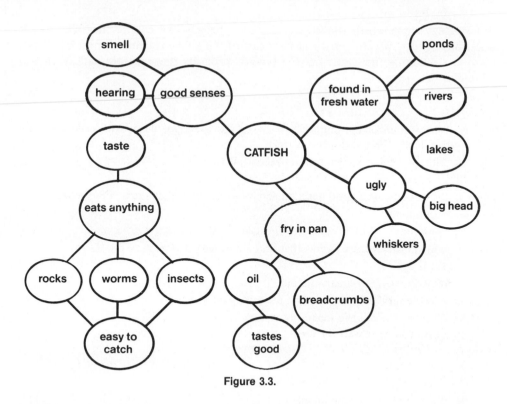

Figure 3.3.

sion. Are they achieving their purposes? Are they using the right strategy in light of their purpose? Are they actively thinking and connecting ideas? Are the Clicking along, or have they hit a Clunk?

Reciprocal Teaching, developed by Anne Marie Palincsar (1984), is a strategy that encourages monitoring comprehension while reading expository text. It encourages students to be active in the process of constructing meaning from text.

The teacher first models the comprehension activity, and then the students attempt the same activity, with the teacher giving feedback on their performance. The teacher takes turns with the students in discussing segments of text. Small groups of students from first grade on can participate in this strategy. Both the teacher and the students read a paragraph. Following the reading, the teacher and the students take turns being "teacher."

The "teacher" must ask the group an important question about the passage, a question that elicits the key issue. Before turns are taken, the teacher models this procedure many times. When the group is ready to begin asking the questions, the teacher gives feedback and guides their questioning. The teacher models, praises correct responses, asks probing questions, and generally gives feedback. The teacher and students can use four comprehension activities: summarize the section that was read, predict what the next section will be about, ask a question about the main idea of the section that was read, or ask a question that helps to clarify the meaning of the passage.

It takes time for both the teacher and the students to become comfortable with this strategy. It is worth the effort, however, because by asking these important questions of text, we are getting at the heart of the active reading-thinking process. Here is a dialogue that indicates the type of progress that can be made with this strategy:

Day 1

S: What is found in the southeastern snakes, also the copperhead, rattlesnakes, vipers— they have. I'm not doing this right.

T: All right. Do you want to know about pit vipers?

S: Yeah.

T: What would be a good question about the pit vipers that starts with the word why?

S: No response.

T: How about "Why are the snakes called pit vipers?"

S: Why do they want to know that they are called pit vipers?

T: Try it again.

S: Why do they, pit vipers in a pit?

T: How about "Why do they call the snakes pit vipers?"

S: Why do they call the snakes pit vipers?

T: There you go. Good for you.

Day 4

S: No question.

T: What's this paragraph about?

S: Spinner's mate. How do Spinner's mate . . . ?

T: That's good. Keep going.

S: How do Spinner's mate is much smaller than . . . how am I going to say that?

T: Take your time with it. You want to ask a question about Spinner's mate and what he does beginning with the word "how."

S: How do they spend most of his time sitting?

T: You're very close. The question would be, "How does Spinner's mate spend most of his time?" Now you ask it.

S: How does Spinner's mate spend most of this time?

Day 7

S: How does the pressure from below push the mass of the hot rock against the opening? Is that it?

T: Not quite. Start your question with "What happens when?"

S: What happens when the pressure below pushes the mass of hot rock against the opening?

T: Good for you. Good job.

Day 11

S: What is the most interesting of the insect-eating plants and where do the plants live at?

T: Two excellent questions! The are both clear and important questions. Ask us one at a time now.

Day 15
S: Why do scientists come to the south pole to study?
T: Excellent question! That is what this paragraph is all about. (Palincsar, 1984)

As students spend time with this strategy, the amount of guidance and feedback that they need lessens. Students, even less fluent readers, can be taught to be active readers and to be metacognitively aware.

After Reading

After reading expository text, students need to be able to recall, reconstruct, and synthesize their reading. The need to make connections between what they have learned so that information doesn't exist in a vacuum.

In the K-W-L procedure, after reading, students discuss the answers to the questions they have asked. They will find that they have some new questions and some questions that remain unanswered. This is the time to send students to other sources. When students are interested and have the "need to know," source books should be available in our classrooms. After reading, we want students to be able to integrate and assimilate information from a variety of sources, including the school library.

After actively reading an expository article and looking for answers to questions, students could map the article according to categories of content. This procedure should be modeled by the teacher with the whole group before students are asked to try it in small groups, and eventually on their own.

The teacher writes the topic on the board and asks the students to identify one of the categories of information that was addressed in the reading. The category is written on the board, and the students are told to think of details that were learned about that category. The details are included on the map. The same procedure is followed for the other categories. Figure 3.4 is an example of a map of the article on catfish that was completed by the same third-grade class.

After the teacher and students map the article according to the categories of knowledge, many types of writing activities can be utilized. Writing after reading expository text gives the students a way to organize and synthesize their thinking and learning.

1. The map provides a good stimulus for writing outlines. The article has been broken down into topics and details, making it easy to begin the process of outlining, even at the third-grade level.
2. The map provides a good stimulus for writing paragraphs. Each branch of the map has a topic sentence and detail sentences. Groups can be formed, each group writing a different paragraph, for example, one about the appearance of the catfish, another about the habitat, and so on.

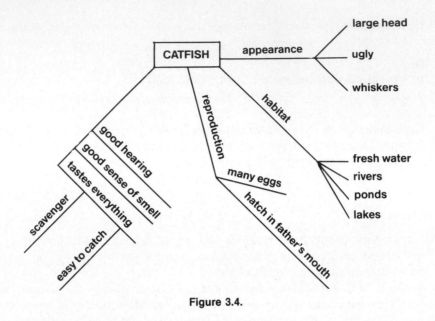

Figure 3.4.

3. The map can provide a structure for rewriting the entire article. This can be especially effective if the original article is poorly organized. Students can see that there is more than one way to write about a subject, and that sometimes what they read is poorly written and organized.
4. The map can serve as the basis for library research. Students might be asked to write follow-up reports on an animal each has chosen. The categories on the map would be the titles on the index cards that students would use to gather their information. The categories would help to organize information from a variety of sources.

One of the most important things students have to do after they read is make connections between what they learned yesterday, what they learned today, and what they will learn tomorrow. Many students do not make connections unless we help them to do so. One strategy that helps students make connections is the construction of categorical charts; these enable students to generalize the knowledge categories across different chapters, articles, and books. Figure 3.5 is a chart that might be constructed after reading three animal articles, one on catfish, one on black widow spiders and one on emperor penguins.

These charts could be used for different areas of learning, such as regions or cultures in social studies and plants or elements in science. In this way we are helping students connect the new to the known.

Students need to continue to answer questions following reading, as we will always be evaluating student performance. However, if students *only* answer questions, we are looking at the product of their learning and not at the process. If we help students to internalize the process, we can assume that the product (their answers to questions) will improve.

	APPEARANCE	HABITAT	FOOD	ENEMIES	MATING	INTERESTING FACTS
CATFISH						
BLACK-WIDOW SPIDERS						
EMPEROR PENGUINS						

Figure 3.5.

Instructional Issues in Expository Text

In this discussion of thinking about expository text, we stressed these critical issues.

1. Our instructional strategies for dealing with expository text should focus on both the content to be learned and the process of reading to learn. We must give the students ways that help them to be active thinkers in the content areas.
2. We need to instruct in comprehension and not simply evaluate it. We need to model the process of getting meaning from text and allow the students the time they need to think actively about the text.

SUMMARY

In this chapter we have focused on instructional practices that give students the chance to be thinkers. Reading is thinking, and only when we are actively thinking about what we read can we construct a rich meaning of text. The more we bring to reading in the form of prior knowledge of content, structure, and vocabulary, the easier it is for us to interact with the text and construct meaning. We view thinking in a holistic sense, and we need to focus our instruction on giving students the opportunities to elicit meaning from whole text.

There is no formula for instruction to maximize students' thinking. Good teaching is not quantifiable. It is not a science; it is an art. Teachers are decision makers, making hundreds of on-the-spot decisions each day. Good teachers make these decisions with their goals and theory in mind. What we are suggesting is that teachers should think about reading instruction in terms of what should be done before, during, and after reading. Instruction should be informed by what we have learned about reading being a holistic, interactive, constructive, and strategic process.

Before reading we should use those strategies that activate schemata and enable students to set their own purposes. During reading we should focus our instruction on helping students use metacognitive strategies that enable them to think and demand clarity of text. After reading we need to give students opportunities to use writing to recall, reconstruct, and synthesize what they have read.

4

The Breadth of Mathematics

In the last decade or so, the cognitivists have brought about a clear focus on mathematical thinking and problem solving. We now see the student as actively constructing meaning, connecting new information to existing knowledge structures, and creating new relationships among structures. See, for instance, the writings of Carpenter et al. (1982), Carpenter (1985), Ginsburg (1983), Nesher (1986), Resnick and Ford (1981), Schoenfeld (1983, 1985), and Silver (1983). Before looking at what the cognitivists have learned about the intellectual processes involved in mathematical thinking, we need to look at the knowledge domain of mathematics.

Mathematics has two main aspects: pure and applied. Pure mathematics refers to the beautiful abstractions of the symbolic language of mathematics, its concepts and theories. Applied mathematics refers to the useful and powerful ways in which mathematics can explain the physical world around us.

If you look at the history of math, you'll see over and over again how some brilliant person was looking at a phenomenon in the real world and tried to make sense of it through the known mathematics of the day. A new and original form of mathematics was created to deal with the particular situation. Then this new idea was spun off into an elaborate and highly *abstract* formulation to address many other problems or situations. For instance, a mathematician was asked by a famous nobleman and gambler to figure out why he kept losing a particular bet in a dice game. The analysis led to probability theory.

Though different in many ways, pure and applied mathematics help each other. To put it simply, mathematicians frequently find new applications for the marvelous abstractions of mathematics, and problems in the real world of science, technology, art, and architecture have been the genesis of conceptual breakthroughs in mathematics. The two aspects of beauty and utility are mutually beneficial and supportive. Pure mathematicians develop new abstractions, formulate theorems, and illuminate connections between branches of mathematics previously thought separate. Applied mathematicians use these abstractions to wrestle with a myriad of real-world situations, such as scheduling airlines' flights, launching the space shuttle, and predicting how old the typical business executive will be when she dies.

What mathematics do we teach in schools? The curriculum is heavily weighted toward the abstractions of pure math. Various curriculum reforms have been overly concerned with what concepts and topics to include in the elementary school. Insufficient attention has been paid to providing *meaningful contexts* students might understand and be motivated to think about. For us, an essential ingredient for motivation and understanding is the real world and its situations, problems, and phenomena. These are the grist of thinking mills.

We are not merely saying that there needs to be a better balance between concepts and applications since that usually means that once the child understands the concept, he can apply it in a real situation. We believe that true conceptual understanding can be enhanced by wrestling with real, particular problems in which the concepts may be *inductively* understood and appreciated. Actively attacking specific problems mathematically allows the student to think about and use the mathematics he knows. The teacher then uses these experiences to *build bridges* to the concepts and develop a deeper level of meaning and understanding.

Consider the concept of "area." How would it be taught so that students really understood what it means? The usual heavily deductive approach encouraged by most textbooks gives an explanation of the concept and a few examples of how you calculate it; then the students apply the concept to a group of exercises. The emphasis is on the *procedure* to calculate the area, and thus the concept of area that most students form is highly procedural: "Area is what you get when you multiply the length times the width of a rectangle and say 'square feet' (or inches) afterward." They may get the right answer, but what is their conception of area?

A more meaningful approach would be to start with existing schemata, for instance, square floor tiles and a rectangular or square room, perhaps the classroom. Ask how many tiles are needed to retile the entire floor? The key conceptual shift is moving from one-dimensional, linear measurement to two dimensions, thinking in squares instead of lines (like inches or feet). The students may actually count squares or realize that they can use their knowledge of multiplication to figure out how many tiles would be needed. After this simple introduction, you can give groups of students an example of a new tile that will be used; it is 1 foot on each side. They can then use this basic measuring device to determine how many of the new tiles would be needed to cover the floor, or the floors of other rooms.

If their multiplication knowledge is sound, they (or some of them) will realize that measuring the length and width of the rectangular room (with a ruler or tape measure) will be easier than (though perhaps not as much fun as) placing the sample tile on the floor. After they have experimented, they should discuss, with your help, how the linear measure of the length and width is related to the number of tiles.

One way might be to ask them how many tiles it would take to cover some absurdly large area, like the gym or the playground.

Next, you can move them from the concrete experiences with the real world to the more abstract notions of area. Just as foot is a standard (and familiar) measure of distance, their tile is a standard measure of area: a square foot. So instead of saying it would take 600 tiles to cover the classroom's floor (20 feet by 30 feet), we can say our floor is 600 square feet. This is a simple conceptual hop, not a big jump, because of the experiential groundwork you have laid. Finally, you move to the symbolic and procedural aspects of 20 feet × 30 feet = 600 square feet, or the formula length × width = area ($l \times w = A$). These representations should be last, not first, as often happens in texts. They are ways of abstractly representing a concept.

Most children will not grasp the meaning of a concept (like area) without a fair amount of work that ties the concept to their prior knowledge and some situation that motivates them to think about the concept itself. A few may be able to understand the concept from an initial, rather abstract explanation. It may be their natural talent or it may be that they have had some prior experience that they can use for their own construction of meaning. But most students need you to establish some framework, to activate some relevant schema to help them make the bridge from where they are now in their thinking to an incorporation of the new idea.

This little example of floor tiles gives a basic understanding of the concept of area, introducing it in a meaningful way. To broaden the concept in the students' minds, other examples and activities are needed, for instance, varying the shapes of the areas being measured and the units of measure (square inches, square centimeters, square meters, square miles, etc., perhaps introducing the concept of acre later on). Also, students could profit from representations and drawings, such as on graph paper. Such additional experiences all serve to build a more generalized and abstract concept of area.

A key idea that we will frequently mention in this chapter is the need to permeate the curriculum with the real-life situations, phenomena, and relevant problems of high interest to the students that can be addressed by applied mathematics. We can use initial understanding of concepts from special cases in applied mathematics as the "beachheads" for meaningfully expanding and generalizing these concepts to greater levels of abstraction in pure mathematics.

A major part of understanding mathematics involves active construction of meaning, allowing children to assimilate information into their existing schemata and modifying their schemata to create new structures and relationships (as we tried to show with the example of area). These processes will occur only when students are allowed the time to engage in what Piaget calls "reflective abstraction," creating and coordinating relationships between objects (and in older children, among ideas, concepts, and experiences). See the article by Kamii (1982).

Yet there is a serious obstacle to be overcome in our schools. Textbooks and adopted curricula tend to push children into *premature and excessive symbolization*. In every grade, students are asked hastily to "learn" how to do operations with symbols and algorithms (mechanical computational procedures). The bombardment of abstract symbols and dimly conceived procedures thwarts the reflective thinking essential for understanding. The mind shuts down.

Researchers have found that children come to kindergarten with some simple but basically sound problem-solving procedures that they abandon for relatively meaningless and mechanical procedures they are taught in school (Carpenter, 1985). Experiences with counting and ordering objects have given a good intuitive basis for understanding numbers and relations. School starts the process of representation with symbols. The forms of symbolic representation must be linked with understanding and meaning. Alas, there are a variety of places where these linkages can break down, the first of which is the connection between the symbol and what it refers to in a concrete context (What does the symbol " + " refer to in 2 + 2? Or what does the symbol "2" refer to?)

Throughout school, children encounter a staggering display of mathematical symbols and procedures for manipulating them. Symbols are the heart of mathematics. But when and how fast must they deal with which symbols and procedures? How do we ensure the *understanding* of the procedure? Every teacher we've worked with initially teaches for understanding of the concepts and procedures. She may use a number of different approaches and strategies to help all the students truly understand what is going on in a procedure. But the sands in the hour glass eventually run out. Then she decides to settle for getting those students who don't fully understand to memorize the way to do the procedure, the way to get the right answer. Maybe it will become clear to them later. Maybe we'll get back to it. But for many students, a rope ladder has been built with cobwebs. As they climb higher in the curriculum, they really have only a slim chance of ascending.

WHAT IS TO BE DONE?

How do we encourage students to construct meaning in math? How can we give them enough time for reflective abstraction? How can we give them the right balance of concrete experiences (with time for reflection) and symbolic representations? We will elaborate on our major idea of interweaving applied and pure mathematics with three suggestions: (1) linking conceptual and procedural konwledge through existing schemata, (2) using a problem-solving framework, and (3) encouraging metacognition.

Linking Conceptual and Procedural Knowledge

From the example of area, you can see that there is a difference between understanding the concept and calculating a quantity from a known procedure. Yet both are important. A teacher must not only provide experiences that build sound conceptual knowledge but also show how to use it. Both kinds of knowledge require understanding and meaningfulness and can reinforce one another. Although we believe procedural knowledge is essential, don't forget our previous statements about the hasty and dominant use of procedures and symbolization in texts. The art of teaching requires the right sequencing and blending of the conceptual and procedural.

Let's take a simple example to illustrate. When a child is asked to subtract 14 from 21, how does she think about the task? It is usually written as

$$\begin{array}{r} 21 \\ -14 \\ \hline \end{array}$$

In school, we usually teach children *one way* to do this task and get the right answer. We teach a procedure for borrowing that can be memorized without much understanding. But there are several different ways a child may think about what is going on in real life:

- I had 21 jelly beans and I ate 14. How many do I have left?
- I have 21 jelly beans; you have 14. How many more than you do I have?
- I have 14 jelly beans and I need 21, how many more must I get?

These are three different situations, despite the fact that they can be represented symbolically in the same way. Children could use various personal strategies to figure out the answer.

In contrast, when asked to deal only with the symbols (21 − 14), what must the children know? To get the right answer, all they need to know is a set of rules for the procedures, such as borrowing 10 units from the 20 to create an 11 from which to subtract 4, and so forth. However, if we want them to understand both the procedure and the underlying concepts, much more is needed. For instance, they should know that the 2 means two 10s, or 20; that the 1 in 21 is not the same as the 1 in 14—our base-ten system has specific place values. They must understand that 21 can be as readily seen as 20 and 1 or as 10 and 11, thus allowing easy subtraction of the units digits. Procedural knowledge means understanding *why* a rule works, not just how to get it to work. Conceptual knowledge of our base-ten system and place value is much more than merely memorizing that the 2 in 21 means two 10s; rather, 10s and units can be grouped and regrouped at will and our symbols are merely a convenient recording of the total amount.

In order to understand our base-ten system, young children must develop appropriate schemata by counting objects and arranging them into groups of tens and hundreds. We probably underestimate how much practical experience with such manipulatives is necessary for a child to construct in his own mind this convention that we have adopted. For decades teachers have used a host of manipulatives, such as Cuisenaire rods, to build this kind of experiential basis for understanding. The excellent curriculum, Math Their Way, is the latest in this genre.

Most children develop a money schema fairly early. This prior knowledge and motivation to understand money should not be ignored. Using pennies, dimes, and dollars, you have a simple but powerful context for addressing place value and the little subtraction problem above. A key issue in place value is realizing that ten 1s and one 10 are the same quantity. It is a problem of equivalence. They are reversible. Work with manipulatives is geared to helping the child make this connection. After it is understood conceptually, through some actions in the real world, then it can be represented symbolically. To do so beforehand is counterproductive.

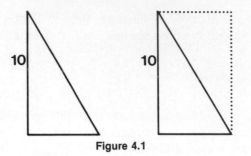

Figure 4.1

Let's take a more difficult example. Imagine that you are trying to teach students to apply their understanding of area to triangles. Their concept of area was developed through a schema of squares and square tiles, and they have used this understanding to find the areas of squares and rectangles. Most texts simply aim for procedural understanding of the areas of triangles through the formula 1/2 *bh* (half the base times the height). Students memorize the formula and merely plug in the appropriate numbers to calculate the area of any triangle. But what does the formula represent and why does it work? Here is a very simple visualization that should *precede* the formula. Imagine trying to figure out the area of the triangle in Figure 4.1.

This is a special kind of triangle, a right triangle. It clearly shows why 1/2 *bh* works in this case. It is half of the rectangle that would be formed by those two sides. Then try a different kind of triangle, such as the one in Figure 4.2.

In this case, cutting the isosceles triangle in half and sticking one piece onto the other to make a rectangle will also illustrate why the formula works. Have the students try cutting and moving pieces of other isosceles triangles to illustrate the idea. With this experiential basis, the formula will make sense and be more readily applied to unusual triangles (e.g., scalene).

If you want to have fun with the concept of area, put it into a really meaningful context like pizza. Some restaurants cut it into pie slices; some use gridlike cuts. Get pizzas of the same total size that are cut in different ways and compare the areas of the slices. Make cardboard copies of the pizzas showing how they are sliced. You will have some pretty wild shapes: pie slice quasi triangles, rectangles, squares, arc-like pieces, and so on. Find the largest piece, and rank order the others. How do

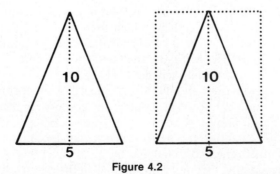

Figure 4.2

you know which are larger? What are their approximate areas? Students can estimate based on their understanding of triangles or you can introduce the concept of "pi" and wrestle with areas of circles and partial circles.

In these cases, you are trying to create both conceptual and procedural understanding and linkages between them. We have found that these tasks can be best accomplished when you purposely build on students' schemata, using examples and explanations from already-meaningful and motivating contexts.

Using a Problem-Solving Framework

A very heartening situation in the state of mathematics education today is the shift toward problem solving. We have listed a fair number of resources on teaching problem solving at the end of the chapter. If properly addressed, a problem-solving approach to mathematics can inspire complex thinking and positive motivation. This trend is even present in textbooks, where the obligatory "story" problems, tacked on at the end of a chapter, are now being integrated into the fabric of each chapter. A good beginning!

Traditionally, teachers have been led to think of mathematics as a mixture of facts, concepts, and applications (with story problems being a kind of application). Earlier, we stated that we do not see problems as being something that occurs after conceptual knowledge. Mathematics (and life) does not fall neatly into a linear progression as follows: First learn the math facts; then learn the concepts; then apply this knowledge in the real world through problems. Although we did urge great caution in ensuring that a conceptual basis was laid before introducing extensive symbolization and algorithms, problem solving is not the end product of instruction; it may just as readily be the beginning.

We see a more cyclical, dynamic process in which a student's existing schemata drive understanding by always relating the encountered to the known. If "problems" are posed in rich, meaningful contexts, problem solving can *initiate* understanding, foster clarity and conceptual understanding, and provide motivation for constructing symbolizations and procedures. In fact, problem solving is probably the best example of *thinking* in the mathematics curriculum.

For example, imagine a fourth-grade class with twenty-eight students. When they do problem solving, they usually break into seven groups of four. One day, when two students were absent, instead of merely telling the students how to form groups, we explained the "problem" to the class and asked them to work with the person next to them to figure out how we could arrange the class into groups of three or four students. After a number of false starts ("We could have thirteen groups"—thirteen groups of two were not what we wanted), they focused on finding some groupings that fit the criteria (putting all twenty-six students into groups of three or four). They did find the two possibilities: six 3s and two 4s or two 3s and five 4s. Then they decided to use the latter because it had more groups of four (their usual arrangement).

We did more with this spontaneous problem at the time; it is from a class of problems we will show later. (Do you remember the kangaroos and the dingoes?) It serves as an example here for what we are after: problems that mean something to the students, problems they are motivated to attack and ones that they can "get their minds around." But also notice that the answer is not obvious.

For most students, story problems are an occasion simply to figure out what operation to perform on the two numbers in the story. They have concocted some fairly outrageous repertoires for solving story problems. They don't really read the problems; they look for the two numbers and then automatically follow a procedure: "If one number is a lot bigger than the other, I divide the smaller one into it." But what operation would you use with the numbers 26, 3, and 4? Problems of this kind can get students to stop and think.

A great many story problems in texts are one-step translations of arithmetic operations. They involve understanding what is going on, determining the proper operation, and doing the calculation. For example, "If pens cost 29 cents apiece, how much would three pens cost?" Problems like this involve reading comprehension and require realizations that one pen costs 29 cents and the desired goal is the total cost of three such pens. Such problems are quite different from the problem of twenty-six students in groups of three or four. The pen problem involves a simple operation based on initial understanding; the problem of the twenty-six students can be attacked in many different ways after it is understood. There are several very different types of math problems that we will discuss in a later section of this chapter.

Most teachers of problem solving teach some version of a process with four phases originally suggested by the famous mathematician George Polya.

- Understanding the problem
- Devising a plan of attack
- Carrying it out
- Reviewing

The first phase is critically important. Understanding the problem cannot be overemphasized. It is a very complex task, involving

- Understanding the language and vocabulary used
- Understanding the initial conditions of the situation
- Understanding the desired goal(s) and constraints
- Forming some kind of "representations" of all of the above
- Examining your assumptions about all of the above

These all relate directly to what schemata become activated. Meaningful understanding of each depends in large measure on the context of the problem. How much prior experience and knowledge that can aid understanding exist in memory? For each student, understanding is a *process* of constructing representations of various aspects of the problem.

For example, consider a relatively simple subtraction problem such as "Annie has twelve guns; five are rifles, and the rest are pistols. How many pistols does she have?" How does the child think about guns, rifles, and pistols? What schemata pertain to these three terms? What kind of representation of the three terms is necessary to attack this problem? The child would have to know that "gun" is a general category (or concept) that contains a variety of special types, of which rifles and pistols are two possibilities. Rifles would have to be distinguished from pistols through some imagery. Then comes the representation that Annie has twelve of these things, five of which are the rifle type. Incidentally, did your mind leap to the Annie Oakley schema? What response would a girl having guns produce in your class? Schemata do funny things.

In more complex problems, conceiving of the initial situation, constraints, and goal state is significantly more difficult. Consider the following:

> I have thirty students in my classroom. They have sworn that they can each keep a secret for one full day. On Monday at 9:00 A.M. I tell a secret to two students. They must keep the secret until Tuesday at 9:00 A.M., when they may each tell two other students (who must keep the secret until 9:00 A.M. the next day, when they can each tell two more students). If these students do keep the secret for one day, on what day will the entire class know the secret?

How did you conceive the problem: the initial conditions, the constraints, the goal? How did you represent all these in your mind? Did you sketch some on paper? The process of thinking about what is happening and working on the problem is probably more important than the answer. What assumptions did you make? If we assume that the two students who are initially told the secret keep it for a day and tell a total of four more on Tuesday, and these four tell eight more on Wednesday, then these eight will tell the other sixteen members of the class on Thursday ($2 + 4 + 8 + 16 = 30$).

The second phase of problem solving is planning how to attack the problem. Obviously we have already started talking about this phase, which relies in a crucial way on the understanding and representation of the problem. Students go through a set of mental actions to search for possible ways to attack the problem, often called problem-solving strategies. In the preceding problem, should we draw a picture, act it out, make a list of the numbers of people? Students can be helped to think the problem through: Is this strategy likely to help me get what I want?

There are a great many books for teachers that illustrate various strategies and how to teach them to students. In a later section of this chapter, we will show some of these strategies. Also, see our list of resources at the end of the chapter.

The third phase of problem solving is carrying out the strategy, actually working on the problem. During this phase, it is important for the student to engage in self-monitoring to ensure proper execution: "Am I using the strategy the right way? Am I following the right progression? Am I getting closer to the solution?" "Where am I now? Is this where I thought I would be? Have I chosen the right strategy?" This is not obsessive self-doubt but rather a careful rethinking of the strategy. If it is not an effective strategy after all, then the students should specifically think "What did I get out of this approach? Did I learn anything new that can be used in my next attempt?" Then they can go back and rethink their assumptions, representations, and understandings.

As you can see, self-monitoring for executing and evaluating progress is an essentially metacognitive process. It involves a stepping back and looking at what you are doing, thinking about your own work. It is a key ingredient of problem solving that students can learn with practice and help from the teacher as well as from their peers.

In the final phase, when a solution has been obtained, it is important for the student to review the initial conditions, constraints, and goals to make sure that the "solution" fits. An invalid assumption, a misunderstanding of the problem, or an erroneous step along the way can cause an "answer" that violates something in the problem. You can make this reviewing phase very meaningful for the class by encouraging even broader reflection on the assumptions and strategies they used.

In many problems, a clear initial *understanding* will allow students to roughly judge the reasonableness of their answers. In the keeping a secret problem, Tuesday is an unreasonable answer (unless you assume that the students will not keep quiet for twenty-four hours). For most problems involving computation, there are basic upper and lower limits that bound reasonableness based on initial understanding of the problem. Helping students to think about these limits before embarking on a solution is very worthwhile. For instance, in our problem of arranging twenty-six students into groups of three or four, clearly we are not going to have seven groups of four (because that was what we used before two students were absent) and we won't have as many as thirteen groups (because we don't want pairs). Even without checking through specific calculations, we would know that the answer of "two groups of three and eight groups of four" must be wrong. And so should your students (with practice).

As we stated earlier, we believe that a crucial ingredient for mathematics in schools is dealing with the real world, with situations, problems, and phenomena that have some bearing on the lives of the students. We might call these *personally meaningful contexts* for problem solving. They would draw on the existing schemata of the students. They would be intriguing and provocative, stimulating thinking, and inherently motivating.

Although the newer texts have a better class of problems than those of yesteryear and there are more resource books around than ever before, we feel that teachers are still going to have to develop good problems for their own particular students. Their schemata, personalities, learning styles, or what-have-you are just not the same as any other group of students. Natural opportunities for problem solving must be seized on and created. Absent students (as above) allowed new arrangements to be conceived. How about a broken audio-tape cassette? How long would the tape be if unwound? How would you attack that problem before unwinding and measuring?

Encouraging Metacognition

We have already mentioned several key places in problem solving where metacognition should be encouraged. The general concern for metacognition in mathematical thinking goes to the very heart of what "mathematizing" is. Our culture has a very misguided notion about what doing mathematics means. Somehow we feel that quickly coming up with the one right answer is what is called for in math. We have standardized achievement tests that cram a horrendous number of "problems" into a short space of time, and we call that a measure of what has been learned.

A student who is knowledgeable and competent in mathematics is one who when confronted with a problem for which there is no obvious solution will use the resources available. She will *persist* in trying to understand the problem, in conceiving of ways to represent it, in looking for ways to solve it. These processes are as true for a first-grader as for a Ph.D. in math. The absolute level of difficulty is irrelevant. This persistence to use everything available—schemata, solution strategies, whatever—and to consider carefully and discard ineffective representations and strategies, is what is crucial. These are primarily metacognitive processes. See Schoenfeld (1983, 1985).

You can teach students to use a variety of metacognitive "prompts" in problem solving. In the understanding phase, they can ask themselves, "Have I ever encountered any similar problems? What do they really want here? What information is irrelevant? What are the different assumptions I could make?" In planning strategies, they can ask, "What will each of the strategies I have learned get me? Which strategies seem more likely to work, given my assumptions?" They can develop the self-monitoring of solution evaluation previously described.

You can teach these processes and have students practice them in small groups, very much like the reciprocal teaching in reading and the cooperative learning techniques. When the students are in their groups, you act as a roving consultant, moving among them, listening to what they are doing, but only assisting when all members of the group want your help. If one member has a question, he should learn to rely on the thinking of the rest of the group, not turn to you. When members of small groups discuss plausible choices, they see one another struggle. Their anxiety and insecurity lessen as they realize that they are not alone in their doubts.

You can discuss problems with the whole class, examining assumptions students made and strategies they tried. You can give them specific guided practice in particular strategies so that they see the need for each strategy and how to use it. With discussion of all of these elements, more thoughtful awareness of the thinking processes will emerge. Practice individually and in small groups will solidify the capability.

And yet, behind all these thinking processes is the belief within each student that persisting is worth it. If the basic affective feelings, attitudes, and beliefs have not been positive, no amount of discussing or choosing "meaningful" or interesting problems will foster the persistence of thoughtfulness. Metacognition is directly linked to affect. How do I feel when I think about my own thinking? Do I believe that I can succeed if I persist? Recall what we said earlier about students who have confidence in their own thinking. They have more tolerance for setbacks and minor frustrations than those who lack confidence. They feel challenged and not defeated. They believe in themselves and their ability to figure out eventually what is going on.

Perhaps then a major purpose for our mathematics program should be to foster these feelings and beliefs. If students spent more school time working with others on potentially meaningful problems to be addressed mathematically, if they were encouraged to take the time to think through a problem, if they encountered many different problems and practiced many different ways to attack them, if they were given consistent encouragement that these problems were within their grasp, if they discussed their ideas and how to become more aware of their own thinking as they worked on these problems, if these processes of problem solving were valued more than the speedily derived one right answer, how would students feel about themselves as "mathematizers" after six years?

THE ART OF PROBLEM SOLVING

In this section we will look at problems and strategies for working on them. As already stated we believe that you should arrange "good" problems for students to attack mathematically. Some criteria of good problems for us are these:

- Initial conditions and desired goals are set in a meaningful context for the students.
- There is no obvious solution to attain the goals.
- The students should be motivated to pursue the problem.
- Working on the problem should involve mathematical thinking and knowledge that is appropriate for the students' levels.
- Discussion of solutions should allow the teacher to build on the problem to explore key concepts and processes in mathematics.

These criteria would urge you to minimize the use of drill exercises for computation since they involve no context and little thought. Also note that what is a problem for some may not be for others. For instance, consider this problem: "Betty bought three doughnuts for $1.20. How much did each doughnut cost?" Although it may require appropriate thought for one group of students, it might be seen as an obvious division operation by another group. For the second group, this is not a problem at all; it is merely a thinly disguised computational drill.

You will occasionally run across problems that are based on spotting the hidden assumption or using some trick to solve them. Often these are called puzzle problems. Exercise caution in using these with students. Look at the problem to see if it involves mathematical thinking or concepts. When discussing the problem with the class after they've worked on it, will you be able to extend their understanding of mathematics?

We realize that the criteria that speak of meaningful contexts and motivation are not necessarily simple. A classroom of children contain a wide diversity of interests, prior knowledge, and the like. It is unlikely that any one problem or context will be equally appealing to all the students. However, your attempt to create meaningfulness through a variety of activities and problems will produce the positive climate necessary for students to be willing to engage in substantial thought.

Types of Problems

We see three broad types of problems worth considering:

- Translation problems
- Process problems
- Applied problems

Translation problems involve translating the words of a story problem into some kind of mathematical sentence or operation. These problems can vary from simple, one-step problems (as we've shown) to complex, multistep problems such as

> Each case of soda has twenty-four cans. A delivery truck can hold ten cases on each rack, and there are twenty racks in the truck. If the local convenience store sells 2,000 cans of soda each month, how many truck loads should be delivered in a month?

Clearly, the student would have to represent somehow what is going on in this problem. Adequate conceptualization would be very difficult for some children and simple for others.

Process problems cannot be readily translated into a mathematical sentence that could be used directly to solve the problem. You would have to create a process for working toward a solution that uses some strategy like making a table or chart.

Recall the problem of the dog tied to the barn (20 feet by 30 feet) with 20 feet of rope. Should the rope be tied to a hook on the corner or the middle of the long side of the barn for maximum running room? It would be most difficult to work on this problem without drawing a picture. Once the pictorial representation is constructed, some basic geometrical knowledge could solve the problem.

Process problems can vary greatly in their complexity and underlying concepts. The previous problem and the pet store with kangaroos and dingoes are two examples. Process problems provoke thinking to understand and represent the conditions and goal(s) as well as to work toward a solution.

Applied problems cover a lot of territory. They are powerful contexts for using mathematics for understanding, organizing, and making sense of information from the world. Consider the following applied problem:

> People in the United States consume vast quantities of soft drinks. According to *Beverage World* magazine, in North Carolina 39.9 gallons of soft drinks a year are sold *for every person*. That is the high for the fifty states; the low is 20.6 gallons in Wyoming. What do these statistics mean? How were they calculated? How might the information have been collected? How much is 40 gallons in terms of 12-ounce cans? Do you drink that many cans in a year? How about 20 gallons? What do these work out to in months, weeks, days? If 40 gallons represent the overall total sales divided by the number of people, what does this suggest for the people who bought and drank less? Are there some people who never drink soda? How

about those who drank more? What are all the different kinds of soft drinks on the market? Are there different types (e.g., quinine water or cola)?

Although some of these questions could be posed directly and worked on in class, others might require a little research or data collection. Different types of stores sell soft drinks; what do they stock? What are their big sellers? What about the actual consumption of the students? They could keep journals of everything they drink during a week or a month. These data could be tabulated for individuals and for the class, and consumption of various beverages could be compared. The data on soft drink consumption of the class for a week could be projected (extrapolated) to a year's worth to see how they compared with the high and low state figures. And so on.

In applied problems, students have opportunities to collect and analyze data from real situations. They can make their own graphs and charts and make estimates, measurements, and calculations—experience the value of mathematics to understand the world around them. The teacher can carefully use these examples and illustrations to build a solid conceptual understanding of key aspects of mathematics as well as its usefulness.

Applied problems can vary greatly in their complexity. Some textbooks include applied problems that are rather narrow, such as extracting information from a table, schedule, map, or menu and using it in computations. The table may have some interesting numerical data, but the cognitive processes involved are more like those we are calling *focus* than the more complex thinking needed in an *investigation* like the applied problem above. Some educators refer to these more open-ended and complex applied problems as situational, real-life, or nonroutine problems.

Problem-Solving Strategies

Quite a number of excellent handbooks illustrate various problem-solving strategies and how to teach them. We will not try to summarize them. Instead, we will list these sources at the end of the chapter. They can provide a much more detailed description of what can be done to help students. Here we will just mention some of the points to keep in mind as you are teaching for thinking. Some worthwhile general strategies include these:

- Use objects to represent the problem.
- Act it out physically.
- Draw a picture or diagram.
- Make a table, chart, or organized list.
- Simplify the problem and solve that version.
- Work backward from the goal toward the start.
- Make a guess and check its accuracy.

Each resource book will have a somewhat different list of strategies for you to help your students learn. It is important to remember that every strategy uses some kind of logical reasoning (the thinking we've discussed as focus and pattern). All require that you try looking at the problem differently, checking assumptions thoughtfully. Many also encourage looking for numerical patterns. These three are often cited as being separate strategies, yet they are intimately interwoven.

It is important that you think of strategies as *tools for thinking*. Some students have definite preferences for the strategies they habitually use. Although there may be some innate inclination for some approaches (e.g., visualization, as in pictures or diagrams), it is more likely that these preferences are based on understanding and practice. Thus, there is a major role for you to play in introducing different strategies, arranging situations in which specific strategies are particularly effective to motivate their use, and giving lots of practice. When students are relatively comfortable with a wide variety of methods, they should be encouraged to use whatever approach they want.

These strategies are especially valuable for attacking process problems. The wide variety of contexts, concepts, and thinking students can encounter in process problems makes them ideal for understanding strategies and developing proficiency in their use. You should select some of the resource books at the end of this chapter to supplement your curriculum. They offer a good bridge to the more complex and open-ended applied problems.

Some educators would have students learn to recognize problems by "type." *We disagree.* This idea appears to be a holdover from old algebra texts with motion problems and mixed-nuts problems and the like. Although some strategies are more useful for some process problems than others, the worst we could do is to train students to choose reflexively a problem-solving strategy based on a quick analysis of a problem's features. That would definitely short-circuit thinking. We would much rather you help students spend thoughtful time in the understanding phase. Also, your guided practice with various strategies can point out significant differences in how to think about different problems.

Many educators are finding that teachers must explicitly teach students how to use each particular problem-solving strategy. For instance, Cathy Cook (1987) encourages teachers to use different types of lessons for students to

- Develop skills in the four phases of problem solving
- Experience a need and desire to use *each* strategy
- Understand how to execute *each* strategy
- Practice solving problems with *each* strategy
- Select and use a strategy that will probably work

In the next three sections we will illustrate some of the strategies as we show examples of problems that you might adapt, modify, and incorporate into your program. In the next section we will discuss problems from the curricular areas of numbers and measurement. We will follow with problems from noncomputational areas of math. These are very important to demonstrate to students that mathematizing is more than doing computations, no matter how meaningful. We will conclude with problems showing relationships. Since textbooks have no small supply of translation problems for you to use, we will offer process and applied problems as our examples.

Numbers and Measurement

Probably the best way for students to deal with numbers and to understand arithmetic operations conceptually is to measure. Our world is full of things and ways to measure them. We count quantities; we tell time; we determine price, distance, temperature, and a host of other phenomena. All these offer marvelous opportunities for children to understand both phenomena and numbers. Also measurement activities can utilize estimation and various representations (graphs, charts, maps, etc.) to enhance thinking.

We have already mentioned the value of manipulatives. You can provoke through physical representation strong conceptual understanding of arithmetic operations in students before proceduralization. Here are several different ways to have students think of multiplication.

---

1. Arrange the students into groups of three or four and give each group twelve large Lego blocks (they are probably better than wooden blocks because they hold together). Ask the children to arrange the blocks into stacks (straight up, one completely on top of another) so that there are the same number of blocks in each stack. If they find one possibility, they should try to create others. They should make a two-column list of what they find:

HOW MANY STACKS?   HOW MANY IN EACH STACK?

When they have found all they can, discuss with the class what they found, making sure that everyone realizes all the possibilities. You can ask them, "How do you know if you have found them all?" Make sure they note that one stack of twelve blocks is different from twelve stacks of one block (and similarly for other combinations). You can make an organized list on the board to illustrate the "pattern" and how the pattern "flips" after three 4s:

HOW MANY STACKS?   HOW MANY IN EACH STACK?

HOW MANY STACKS?	HOW MANY IN EACH STACK?
1	12
2	6
3	4
4	3
6	2
12	1

Next, take one block away and ask the students to repeat the task. Have each group record its answers. Then take another away, and so forth down to one block. You can provide a special recording sheet that will make the distinction among the total blocks they are stacking easy to see. You can quickly move them through these total blocks; you do not have to put everything on the board.

At some point most groups will catch on to the idea of carefully checking for patterns. Many will see that they don't have to work out the stacks physically; they can imagine the possibilities.

After they have worked out all the possibilities, you can ask them what differences they saw from the different numbers of blocks that they started with. Most children will have noticed that when they start with eleven, seven, five, three, and two blocks, they can only make two possible arrangements (one tall stack or the individual blocks spread out). In your postactivity discussion you can lead them to a very real understanding of prime numbers as well as factors. In fact, this activity can introduce multiplication.

2. A related but more complex activity uses pegboards (a 4-by-8 foot sheet, cut into three smaller sheets 4 feet by 2 2/3 feet, golf tees, sets of large Legos, and a large quantity of small objects (such as pennies). Arrange the students into small groups (e.g., nine groups of three or four). Have nine activity centers or tables set up around the room (e.g., three in each of three corners). In one corner, three tables each have piles of forty pennies. In another, three tables each have thirty-six Legos. The other three tables each have forty-eight golf tees (or some kind of pegs). Near these last three tables (perhaps on the tray of the chalkboard) are the three small pegboard sheets. Each group goes to one of the nine tables.

They are told that there are three tasks they have to perform: (1) finding all the ways they can divide the pennies into piles that have the same amount (this should be explained and illustrated with a smaller number like sixteen), (2) finding all the ways to divide the Legos into stacks of equal height (again illustrate with sixteen), and (3) finding all the ways to divide the pegs into rows and columns that make rectangles or squares (explain and illustrate how sixteen pegs could be arranged into rows with the same number in each column and vice versa). Tell them that each group will get a chance to try all three tasks.

At each table are recording sheets set up with two columns (as in the previous example). These sheets are clearly labeled for pennies (piles and number), for Legos (stacks and number), and for pegs (rows and columns). Note that the array of pegs is a bit different, and ask them to distinguish between rows and columns. This might be too difficult for some classes; use your judgment.

Next, the groups get to try each of the three tasks. Allow anywhere from 5 to 10 minutes per task. You have to judge the pacing. Some groups will speed through and need to be asked if they have found all the possibilities. ("Are you sure? How do you know for sure?") Some groups may not find all the possibilities even though other groups have done so. All groups may move to the next task, even if the recording sheets are not actually completed.

All nine groups should move in unison, probably clockwise around the room to the next task station. Obviously, you want a minimum of disruption and lost time. Each group should tackle its second task and use the new, appropriately labeled recording sheet. When given enough time, they can all move to the third and final task. You will probably note that each task seems to take the groups a bit less time.

In the postactivity discussion, you can ask some very open-ended initial questions exploring what the students saw as differences among the tasks. Which one was the easiest, the hardest, and why? What were some similarities and some differences among them? Many children will not immediately realize that they were doing the same basic task because of the three different contexts. Discussing the basis of similarity is important.

Then you can go into a more formal debriefing of each task, asking each group to report in turn on one possibility it had found. If you happen to have nine groups of three, you can have each of the members of a group be the reporter for a different task. You can go through the pattern for each task (forty, thirty-six, and forty-eight) on the board. Usually some students will have noticed the patterns while doing the tasks and suggested to the group that they just write down the possibilities instead of doing them physically (or they could do a physical check).

As you have undoubtedly guessed, this activity is a good introduction to division. It builds on students' basic knowledge of multiplication factors. In the discussion, you can stress how multiplication and division are related; you can emphasize this concept because the students have just had a powerful and very concrete experience with it in three somewhat different forms.

Another analytical tool from our number system that is quite important is signed numbers (positive and negative). Texts often deal with negative numbers solely through a number line. There are a variety of ways that students may have already encountered negative numbers in their lives, for instance, temperature (above and below zero) and wind chill factor), golf (below and above par), and elevation on maps (above and below sea level). Do you have any budding entrepreneurs who follow the stock market (up and down points)? Notice population changes (percent increase or decrease).

A variety of phenomena could be examined, recorded, and charted over time. Easy ones to chart are the high and low temperatures for each school day during the winter (assuming it gets below zero). What if it doesn't go below zero? Why not pick another standard to illustrate negative numbers? How about freezing (32° F.)? Instead of recording the actual temperature, record how many degrees above or below freezing. Or pick the average temperature for that day in your city and record positive and negative differences from that amount. If you want all negative numbers, use the daily temperature at Death Valley as your standard.

Charting and graphing a variety of phenomena are fascinating to children of all ages. Kindergarteners love to see giant bar graphs that show almost anything they know about: how many brothers and sisters each person has; how many of them were born in each month; how many of them like which flavor of ice cream the best. The list is almost endless. It is important to show each individual quantity as a "square" in the bar, not just a bar that goes up with numbers on the side. The children should help you construct the bars. Perhaps they could glue big squares in a pile to represent their quantity (their one vote for the best ice cream or their three squares for their three sisters).

As they get older, students can use charts and graphs to represent or summarize data that they have gathered or found. An activity that has been written up many times elsewhere involves students charting the different colors of the M & M candies in each of their own little bags. Using color coding on bar graphs is a very powerful device to focus attention and facilitate analysis. Earlier we mentioned a class collecting data on their own beverage consumption. These data could be charted and color-coded in many different ways; in fact, after the students have had some guided experience with making charts and graphs, you should let them take raw data and, working in small groups, create their own inimitable graphic representation. This is a marvelous opportunity to allow for projection, the creative extension of what they know.

Units for measuring time offer some intriguing possibilities for activities. For younger grades (K–3), it is important to give them concrete experiences with these units (especially seconds and minutes). You could use a stopwatch to time some students performing various tasks (walking across the room or reciting the alphabet), while others estimated how much time had elapsed. They should also carefully observe the hands on a circular clock as well as digits on a digital clock. They should time events themselves with a stopwatch. This sense of experiencing units of time should be done before asking them to learn how to tell time.

Here is a time activity that can be used with some modification with grades three through six. Try asking the students to suggest all the ways they can think of that people use to describe time. In addition to the obvious seconds, minutes, hours, days, weeks, months, and years, they may suggest decades and centuries. But they may also suggest some unusual notions, such as moment, eon, millennium, generation, or era. You should record every suggestion on the board without correcting it in any way. Note how this is basically a semantic mapping.

Arrange the students into groups of three or four. Have each group list the terms from the board down the left side of a sheet of paper, from smallest to largest. Then ask them to write next to each term how long this term is using some other unit. You can use one very common example: "Week—seven days." When each group has completed the task, you can start debriefing. If some groups finish before others, have them write a second, different unit for each term.

In discussion, take one term at a time and write on the chalkboard what each group wrote. Start with the terms most familiar to them. If there are inaccuracies, allow time for the students to correct them. You may have conflicting "definitions" from two groups. Let them discuss and work out the differences. When you get all the accurate statements you want, you should record them on separate sheets of newsprint for the students to see.

Several kinds of things will come out in debriefing. First, some terms (e.g., *moment*) are not really units of measure but literary or poetic devices. Second, some terms have both popular and scientific meanings (e.g., year and leap year versus a "real" year of 365 days, 5 hours, 49 minutes, 12 seconds), and some are merely popular conventions of our current calendar, such as *month*. A nice follow-up activity would be for groups to devise a more reasonable definition for *month*. Similarly, even though a century may be thought of as any block of 100 years, our demarcation of centuries (e.g., the seventeenth century) is a convention that often confuses students; it bears explanation (along with A.D. and B.C.). A digression into other calendars of Western civilization as well as Hebrew or Chinese calendars could prove fascinating.

Third, you can deal with the scientific units of measure. If they understand equivalence, the students should be able to see that any time they think of 1 hour they could just as readily think of 60 minutes. Next, they should grasp why 2 hours is two of these 60-minute chunks, or 120 minutes. This conceptual understanding of equivalence is absolutely essential for conversions among units. More subtle forms of these equivalences are the fractional relationships (e.g., Hour—1/24th of a day).

These relationships can be used in amusing ways. Students can keep track of their own life patterns: time spent eating, sleeping, in school, watching television, brushing teeth, and so on. Using some assumptions, they can make reasonable projections of these activities for their entire lives.

Many excellent activities involve timing things around us. Students could bring to class examples of schedules or timetables. From these documents, many questions could be asked. Some could be mathematical, such as "What means of transportation could we use to get from our town to Los Angeles (or some other major city) and what difference would it make in traveling time?" Other questions could be more social, such as "Why do we have these events scheduled? Are there some countries that do not do so? What events are not scheduled in our society?"

The *Guinness Book of World Records* is filled with timed events, which students could report on and chart. Imagine a bar graph with time as the vertical axis and bars for flagpole sitting, holding breath underwater, and so forth.

Similarly, a wide variety of sporting events are based on time (e.g., swimming, track, horse racing, and auto racing). You could pose various questions for groups to research and graph. For instance, "How has the time for the fastest-run mile changed over the years?" "Are Kentucky Derby winners getting faster?" "Examine the times for different swimming strokes based on the same distance and compare them over the years." A chart of this task should have several different lines (color-coded), each showing one type of stroke over the years.

And now to distance, another very directly encountered aspect of students' lives. You can probably imagine doing another semantic map with all the ways we think about linear measure: length, height, width, and distance as well as the units we use—not only English units but also metric.

You may also get some of the ancient or poetic measures suggested by students, such as cubit, or context-specific measures, such as hand, furlong, fathom, and parsec. (You never can tell what kids have read or watched.) As with the units of time, these are all worth addressing in some way. Instead of a single list of terms and equivalent units (as with time), you could establish three groups: the traditional English units (inch, foot, yard, and mile), an abbreviated version of the metric (meter, kilometer, and centimeter), and a list of other, more unusual units (which most children probably wouldn't know much about). The students should also try to order each list from smallest to largest before trying to write down equivalences.

You would handle discussions differently depending on the age and grade of the students and your overall curricular purposes (introducing, working with, expanding knowledge, etc.). Let's assume this lesson is to activate the students' schemata and help you see how they are thinking about these different terms. You don't want to emphasize equivalence of units unless there is a good experiential basis for conceptual understanding of the very notion of linear measure and the key units.

You should start with the most familiar phenomena, such as children's heights and obvious lengths of desks and tables. These should be compared for relative length ("greater than" and "lesser than" relationships among them). The idea of absolute length, using a standard measure, can only be appreciated after understanding relative length. The need for establishing standards can be demonstrated readily in the primary grades by asking students how long something is (say a desk) in terms of their hands. After four or five children measure the object in terms of hands, you measure it with your hand. Even if their hands did not yield different numbers of hands, yours is sure to be a smaller number. So, is the object 7 hands long or 4?

The metric system requires similar experiential work, measuring a wide variety of distances (lengths, heights, etc.). Students should work with centimeters and meters to build a strong feel for these distances. Although we do not believe that you should ask them to convert metric and English measurements, if they have established a clear sense of inches, feet, and yards, they can realize that a yard is a little smaller than a meter and a centimeter is a bit smaller than half an inch.

---

1. An amusing activity can reveal whether students have a feel for metric distance. Provide a handout with questions that ask each student individually to estimate in centimeters the following features of his own face:

- Distance between your two eyes
- Width of each eye
- Length of your nose
- Width of your nose
- Width of your mouth
- Distance from your nostrils to your lips
- Width of your face (roughly from ear to ear)
- Height of your face
- Length of your ears

The students should write their estimates in ink so they cannot be changed. When every student has made all these estimates, each is given a sheet of drawing paper and a centimeter tape measure or ruler. They are asked to draw a face based on the specific measurements they listed. Reassure them that the drawing need not be artistic but must accurately use the figures they estimated. Amusing drawings and lively discussions ensue.

Finally with a partner's help, each student uses the metric tape measure to determine the actual measurements and records them next to their estimates. A follow-up discussion can ask which lengths were most "off," by how much and why.

2. You can pose an interesting general question about perimeter and area: "Do rectangular yards with the same perimeter have the same area?" Give students thirty-six toothpicks. Ask them to imagine that these are pieces of fence, 1 foot long, and you want to enclose part of the backyard for your dog. Arrange the fence pieces in a rectangle or square that will give the biggest area for the pooch. Show the example of a 1-by-17-foot rectangle, yielding an area of 17 square feet. Ask them to keep a record

of the rectangles they find and their area. Some students may work somewhat randomly and others more systematically. A pattern does form: 1 by 17 = 17 square feet; 2 by 16 = 32; 3 by 15 = 45; 4 by 14 = 56; 5 by 13 = 65; 6 by 12 = 72; 7 by 11 = 77; 8 by 10 = 80; 9 by 9 = 81 (this is the largest area, and the pattern flips at this point). Quite a remarkable difference between 17 and 81 square feet!

Look at your textbook's chapter or sections on measurement. Build up your own collection of concrete examples that students can use to make the text come alive. Have students work in small groups at measurement tasks. Expect an increase in noise. If anyone asks what is going on or complains, just tell them that students are extrapolating their schemata.

Noncomputational Areas of Mathematics

It is very important for students to realize that mathematizing is not just doing calculations. In fact, numbers may not be involved at all. Mathematical thinking is symbolic and logical but not always numerical. In this section we will provide some activities from three areas of mathematics that you can do with children to foster good thinking without computation. These areas are logic, geometry, and topology.

Here is an activity involving logic for younger children: experience with "attribute blocks" of varying color, size, and shape that can be sorted, arranged, and ordered in many different ways. Our language provides us with labels and our initial concepts as children. Pulling out all the *red* pieces or all the *triangles* are important experiences linguistically, conceptually, and mathematically. Pulling out blocks with two attributes is difficult but valuable: all the pieces that are *red circles* (regardless of size) or all the *big red* pieces (regardless of shape). Two overlapping hoops can be used to create four areas into which objects should be sorted (see Figure 4.3). Be sure to carefully explain or label with cards what each area represents.

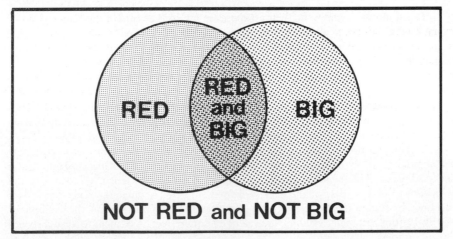

Figure 4.3

These are valuable early experiences for children. Creative Publications and Dale Seymour Publications have catalogues that offer dozens of excellent manipulatives for such activities. (For full information, see the Resources list at the end of this chapter.) These and many of the classifying, sorting, comparing, and contrasting activities we discussed under Focus can provide the intellectual basis for more sophisticated logical thinking.

There are several different types of logic problems. Those most commonly found in resource books are solved with a logic chart. For instance, take the problem of the car pool (page 42). There are five families and five days of the week. Information is provided about whether certain days are good or bad. These data can be attacked through diagrams, charts, logical reasoning, and so on. The problem could be used to show students how to use an organized chart.

	MON	TUES	WED	THUR	FRI
Brown	N		N		N
Schmidt	N	N			N
Randall			N	N	N
Gross	N		N	N	
Opolous	N	N		N	

Notice that we enter the No's (N) but not the Yes's because the No's are definite but we have not settled on any definite Yes's yet.

From this chart we can conclude that the only family that could drive on Monday is Randall. This is a significant point. Perhaps it could have been reached by logical inferences from the story. However, the chart helps us quickly organize the information. Therefore, we can fill in a Yes for Randall on Monday. We can then immediately fill in a No for Randall on Tuesday because they won't drive on that day if they are driving on Monday.

Many of the logic problems in handbooks present a rather direct sequence of inferences that lead, one at a time, to checking off Ys and Ns to find the only possible solution. However, this problem is more open. Notice that at this point, the four remaining families each have two days on which they can drive. This means that there is more than one possible solution to this problem. For instance, if you decide that Brown will drive on Tuesday, putting Yes there automatically makes Gross drive on Friday (the only other day possible) and subsequently Opolous on Wednesday and Schmidt on Thursday. See how the chart shows this quite nicely. Although the two solutions could be found by other approaches, the chart is especially suited for this problem.

Many books have this type of logic problem. This one was relatively simple and could be represented by two dimensions. There are much more complicated problems that require adding more dimensions. Please try each problem yourself to make sure what is required before assigning it, even as "just for fun." We also urge you to go over any problems you assign. It is frustrating for students to work on problems that are much too difficult for their present capabilities, but working out a problem that the teacher does not care enough about to discuss also sends a negative signal.

There are other, less common logic problems that you should consider. For example, four people sit around a table playing cards. People who sit across from each other are "partners."

> The four people playing cards are two men and two women. After the game, Ms. Jones says she does not want to be Bill's partner ever again because he was too silly and didn't concentrate. Betty is good friends with Donna, although she was Frank's partner. Frank sits to the right of Donna. Mr. Daniels sits between Ms. Bloom and Mr. Johnson. What are the people's full names and where are they seated?

You would help students by giving them the diagram in Figure 4.4. Students could enter inferences they were certain of into the diagram, then use reasoning to finish. For instance, the first sentence allows the inference that the partners in each pair are of the opposite sex, thus they can enter Jones across from Bill. The second allows the inference that the other couple is Betty and Frank (but they can't yet put them in since there are two ways they could be seated). It also shows that Ms. Jones' first name must be Donna. The third sentence does show where to put Frank (to Donna's right); students have to imagine themselves in Donna's chair facing the table, an important visualization. Therefore, Betty can be written in, across from Frank, and so on.

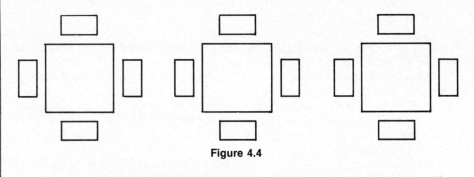

Figure 4.4

Have the students (individually or in groups) make up their own logic problems of this type for each other to solve. They can use their own names or fictitious ones: "Blake and Alexis were partners."

A wide variety of noncomputational activities involve geometry. Three somewhat different approaches are *tangrams, pentominoes,* and *tessellations.* Each involve fitting together geometrical figures onto a plane surface. You can get the basic materials and teaching ideas for all three from Creative Publications or Dale Seymour Publications. We will just sketch them here.

Tangrams use seven basic pieces that can be assembled into a wide variety of figures and shapes, some geometrical and others very imaginative. Figure 4.5 shows the seven pieces in the form of one large square.

You can probably imagine how a few pieces could be shifted to form a rectangle or a parallelogram. A nice question to pose is this: If there is a single little square and a big square formed by all seven pieces, can you form squares from two, three,

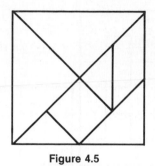

Figure 4.5

four, five, or six pieces? How many different triangles can be formed with various numbers of pieces? How many trapezoids?

Pentominoes are the twelve basic ways that five squares can be fitted together with joined sides. With a collection of squares and graph paper to record their answers, can your students find all the pentominoes?

The twelve pentominoes include a total of sixty squares. In Figure 4.6 they are arranged in a 6-by-10 rectangle. They also can be arranged in several different ways to form 5-by-12 as well as 4-by-15 rectangles. However, there are only two basic ways to form a 3-by-20 rectangle. Also, these twelve pieces can be arranged onto an 8-by-8-square checkerboard in several ways (obviously with four squares not covered). The students can use graph paper to record solutions to these problems or you can provide handouts with appropriate borders.

Another clever problem with pentominoes is to find "triples": Exact replicas of a piece three times as large in length and width can be formed by nine of the other pieces. Notice that increasing both these dimensions by a factor of three increases the area by a factor of nine. Figure 4.7 shows two triples.

Here is a way that even young children can do some good thinking with pentominoes. Have students work in pairs. With his partner not looking, one student selects any three of the pieces, fits them together in some fashion, and traces their perimeter on a sheet of paper. The partner must try to discover how to fill in this perimeter by using any three of the twelve pieces. Often there are many ways to

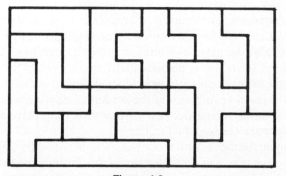

Figure 4.6

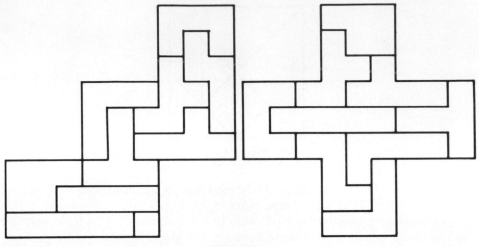

Figure 4.7

make a particular shape, although it may take some work to find a solution. Obviously, with practice, students could use more than three pieces.

A tessellation is a way of "tiling the plane" with repeating geometrical patterns—everything fits together with no holes. Children are quite familiar with floor tiles. Obviously squares will tile a plane surface, as will equilateral triangles, regular hexagons, and rectangles (e.g., bricks). These are examples of repeating one polygon. However, tessellation patterns can be formed by repeating two or more polygons (regular or irregular).

You can purchase basic sets of geometrical figures for students to use in creating and exploring tessellations. You could also provide a few pieces to use as a pattern to trace on paper. It is worthwhile to have these explorations done thoughtfully and carefully and to have students record their findings. Again, there are many excellent resource books now available.

You might also have students actively look for tessellations in art and architecture around them (e.g., their own kitchen floor, as the square tiles "interact" with one another to make different tessellating patterns). Ask them to sketch what they find. They can go on to create their own unique tessellations with a little assistance.

In each of these geometric areas, you have to balance several different concerns. First, with a great many "messy" manipulatives, students have to cooperate with your rules of behavior. We have found that small groups of two or three can work on most of these without two much trouble if they have been learning the essential cooperation skills we've discussed earlier.

Second, as you look at tasks suggested by various resource books, think about level of difficulty. You have to build up the students' experiences in ways that challenge but neither frustrate nor bore; you should make sure there are extensions for those who quickly work through tasks. They should keep track of what they do in some way, making a simple record.

Third, make sure that you debrief adequately. The basic work with manipulatives may be fun and thought provoking, but the thoughts must be discussed. You

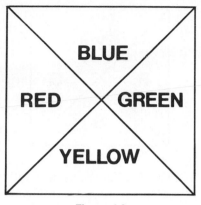

Figure 4.8

should always lead the students in a debriefing that really brings home the key ideas, concepts, patterns, or whatever it was that led you to choose that activity.

The next activity is a bit different and may not even seem like geometry at first. Imagine a square card like the one in Figure 4.8.

How many other cards can you make that use these same four colors once each? The key issue here is whether or not you are allowed to turn that card. If you are not allowed to turn it, these three cards in Figure 4.9 are different from each other and the one in Figure 4.8. (We've abbreviated the colors.) If you are allowed to turn the cards, they are not different; they are the same card with different rotations. That is, they have been turned or rotated clockwise one color.

Notice that in all four examples, red is opposite green and blue is opposite yellow. Can you create some others? If you gave students paper squares, could they draw the diagonals and color in the possibilities? They would find that if you do not allow different rotations of the same figure (i.e., the four are counted as the same one figure), there are only six basically different figures. Can they find them? Try it yourself.

Perceptive students may also notice something interesting (cross-contextual insight). The preceding example had red opposite green and blue opposite yellow. Do you remember the card table with two pairs of partners? There were two ways to

Figure 4.9

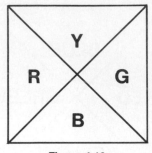

Figure 4.10

have the same partners. In this situation the same colors could be seated opposite but arranged differently. Note the arrangement in Figure 4.10.

Verify that this is not one of the preceding four. No matter how you turn (rotate) it is not exactly one of these. However, it is its *mirror image,* or *reflection.* Observe the relationship between the two in Figure 4.11.

They are mirror images: You can stand them up face to face, just like looking in a mirror. Or you could glue them back to back and they would match. They are also sometimes called "flips," as in "flipping" over.

These are two basic forms of *symmetry* (rotation and reflection). You may also introduce your students to the more common, bilateral symmetry (which may be thought of as a line down the middle of something, with a left and right half being mirror images).

Let's use these nine squares to play a perceptual logic game. Get squares of manila or some strong paper, ten squares per student. Have the students make a nice-looking and accurate version of the six different squares. You can quickly check to see if they have done it correctly by having them make three rotationally different squares, for example, blue opposite red, blue opposite green, or blue opposite yellow. They then make the mirror image for each of these squares. If they set the six on their desks or a table in mirror pairs you (or a partner) could quickly check their accuracy.

Next, have each student put a big black dot on the back of one square and take its mirror image and make two just like it. This will result in three of the same square and one mirror image (with a black dot on the back). They take one of these three identical squares, mark two black dots on its back, and put it completely away

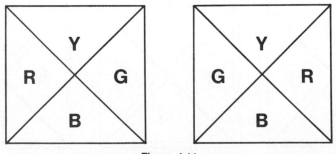

Figure 4.11

(e.g., in their desks). Now they go to another mirror pair, pick one, and make another just like it. Then they do the same with the other mirror pair, making a copy of one of them.

At this point, the students should have nine squares on their desks and another not visible. These nine include three sets of identical pieces and one mirror image for each. The task for the students is to arrange these nine into a 3-by-3 big square so that the sides of touching squares have the same color (kind of like dominoes). Thus, the middle piece will have all four of its sides touching four different squares with colors matching on their sides.

With a little work, most students can find a solution. Provide a recording sheet with the nine squares ready to be filled in. The students can simply write in the colors. Students who finish quickly should be encouraged to find another pattern that uses what they have learned about mirror image symmetry. Of the many varied solutions, one that uses mirror image symmetry is shown in Figure 4.12.

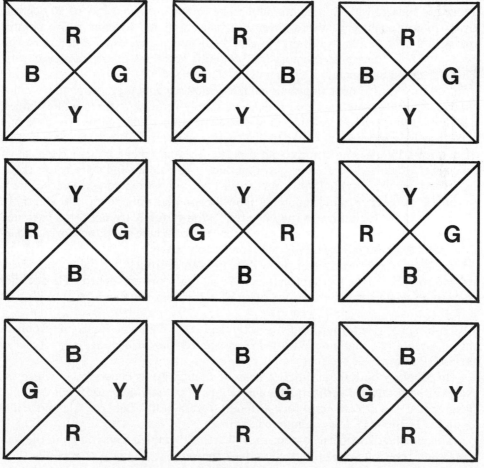

Figure 4.12

Other patterns also show this same mirror image symmetry. In fact, you could pick up the whole bottom row in Figure 4.12 and stick it on the top row (reds onto reds). There are also many solutions that do not show this property. In your debriefing, this difference should be emphasized.

For an extension, or just to tease your students, you can tell them to now take out the tenth piece (the one with the two black dots) and exchange it for the one with the single black dot. Now try it again. It is significantly harder. Why? You cannot use mirror image symmetry any longer because you now have three identical pieces.

This activity will provide an introduction to these two types of symmetry through which a wide variety of phenomena can be explored. Have students look for and record examples of these symmetries in the world around them: in clothing, wallpaper, architecture, art, and so on. In fact, you can readily build some conceptual bridges between tessellations and symmetry.

Older students can be introduced to some more complex aspects of rotational symmetry, especially if they have dealt with angular measure. The color cards used above are squares with four colors, able to be rotated in increments of 90 degrees. Other figures could engender different angular rotations. Imagine a five-pointed star with a pentagon at its center. How many different ways can the points be colored with five, nonrepeated colors (not counting rotations of the same pattern)? This star could be rotated in increments of 72 degrees.

Another kind of noncomputational mathematics is *topology*—sometimes called "rubber-sheet" geometry. Here, instead of simply rotating and reflecting shapes, we imagine that geometrical figures are made of rubber and can be stretched and shrunk as long as we do not change their basic topological properties. This branch of mathematics has some pretty wild aspects, for which none of us have a lot of schemata. However, there is one part that does: places to go and ways to get there.

There are two ways to look at these ideas: Are you more interested in the places or the ways? Imagine going shopping. How do you plan your route? Do you try to go to stores near each other at the same time? You certainly try not to go back and forth across town or back past the same store twice. Where are these stores in relation to each other and where are their connecting streets?

Imagine a night watchman. How does he plan his route? He has to visit every corridor on his rounds (perhaps making sure all the doors are locked). He does not want to go down the same corridor twice if he can help it. How is the building set up?

You can present your students with these two different kinds of problems through real-life situations. With some assistance, they can even make some up themselves. As usual, the first step is representing the problem.

In topology both these situations can be thought of as *networks,* in which the places or points (called *vertices*) are intersections of paths (called *arcs*). For example, imagine that you have to go to four different stores: Aldi's, Baker's, Clarisio's, and Denny's. Figure 4.13 shows a map of the town.

Imagine that you live next door to Aldi's. Starting there, can you go to the four stores and return home without going past the same store twice? Certainly, there are several ways to do so. However, if the problem specified the order in which the

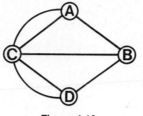

Figure 4.13

stores must be visited, it might prove impossible (e.g., Denny's can't be the last stop before heading back to Aldi's and home since there is no way to get there without going past one of the other two).

Let's imagine the other kind of situation. Instead of the night watchman, perhaps your students will remember the vice-principal from the movie *The Breakfast Club* chasing students through the corridors. Consider a simple set of corridors, such as in Figure 4.14, in each one of which he must travel (in case the students have slipped into a room). Is there a way for him to go down each corridor just once? Assume that he starts at the first intersection of corridors.

Regardless of where he starts, the poor man cannot go through each corridor only once. However, if there were another corridor that linked intersection 1 and 4 (call it "H"), he could accomplish his task if he started at intersection 3 and ended at 2.

The networks of stores and corridors are topologically the same. Both have four vertices and seven arcs, and both could be represented by the line drawing in Figure 4.15.

Despite identical networks, the two problems are quite different. The first is seeking what is called a "Hamilton path," one that goes through every vertex exactly once. Technically, the Hamilton path should end at the vertex it started from, although you don't have to be a fanatic here. The second is called an "Euler path," one that goes through every arc exactly once. As you can see, some networks may have one kind of path but not the other.

Let's try one more network. Try to find each type of path for the network in Figure 4.16. Now imagine having to go to each of many different cities. If you

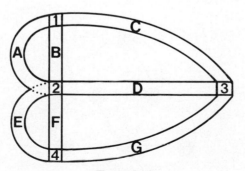

Figure 4.14

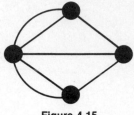

Figure 4.15

wanted to keep your travel time or distance to a minimum, you would want a Hamilton path with the shortest total route. You could work with your students on real-life situations with these conditions. Thus, a traveling salesman might leave New York, needing to go to five major U.S. cities (connected by major interstate highways). Or a family (the Griswolds) might be taking a vacation from one major city to another and want to visit relatives in four other major cities as they go or on their way back. How can these trips include each of the cities while minimizing the road distances?

Have the students make up these kinds of questions by studying maps, choosing cities, and working out travel distances for different routes. Obviously, students could do the same thing with stores in their town, for example. Actually, airline companies have to do very similar (but incredibly complex) versions of these problems. Ironically, the large number of different combinations of possible routes has defied simple approaches, even with computers.

You can find some patterns to the second kind of problem. When you are trying to traverse a network and travel on all its arcs (Euler path), notice how many vertices have an odd number of arcs coming out of it. In our first example of the vice-principal, all four intersections had odd vertices (five, three, three, and three arcs respectively). Then we added another arc, which changed the vertices to five, four, four, and three. Through analyzing examples of networks for Euler paths, your students will see some patterns.

You and your students should concoct a number of situations in which you would want to go on every street, highway, or corridor. Start with those that are not too complex; remember the strategy—find a simpler problem. Use two vertices and two, three, or four arcs; then three vertices; and so on. Use real situations, for example, delivering newspapers or flyers door to door, following trash pickup

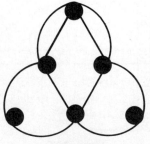

Figure 4.16

routes, inspecting trees for Dutch elm disease, or looking for lawns that need mowing. As before, have students create the problems with you.

For any network students analyze, they should record the number of vertices and arcs and indicate Yes or No for Euler path. You could use big sheets of paper with the diagram included. After a little experience with different networks, your students will probably infer that

- If there are two odd vertices, you can find a Euler path if you begin at one and end at the other.
- If there are more than two odd vertices, you can't find a Euler path.
- If the vertices are all even, you can find a Euler path by starting anywhere (and you'll end up there too).

Try these basic conclusions with more complex networks for your school, town, or state.

Relationships

A major part of mathematics is establishing relationships between entities. We want to help students move from understanding patterns and relations concretely to representing them abstractly. Two basic types of relationships can be seen in a wide variety of situations. The first is a direct relationship (the more of one, the more of the other). For instance, the amount of garbage produced by a city in the United States will depend on the number of people in the city; the more people, the more garbage. There is also an inverse relationship: For example, if we have 1,000 envelopes to stuff and mail out and a person can stuff and lick fifty in an hour, the amount of time needed to do this job would be twenty hours for one person, ten hours for two, and so on. For situations like this, with a fixed task, more people take less time to do the task (the more of one, the less of the other).

As always, we feel it is more important for students to be able to conceive of what is happening than to manipulate the numbers mindlessly. As with even the simplest calculation, jumping in with an arithmetic operation, an algorithm, a formula, or an equation before understanding the problem is dangerous. Although relationships can be symbolically represented by algebraic formulas, they do not need to be for students to understand the problem, plan a strategy, work on the information, and derive a reasonable answer. For instance, here is a set of problems that may relate to students' schemata.

1. Hamburgers cost $2 and hot dogs cost $1. If there are twenty children in the class and ten want hamburgers and ten want hot dogs, how much money will we need?
2. G.I. Joe action figures cost $3 apiece. Muscle figures cost $1 apiece. If you had $10, how many of each could you get? Spend all your money; get at least one of each.
3. Some of the people at a family gathering are thinking about going to the movies. Adult tickets cost $4 and children's tickets cost $2. The people have

only $20 among them. At least one adult must go to the movies. How many adults and how many children could go?

4. Orville was lying on the grass watching a parade of unicycles and bicycles. Unfortunately, because of the crowd, he could see only the wheels. He knew that his brother and two friends were riding their unicycles in the parade. Also, his sister and two of her friends were riding their bicycles in the parade. He saw fifteen wheels go by. How many of each kind of cycle might there have been?

5. Eleven Chicago Bears linemen and their wives are at the Sears Tower and want to go to the top floor. The elevator can take a load of only 2,000 pounds. The linemen each weigh 300 pounds and their wives 100 pounds apiece. If the husbands always stay with their wives, how many couples can go up in the elevator at a time? If the wives all go up first, how many men could go with them in the first elevator load?

6. Nine children from the baseball team and their coach go for Slurpees after the game. The 7-11 store has only two sizes of cups left: the small Slurpee for 50¢ and the large for $1. The coach is dieting and doesn't want anything. He only has $6 to spend on the team. How many Slurpees of each kind can the team members get?

7. The Whamo factory has to mail boxes mixed with glass marbles and rubber balls to customers. The marbles and balls are the same size. Each container can hold fifty of these spheres. The glass marbles weigh 2 ounces and the rubber balls weigh 1 ounce. To get the best rate from the post office, each container should hold a total weight of 80 ounces. How should each container be filled with 50 spheres to get the full 80 ounces?

Though different in some ways, these problems all involve juggling the numbers of two items. Problem 1 starts with a familiar situation. We know how many of each item we want and we know their cost; we can multiply twice and add the products. Students do this frequently. Problem 2 presents a situation that is essentially reversed. They have the amount to spend that must be juggled between two different items of different cost. Because the numbers themselves are not formidable and the situation is conceivable, most children from second grade and up can formulate some reasonable strategy. They can even handle the constraints of spending all $10 and getting at least one of each item.

The other problems vary things a bit; they use different contexts, various sizes and units, and unusual constraints (e.g., husband and wives stay together in problem 5). Problem 7 may seem quite a bit more complicated. It is different only in one respect, it adds a type of constraint, not found in the other problems. If the task were only to juggle the quantities of 1- and 2-ounce spheres to get a total of 80 ounces, this problem would be like the others; there could be several different ways to satisfy the conditions of the problem. But stating that there must be fifty spheres constrains us to one answer (or perhaps no answers that will work out evenly). Ironically, this narrowing of possibilities seems to make the problem more difficult.

Many problems of this type in resource books do add this constraint on the solution to force one right answer. This is obviously not necessary. Multiple solutions to some problems in your curriculum are well advised. Life is rarely so neat and simple.

Did you want to set up an algebraic equation for some of these problems? Did your mind immediately see such a representation? There is no one right way to represent these problems. Thinking in tables, manipulating objects, and writing equations are simply different ways to handle problems. If you want your students when they're adolescents to be able to *understand* simultaneous linear equations (as opposed to just crunching out the algorithmic solutions to them), they need the conceptual foundations in *meaningful contexts* when they are younger.

Laying this foundation means more than giving one or two process problems of this type. It means having students wrestle with a dozen problems that vary in ways like these, with different meaningful contexts and different kinds of numbers. At first, the students will not realize that they are the same essential problem. Along the way, you will have to illustrate the basic conceptualization of varying two quantities under different conditions. You must help them make the connection that generalizes thinking across contexts.

There are other valuable things you can do to lay the foundation for symbolic representations of relations. Obviously, providing many varied and rich experiences with patterns is crucial. A good number of resource books give many process problems such as these: If you have forty-five boxes to be stacked in a kind of triangular pattern (one on top, two next, then three, etc.), how many boxes will be on the bottom row? There are many variations of stacking boxes, arranging bricks, and so forth that can be attacked through diagrams, tables, and other strategies.

A good way to illustrate relationships for younger students is through a two-pan scale or a balance beam of some kind. You don't even need a set of accurate weights to start children on the right conceptual foot. Imagine weighing potatoes in terms of a number of wooden cubes. Just make sure that the cubes are all the same size and weight; then they become your standard. With younger children, once you establish that any single potato can be matched to a number of cubes, you have given the conceptual start for the meaning of equal and equations. A potato that "is" five cubes can be marked "5" and used to form other relationships. A giant potato might be balanced with the 5 and the 7, and so on.

The modest two-pan scale should not be underestimated for its power to provide a schema for number sentences. Imagine the situation shown in Figure 4.17. On one side two known quantities (two weights of 5), on the other a known 7 and an unknown. This simple situation can be used to help students understand several related ideas. For instance, "7 plus what equals 10?" can be seen as "10 minus 7

Figure 4.17

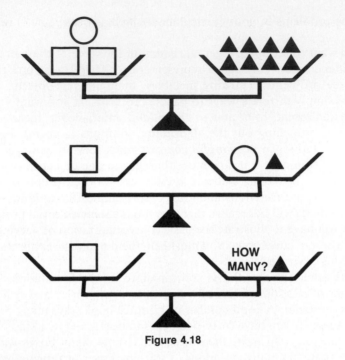

Figure 4.18

equals what?'' Even younger children can see that if you want to get the potato all by itself on one side of the scale, you take the known 7 off; but that operation would make the scale unbalanced. Therefore, you must also take 7 off the other side as well. Establishing this metaphor for equations through repeated experience early in school enables conceptual understanding of symbolic representations and procedures later.

Figure 4.18 shows a problem that you and your students can solve in a variety of ways. Try to work this out in several different ways, such as substituting equivalent quantities on the scales.

You and your students can create many different problems that use many different kinds of objects, for example, fruit: Imagine apples, bananas, pineapples, and melons being used in the preceding problems instead of geometrical figures. Notice how these problems emphasize thinking about the relationships and not merely calculating numbers. (You should get 3 for an answer to the problem in Figure 4.18.)

Another kind of problem (and branch of mathematics) can be an excellent source of thinking: different arrangements of objects (combinatorial mathematics). We were using this kind of thinking when arranging four different colors on square cards. Here is another example: Imagine a dish that will hold two scoops of ice cream. You have three traditional favors from which to choose: chocolate, vanilla, and strawberry. How many different arrangements of the two scoops could you possibly get? Draw a picture, make a list, or do whatever makes sense.

1. Vanilla
   Vanilla

2. Vanilla
   Chocolate

3. Vanilla
   Strawberry

4. Chocolate
   Chocolate

5. Chocolate
   Strawberry

6. Strawberry
   Strawberry

Now imagine that these scoops are placed into a cone in the order they appear above. How many different arrangements can we have of these three flavors in cones? There are these six combinations above, but wait—there are some more:

7. Chocolate
   Vanilla

8. Strawberry
   Vanilla

9. Strawberry
   Chocolate

Numbers 7, 8, and 9 are different from 2, 3, and 5. There are nine different *permutations*. Although these two labels (combinations and permutations) are not crucial, an understanding of these conceptually different arrangements is. In a sense, it is an analogous issue to our interest in distinguishing between rotations and reflections. Are we in a situation in which we need to make the distinction? With a dish of ice cream it doesn't make any difference which flavor we put in first, but in a cone, perhaps it does. Some people are very particular about their favorite foods.

You can extend either of these ice-cream problems into more flavors or more scoops in many creative ways. You could even look for patterns that form as you expand. For instance, with the dish problem keep two scoops constant and ask, "How many arrangements are there with one flavor? With two? With three, four, five, six, and so on? What is the pattern? What happens if you want a banana split with three scoops? Does it matter which flavor is in the middle?" If it does, you'll be dealing with more possibilities (permutations); if it doesn't, fewer possibilities (combinations).

You can vary the context of these problems by having the students suggest or find things around them that can be arranged in different combinations. For example, what are the different items that can go on a pizza besides basic cheese? How many different combinations can you get with six different items put on two at a time? This is the same problem as two scoops of ice cream taken from six flavors. You can later vary the pizza problem to look at all the different ways to put those six items on a pizza: two at a time, three at a time, and so on. There is a very different pattern to this problem.

In these problems, there is no one right way to attack or represent the problem. Some students like to draw pictures, some use a counting strategy, and so on. What you want is a good problem-solving process. Getting all the possibilities and coming up with the exact answer is *much less important* than developing intellectual habits of problem solving, especially carefully thinking about what is going on and representing it accurately. Also, in these combinatorial problems, a major intellectual task is coming up with a good procedure for generating possibilities that helps you see if you have found them all. Being able to generate and check all the solutions to any multi-answer problem is very difficult for students.

A major teaching task is helping the students move from a list or table that merely *records* possibilities they have generated to an *organized* list or table that by its structure generates possibilities and/or suggests patterns. For instance, what are all the ways to arrange the letters *A, B, C?* We could merely start to randomly generate possibilities. Or we could do it in a structured fashion. Let's try to keep it alphabetical, starting with *A* first. That gives us *ABC* and *ACB*. With *B* first we get *BAC, BCA. C* first gives us *CAB* and *CBA*. Are there any others? No, because we have generated every possibility when putting each letter first.

As with so many other aspects of teaching for thinking, you can frustrate students by pushing too hard or too quickly for this kind of systematic generation and checking. It is important, but not as important as their feelings and beliefs about themselves and their abilities to think things through and work out possibilities.

A good source of problems is the raw data from recorded measurements or counts of objects and events. Statistical data are all around us. Skim through an atlas and you'll find data on population, heights of mountains, lengths of rivers, land and sea surface area, and much more. Check an almanac and you'll find statistics on production of crops, consumption of milk, nutritional value of foods, numbers of people speaking various languages around the world, immigration to the United States over the past 150 years, and on and on. Any of these could inspire an activity.

Students can handle three kinds of statistics: frequency, percentage, and mean. Frequencies, discussed earlier, can be found in many meaningful contexts. Bar graphs and other simple devices for representing frequencies can be constructed by any age (with some assistance) and can provide practice in seeing relationships among items (comparing/contrasting) and drawing inferences.

The concept of percentage is closely allied to our decimal system. Yet children deal with percentages in strange ways much younger than when they meet them in school. Consider the statistics from baseball. Wins and losses are routinely discussed among children in terms of percentages. The misnomer of "batting average" is actually a three-place decimal equivalent of percentage (not average as arithmetic mean, at all). When they sat someone is hitting 300, they mean .300; he got a hit 30 percent of his times at bat. They are not fully aware of the concept behind these statistics, which could provide a powerful schema for understanding. What other statistics using percentages are available for students to consider? Percentage of U.S. adults over 20 who smoke?

There is a type of problem that we trust you will find intriguing since it is a bit unlike what you've seen in this chapter. *Fermi questions* (or problems) get their name from the famous physicist Enrico Fermi, who was known for his uncanny ability to generate reasonable approximations for seemingly impossible mathematical problems or questions. In these problems, there is no right answer. Practice with Fermi questions will greatly help students learn to attack applied problems from real-life situations. For instance, how many drops of water are there in Lake Michigan? It may seem that insufficient information is available. However, when reasonable assumptions are combined with simple calculations, one can narrow the range of values within which the answer must lie.

With younger children (grades K–2), you can emphasize the idea of "coming close" rather than getting it exactly right. With older children (grades 3–5), the concept of approximation may be used. With older children (grades 6–8), the teacher might introduce the concept of order of magnitude (the power of 10 of the number that fits the value). This concept can be introduced if the notation for place value has included exponents.

With each of these concepts, the teaching emphasis is on the process of problem solving, the decisions made along the way that lead to reasonable answers. Students should be helped initially to think through ways of attacking the problem and determining the kinds of assumptions that they would have to build into the process. The actual calculations become secondary in importance. For instance, take a question for primary children: How many tennis balls can you carry across the room at one time without using any devices (bags, baskets, etc.)?

First, you should have the class examine a tennis ball. Then the class should discuss what it means not to use any devices. When a clear conception of the question has been established, you could have the class, or small groups of three or four, brainstorm places on the body that could be used for carrying tennis balls or ways to carry them. It is this process of conceiving of possibilities that is key. Will some students assume that you cannot use your clothing (e.g. stuff tennis balls inside your shirt, pockets, etc.)? Will some assume that the balls must be carried in your hands? When assumptions have been clarified, either through consensus of the class or your suggestions, the students can generate reasonable answers. For a finale, you could provide tennis balls to allow experimentation under different assumptions.

Let's take a somewhat more difficult question: How many golf balls will fit in a suitcase? If you use the same general tactic, the students might first discuss how big a golf ball is. If they assume that it is about an inch in diameter, they can envision that one golf ball will fit into a cube space 1 inch by 1 inch by 1 inch, or 1 cubic inch. They could look at a golf ball but should not actually measure it. Next, the class might be broken down into small groups to decide on how big the suitcase would be. You should let each group decide on the dimensions of its suitcase. These dimensions might vary from those of a briefcase to those of a steamer trunk. If one assumed that the suitcase were 30 inches by 8 inches by 24 inches, a good approximation would be 6,000 cubic inches. (An estimate might use $30 \times 10 \times 20$.) Thus, about 6,000 golf balls would probably fit into this suitcase. The 30-by-20-inch base would hold 600 balls; the height of 10 inches would yield ten layers.

Even if more tightly packed than in the 1-cubic-inch spaces, the number will probably not exceed 8,000. If we were to use 6,000, we could write that as 6×10 to the 3rd power. The answer certainly is between 1,000 and 100,000; 10,000, or 10 to the 4th power, would be a reasonable approximation.

Here are some Fermi questions you could modify to fit different age groups. They are roughly in increasing difficulty.

1. How many balls can you keep in the air at one time (simultaneously), if you throw them up one at a time?
2. How many jelly beans could you hold in both your hands cupped together?
3. How many steps will it take to walk across the classroom?
4. How many pieces of popcorn do you get in a large container at the movies?

5. How many students would fit in this room if we took out all the furniture?
6. How many fully inflated basketballs would it take to fill the gymnasium?
7. How many breaths do you take in a year?
8. How many sheets of tissue paper would it take to make a stack up to the ceiling of this room?
9. How many meals will you eat in your lifetime?
10. How many raindrops will it take to fill a cup?
11. How many gallons of gasoline will it take to drive from Fairbanks, Alaska, to Miami, Florida?
12. If the total amount you earned in your life were given to you at a rate of so much per hour for every hour of your life, how much would your time be worth?
13. How many words are there in the *World Book Encyclopedia?*
14. What is the surface area of the skin on an adult human's body?

As you can see, the assumptions you make are key. Problems 10 and 14 have been considered by experts: Their guesses are 4.6 × 10 to the 5th power, and 1.7 × 10 to the 4th square centimeter.

Evaluating Students' Problem Solving

It should be clear by now that we want students to develop

- Positive attitudes and beliefs about themselves and mathematics
- Their abilities to think mathematically, to use problem-solving strategies, and to monitor their own thinking
- Their knowledge of mathematics and concepts in related areas

Standardized testing to evaluate students' performance will gather information on only a small part of these concerns. If you want to determine how your students are progressing in their development in all these areas, you (and perhaps your school) should use a variety of evaluation procedures. Charles, Lester, and O'Daffer (1987) have written an excellent and readable booklet that offers several alternatives to standardized testing.

Both formal and informal observing and questioning of students while they are engaged in problem solving can provide valuable information. For instance, observation checklists can point out specific things to look for. Students can use a variety of techniques to assess their own progress, such as simple reports and inventories.

Perhaps the most intriguing form of evaluation Charles, Lester, and O'Daffer suggest is for teachers to assess students' work in problem solving more analytically than the traditional, simplistic right or wrong. They offer several schemes for assessing and scoring students' written solutions in terms of the first three phases of problem solving: (1) understanding the problem, (2) planning a solution, and (3) working out an answer. For instance, students may receive points in each of these three areas. Thus, if a student's work on a problem exhibits a clear understanding of the problem and a valid use of a strategy, significant partial credit would be awarded, even if a correct answer was not obtained. These approaches put the emphasis where it belongs—on thinking.

CONCLUSION

We are only temporarily leaving mathematics as this chapter ends. Just as with reading, mathematics is a way of thinking and understanding our lives and our world. It is a set of tools, a pair of glasses, that we can use. There are many aspects of the sciences and social studies that rely on mathematics. These areas can be rich contexts for meaningful problems and concepts from mathematics. The habits and feelings that go along with thinking can be nourished in many ways.

Here are some resources that will help you focus your mathematics program on problem solving.

RESOURCES AND FURTHER READINGS

In addition to those works cited directly in the text, you will find more information about the topics covered in this chapter in the following works:

Baratta-Lorton, M. (1976). *Mathematics their way.* Menlo Park, CA: Addison-Wesley.

Burns, M. (1987). *A collection of math lessons.* New York: Cuisenaire Co.

Charles, R., and Lester, F. (1982). *Teaching problem solving: What, why, and how.* Palo Alto, CA: Dale Seymour Publications.

Cook, C. (1987). *Problem solving and critical thinking in Mathematics: A professional development project for elementary and middle schools.* Aurora, IL: Corridor Partnership for Excellence in Education (1500 West Sullivan Rd., Aurora, IL 60506).

The following catalogues may also prove useful:

Creative Publications (5005 West 100th St., Oak Lawn, IL 60453).

Cuisenaire Co. (12 Church St., Box D, New Rochelle, NY 10802).

Dale Seymour Publications (PO Box 10888, Palo Alto, CA 94303).

PART THREE

The Sciences and Social Studies—Vibrant Contexts for Meaningfulness

The following two chapters will address two areas of the school curriculum that are vital parts of students' lives. The sciences deal with natural phenomena occurring all around them and within their bodies. The social studies involve the human phenomena in which they participate every day of their lives. These two arenas of life offer exciting possibilities for students to understand and use all the cognitive processes of literacy and mathematics. In the previous two chapters we have been discussing the thinking involved in these abstract, symbolic, communication systems and urged that you teach this thinking in contexts meaningful to the schemata of your students. For elementary school students, the natural sciences and the social studies provide the best possible contexts you could hope to find.

5

The Natural Forces of Science

INTRODUCTION

What we think of as "science" is a collection of sciences, each with enormous knowledge bases. They represent the accumulated wisdom of scientific inquiry over two or three dozen centuries. Each science has its own domain, each a particular focus. Yet they all share roughly the same mode of inquiry to generate new knowledge, what we might call *scientific thinking*. Thus, we see physicists investigating nonliving matter and energy; biologists, living systems; astronomers, the heavenly bodies; chemists, the substances that make up our existence; and so on.

Each of these domains within science has amassed a staggering amount of information over the centuries. At the most basic level we can think of the data as facts and inferences about the facts. In our attempts to make sense of our experiences and these data we have formulated hypotheses and concepts and, more grandly, principles, laws, and theories. More recently, philosophers and historians of science speak of "paradigms" that transcend theories.

Note that all these ideas that go beyond the most basic level of factual data are thoughtful attempts to explain the phenomena we observe. These bodies of knowledge represent our current understanding of these things. Our scientists are making meaning; they construct explanations. However, most of us nonscientists do not spend much time consciously trying to comprehend fully the phenomena around us: the changing colors of leaves in the fall, the forming of storm clouds, the darkening of bruised skin. It is quite an irony that although we are almost constantly confronted with the phenomena scientists study and have an immense store of experiences, most of us spend little time purposely reflecting on what is going on around or within us.

How do we think about these scientific phenomena? Cognitive researchers are finding that students come to the classroom with a variety of intuitive conceptions or naive theories about the phenomena around them (Anderson and Smith, 1987; Carey, 1986; Linn, 1986). The schemata students have constructed from their experiences with the world help them to organize their reality, to explain and interpret happenings, and to conceive regularity and order in their lives. We humans will seek to create meaning, even with scant information. Yet most of us do not seem to move beyond very superficial understanding of these natural phenomena; we settle for on-the-ground, pragmatic interpretations and commonsense explanations.

Much of this commonsense knowledge is actually erroneous. The naive theories contain misconceptions about phenomena that can dramatically interfere with understanding. For instance, students might not be able to make distinctions between dead and inanimate, heat and temperature, weight and density. They may believe that

- Sugar ceases to exist when put into water.
- Styrofoam is weightless.
- Shadows are made out of matter.
- Light from a candle goes further at night than in the day.
- A worm is not an animal.
- Heavier objects fall faster than lighter ones.
- Electric current is used in a light bulb.
- Gravity requires the presence of air.
- Coldness causes rust.
- Soil, water, and fertilizer are food for plants.

See the book *Children's Ideas in Science,* edited by Driver, Guesne, and Tiberghien (1985), for elaboration of such naive conceptions in children ages 10 to 16 and how they influence the learning of science. In fact, all of us nonscientists probably have some naive theories or misconceptions about various aspects of natural phenomena. It is a good idea for all of us to do some background reading in areas we have to teach.

Misconceptions such as these can inhibit students from comprehending (or even seriously considering) the concepts of the curriculum. For example, Eaton, Anderson, and Smith (1984) carefully examined the conceptions of over 100 fifth-grade students as their two teachers attempted to teach them the concept of reflected light and its key role in our vision. Despite four to six weeks of instruction, using good textbook passages and presentations of the scientific explanations of the phenomena, discussions, demonstrations, and hands-on activities, virtually all students persisted in some form of their original misconception: that we see because light shines on things and brightens them. These students were intelligent, attentive, and motivated. Their teachers seemed to do everything right in presenting and discussing the scientific conception; however, they did not identify and directly address their students' fundamental misconception.

We should assume that in the science curriculum, students are not blank slates. They have prior experience, knowledge, misinformation, and misconceptions. Students will always attempt to link new information to established schemata in some way. Your task as a teacher of science may be less providing a new schema than perhaps dislodging and dramatically altering an existing one, one that is not just incomplete but fundamentally wrong. In a sense, you have to get the students to consider seriously two rival conceptual frameworks.

Misconceptions cannot be eradicated by simply presenting new information. The existing ill-conceived schemata are used to make sense of anything you present. That is, new information is most often assimilated into existing schemata without pronounced change in the way the knowledge is structured; new information is added on to what is already there. For instance, in the lessons on reflected light just mentioned, the text discusses sources of light shining on things that one sees; although true, this statement fits in nicely with the students' misconception. Later, the text states that shadows are formed because light travels in straight lines and cannot pass through opaque objects. Since it does not explicitly state that some light bounces off the opaque object, nothing contradicts the misconception. Unless the teacher directly confronts the misconception, there is little hope of its being changed.

New concepts usually require the restructuring of existing knowledge in some way, some kind of cognitive reorganization to deal with this new way of conceiving something. Students have invested time and energy in building their knowledge structures; schemata are not assembled and disassembled willy-nilly. Some schema are extraordinarily deep-seated and resistant to change. Why would someone be willing to restructure her way of thinking about something? What would induce her to modify or replace schemata? When teachers present new concepts quickly and abstractly, they offer little inducement for students to change their schemata.

Misconceptions, naive theories, and ill-conceived schemata in science will be stubbornly held on to unless students are *actively engaged* in wrestling with phenomena, problems, or questions. Students must willingly commit themselves to the cognitive struggle of restructuring. They must become motivated to confront actively the inconsistencies or contradictions between their misconceptions and the phenomena. If students perceive an inconsistency and accept the intellectual challenge of resolving it, the teacher may be able to provoke the cognitive restructuring to more sophisticated conceptual understanding.

Posner et al. (1982) suggest four criteria for changing students' misconceptions:

- They must become dissatisfied with their existing conceptions.
- They must achieve a minimal initial understanding of the scientific conception.
- The scientific conception must appear plausible.
- They must see that the scientific conception is useful in understanding other examples of phenomena.

The major purpose of this chapter is to illustrate some strategies and approaches that are likely to accomplish these four criteria. We contend that the best way for students to acquire the rich conceptual structures of scientific knowledge is by engaging in those very processes that created it. They must experience the processes of creating meaning that will lead to restructuring schemata. Students can become more proficient in these cognitive processes by practicing them.

We do not seek a stark dichotomy between the conceptual content of science and the cognitive processes that construct it. They are intertwined, and teaching science means addressing both in an integrated fashion. The ideas and concepts we use to think about phenomena guide our intellectual processes, and yet through these processes we create meaning. This dynamic flow is stimulated, provoked, and monitored by the teacher.

As we asked in the chapter on mathematics, are the concepts so incomprehensible? Is scientific thinking so difficult that it's beyond the capabilities of most of us? We do not believe so. Let us briefly examine the nature of science and scientific thinking before suggesting approaches to teaching them.

WHAT IS SCIENCE AND SCIENTIFIC THINKING?

Traditionally, the knowledge domains of the sciences have been divided into life sciences and physical sciences, following the distinction between living and nonliving systems of matter and energy. Thus, one can readily see biology as the quintessential life science. Zoology is the study of creatures of all kinds, and botany is the study of plant life. Ecology and environmental science may be seen as recent additions to our knowledge domains, being concerned with relations between organisms and their environments.

Physics is considered the king of the physical sciences. As with the other sciences, it has many branches or fields (acoustics, optics, mechanics, thermodynamics, etc.). Chemistry, the study of the elementary and compound substances, has traditionally been divided into organic and inorganic branches, reflecting our basic distinction. In this century, we have seen the incredible advances in chemistry through the application of principles of biology (biochemistry) and physics (physical chemistry).

Physical science has also included astronomy (celestial bodies and phenomena), geology (our planet, Earth), and meteorology (our atmosphere and weather). In recent decades, these three have come to be thought of as earth sciences.

School districts make decisions about which sciences they want students to encounter at different times in their academic careers. Rather than suggesting a rearrangement of your curriculum, we will assume that you have some kind of curriculum guide with text (and perhaps some materials) with which to teach concepts from some of these sciences. Some districts (and texts) purposely deal at each grade level with selected concepts from each of the major branches (e.g., physical, life, and earth sciences). Whatever your district has decided, you have some starting point for the key concepts (and maybe principles, laws, and theories) you will have to address with your students.

In each field, scientists engage in some form of *systematic empirical inquiry*.

There are somewhat different ways to describe what that inquiry is. For most of us, what comes to mind is something called the *scientific method*. Perhaps you think of it as performing experiments, testing hypotheses, determining a way to measure something, deciding what variables to control or hold constant, or analyzing the results with statistics. You may recall working in the laboratory, conducting experiments, following the directions from the lab manual to the letter in order to get what you were supposed to get.

Actually the scientific method is much broader than this experimentalism. It does involve systematic inquiry into some question, problem, or phenomena, but not always through formal experiments. For instance, the scientific inquiry of astronomers could hardly involve manipulating variables in an experiment. Each of the traditional branches of science has its own particular focus. Different phenomena require somewhat different approaches. Some can be controlled and manipulated through experiments; others must be observed as they occur in nature without intrusions by the scientist. There are at least two somewhat different kinds of phenomena that are not studied experimentally. In one, control is impossible (as in astronomy or paleontology); in another, control is undesirable (as in studies of wildlife in their natural habitat; we could study them in a zoo or laboratory, but their behavior would not be the same as in the wild).

Even with experimentalism, the experiment is not the beginning. Where did the ideas for the design originate? The hypotheses? In all our domains, with their vast data, there is an accumulation of recorded observation of phenomena. There is a foundation of centuries during which scientists watched, listened, smelled, tasted, and felt things; took notes; and thought about what they had experienced. In some cases, they then tried something to see what would happen (e.g., dropping various objects off the leaning tower of Pisa). Therefore, what we might call *naturalistic observation* is a major part of conducting an inquiry. Being able to observe and record observations are essential aspects of science.

On a parallel track is *mathematical measurement*. Many inquiries require the simple counting of phenomena; others, more complicated measuring. Furthermore, measurement requires intruments that can range from simple devices (e.g., rulers or graduated cylinders) to incredibly sophisticated apparatus. We also have devices that extend our ability to observe phenomena, such as telescopes, microscopes, and cloud chambers. Finally, we have devices that dramatically act on matter (e.g., atom smashers).

As we consider the intellectual processes involved in conducting an inquiry, bear in mind the preceding distinctions. We can study phenomena as if they exist naturally without our manipulation through direct observation and recording, which might involve simple counting. We can set up a situation or simple experiment for us to observe and record what happens, which also might involve mathematically measuring phenomena in some way.

The American Association for the Advancement of Science (AAAS) developed curricula (1975) in which it suggested thirteen intellectual processes used in science. Eight of these were seen as basic (for grades K–3), five as more involved and integrated (for grades 4–6).

Basic

- Observing
- Using space/time relationships
- Classifying
- Using numbers
- Measuring
- Communicating
- Predicting
- Inferring

Integrated

- Controlling variables
- Interpreting data
- Formulating hypotheses
- Defining operationally
- Experimenting

Instead of analyzing this list, think about what we want students to do. What are our goals? They are two-fold: We want the students to attain rich, powerful conceptual structures for understanding phenomena, and we want them to be able to become proficient in the intellectual processes that constitute scientific thinking. These goals are intertwined and equally important.

TEACHING SCIENTIFIC CONCEPTS AND INQUIRY

How have science educators of the past handled the twin goals of teaching concepts from the sciences and the process of scientific inquiry? Some have referred to *sciencing* to convey the inseparable nature of content and process. Ironically, for over 20 years, there have been those who have clamored for a more active engagement of students in the process of *doing* science, that is, conducting an inquiry. Despite a dozen major curriculum reforms that sought to integrate content and process (or just to make sure that students were introduced to the processes of inquiry), today it is still commonplace for schools to rely heavily on textbooks. Most students experience science as some information that they read about. The concepts of science seem like a giant vocabulary list.

Many factors foster a textbook orientation to science. Most elementary school teachers do not have a strong background in science and may well have some anxiety about "getting over their heads." Many school districts do not truly value student-conducted inquiries; materials and kits may seem an unnecessary expense. The school day is certainly crowded, with many subjects to teach. An emphasis on reading and math has frequently relegated science to "whenever we can fit it in." Finally, conducting an inquiry with equipment, materials, substances, and thirty children is not always rewarding. It takes time to set up and clean up. Things may not work right. Some children will understand and others won't. And maybe the children will get out of control or break the equipment.

Obviously, if you are in a district or school that does not support student-conducted scientific inquiry, we can only give you reasons you might use to convince administrators to change their minds. However, if you have even mild support, you may profit from our illustrations of what can be done.

First, we are not critical of science texts, which are a valuable resource. Assuming they are current and well written, they can provide basic organization to the knowledge you want students to acquire. Also, your classroom should have refer-encc and trade books that supplement the text. We would hope that your school library could provide additional reading on topics you are addressing. The drawback of texts is that they are static and lifeless if not connected to life experiences. Also, they may be too brief and too abstract, without the richness and examples needed to engage the students.

The inquiry process is obviously essential, but it too can have drawbacks if done incorrectly. Can you remember following the lab manual, like a cookbook? If it emphasizes procedures to be rigidly plodded through to arrive at a finding that was obvious, the process is a charade, contrived and meaningless. On the other hand, if the process of inquiry has little or no structure, students can flounder and become frustrated, their thinking sloppy.

We have exaggerated these two extremes for effect. The point is that the pro-cesses of inquiry require a certain amount of structure or guidance for the students. The degree of structure will vary according to the ages and capabilities of the stu-dents. First-time inquirers in September will need more structure and guidance than they will in May. As with most things in life, fruitful experience in science develops proficiency. If we are to create independent thinkers and inquirers, they must have the appropriate experiences, geared to where they are in their development. Further-more, these experiences must be debriefed, thought about, reflected on, and dis-cussed. There must be a continuing cycle of action and reflection. Debriefing must explicitly tie together the processes of inquiry with the appropriate scientific concep-tions.

Recall our earlier discussion of Posner's four major criteria for changing con-ceptions: provoking dissatisfaction with the old, promoting initial minimal under-standing of the new, making the new appear plausible, and seeing the new as useful. To accomplish these, Anderson and Smith (1987) suggest that teachers of science must *present information*

- To contrast explicitly students' own conceptions with the scientific alternative conception
- To apply the scientific conception to specific phenomena
- To emphasize repeatedly the crucial conceptual point so that it doesn't get lost in a list of facts

They urge teachers to use *hands-on activities* with real-world phenomena

- To create dissatisfaction with existing conceptions
- To illustrate how the application of the scientific conception is plausible and useful

They urge careful *questioning* that pushes for explanations of specific phenom-ena (avoiding simple recall). Questions can be used

- To diagnose and challenge students' misconceptions
- To diagnose students' understanding of new conceptions
- To provoke students to use and apply conceptions

To address both scientific concepts and thinking, we propose a general approach that balances the concerns we have expressed. We see eight roughly different phases of science teaching:

- Diagnosing existing schemata
- Confronting schemata
- Exploring phenomena
- Generating opinions
- Conducting systematic inquiry
- Debriefing explanations and concepts
- Debriefing cognitive processes
- Broadening schemata

Before discussing each of these ideas, let's look at an activity that we began in the previous chapter.

Ask the students if they have ever gone down a hill in a wagon, on a bike, or on a skateboard? Did they ever ride a roller coaster? What did it feel like? How did they get started? Was it a long way down? Did they feel themselves going faster and faster? You could have them write about one of these experiences and discuss it with the class.

Tell the students to bring in to school the next day several simple objects that roll. They cannot be toy cars and the like but rather basic objects like balls, tubes, and spools. You should have a supply of things also that includes several solid spheres (balls, marbles), hoops (tape rolls), and disks (solid wheels). The next day, review the assembled collection, asking the students to compare and contrast the items. Make one list of all the items, with appropriate names and who contributed which item.

Ask students to predict which objects will roll fastest down a hill. Then ask them why? Allow students time to discuss and debate with one another. Write down their predictions and explanations on newsprint.

Next, working in small groups, the students should categorize the objects. When they have categorized their list in several different ways, share these categories with the entire class and also list them on newsprint. Ask students if any of these categories will roll faster than others. If some believe so, ask them to explain why? Again, write down any such predictions and explanations on newsprint.

Present the students with two unopened soup cans of the same brand: tomato and vegetable. They should be the same size, shape, and weight, but don't mention anything about weight; tell them if they ask, but don't volunteer. You should set up some kind of inclined plane of at least 8 feet (longer, if possible). The incline should be straight and not too steep. It should be smooth and free of bumps and gouges. For instance, we have used rectangular tables with books raising one end.

Now pose this question: "Which soup can will roll down the incline faster, or will they be the same?" Ask the students to predict and to say why they think so. If they are not sure why, ask them to think of what would make a difference. You need only pose questions and not give answers. Roll the two cans at this point and let the students see which reaches the end first (the tomato). Most students are surprised that there is a difference and want to figure out why.

Ask the students to explain why the tomato can won. (We are not going to tell you yet.) Ideas and explanations can be listed on the board, without your evaluation. Students are not competing for the right answer or for your approval. All conceptions are valuable at this point; in fact, there are several layers of explanation possible. Ask students to compare these explanations to those they previously expressed about all the objects that roll. What are their conceptions and schemata? You will have to contrast explicitly the scientific explanations of the phenomena with these existing conceptions.

The students should now conduct some explorations with their collection of things that roll to help them understand the factors that might be involved. You should tell them that experimenting with these items can help them explain what they have just seen.

Conduct some kind of competition between items, for example, a paired elimination. Be sure to record on the board which objects won and lost. A fair competition would pair every object against every other one (a nice combinatorial exercise). This kind of playful exploration is very useful. Students will note how important it is to release both objects simultaneously, to ensure a clear surface, and so on. Since they have thought about differences and categorized the objects, they may get an inkling of some pattern to the results.

Students should discuss what they have observed and what patterns, if any, they have noticed. These ideas should be written on the board. There will undoubtedly be differing opinions about what happened and what can be inferred. That is fine. Encourage the students to discuss their differing ideas (without rancor). It is good for students to help one another draw conclusions or point out erroneous inferences.

In general, solid spheres will go the fastest, followed by solid disks, with hoops last. Hollow spheres, hollow disks, and hoops with spokes are usually a little faster than hoops but not as fast as either solid disks or spheres. Surprisingly, this pattern holds regardless of weight, which was probably a major misconception held by the students. Several of the obviously heavier (and perhaps bigger) objects did not roll quickly. Emphasize this discrepancy with the class.

The next phase should be a more systematic data gathering, with more of a design. The best way is to have a stop watch with hundredths of a second to record individual trials. Once again, there are some excellent opportunities for students to discover the need for careful procedures. For instance, if one person releases an object and another starts the watch, were they synchronized? Allowing students to realize what kinds of controls must be built in is infinitely better than you (or a manual) telling them what they should do. Repeating trials until they have good procedures is valuable. You could have several different groups simultaneously conducting trials if you have several stop watches.

A key aspect of the design of this experiment is for students to think through what they are expecting, based on their explorations. That is, what are the conceptions and factors they want to investigate. This is a good place for you to provide appropriate structure for their work. Because weight seems to be a puzzling factor, you should have available some kind of sensitive scale. Allowing the students to do the weighing is excellent experience. Then let them compare the rolling times of similar objects of distinctly different weights (e.g., solid spheres of different weights). The times will be nearly identical. Differences will be due to experimental factors, which should be discussed.

For the next experiment, we suggest that you encourage students to limit the objects they use to about a dozen that fall within a narrow range of weight, with four from each of the major categories (solid sphere, solid disk, hoop). Repeated trials for each object can be averaged, or you could have three trials and discard the high and low times. A summary chart can be made on the board or on newsprint.

From these observations and measurements, students should be able to infer the pattern that spheres take the least time, followed by disks, then hoops. Ask them to apply this pattern to the soup cans. They may infer that the tomato is more dense and solid, like a disk; the vegetable is more liquid and becomes like a hoop when its contents are thrown to the sides as it rolls. Will some students have a conception of centrifugal force (even if they don't know this term)? You might want to get a clear cylinder that could be tightly capped. Fill it with vegetable soup, roll it, and observe what happens.

The students probably do have some schema that relates to centrifugal force. Swinging one another around or various rides in the amusement park provide examples of this phenomenon. Can they think of some specific examples?

Thus, one level of explanation for the tomato soup can beating the vegetable is that it is more disklike and the other hooplike. Note that the vegetable does not start out like a hoop; it becomes a hoop as it rolls. Classes have noted that vegetable soup initially starts rolling faster down an incline but that tomato will catch up within a few feet, pass it, and win by a few inches in a ramp about 8 feet long. But why would a disk beat a hoop? That is another layer of explanation that you might address with older students.

Ask the students to compare and contrast the disks and hoops that they rolled. If the items are of the same approximate weight, the students should be able to see that either the hoops are made of fairly dense substances or they are quite a bit bigger than the disks. Some of the hoops may be made of heavy metals and have small diameters; others, of lighter plastics with large diameters. Thus, there is another factor that the students might consider: the diameter of the rolling object. With the soup cans, this was the same, but it was not in the dozen objects the students rolled.

A key concept operating here is the center of gravity. To illustrate this concept you can have students put their backs against their chairs, feet firmly on the floor, arms across their chests, and try to stand up. They must try to keep their backs against the backs of their chairs. It is quite impossible. If you relax that restriction, they will lean forward a bit and stand up. Why?

As another illustration, have a student stand beside a wall placing his right shoulder and cheek and right side of his right foot against the wall. Now tell him to lift his left foot while keeping these three body parts against the wall. He can't; why not? Have the rest of the class try.

Here is another example for the students to try: They open a door and stand perpendicular to it with the toes of their two feet on either side of the door. They inch closer until their nose and chest are against the edge of the door and their toes are past it. Keeping nose and chest in place, they try to rise up on their toes. They cannot; why not?

In each of these tasks, the rules prevent you from putting your body's center of gravity directly above the force you want to exert. For instance, when seated in the chair you want to rise up, with the force emanating from your legs, but your center of gravity is not above them. It is about a foot or so back in the seat of the chair. From your vast experience with rising from chairs, you automatically lean forward to get your center of gravity *directly above the force* that you will exert. We do this without thinking; it does not provoke reflection until considered with these seemingly silly activities. Ask the student, "Where is the center of gravity for the rolling objects?" It is midway along the line of the center of the circle formed as the object rolls on its circumference.

These examples illustrate the vertical sense of the center of gravity, but there is also a horizontal sense. Tall, thin objects are easier to knock over with a horizontal force than short, wide objects (or people). The surface area of the base relative to the height must be considered if you are to think about the center of gravity. Now imagine two identical rectangular boxes (such as those that a single bottle of liquor might come in). Imagine gluing two identical large, wooden blocks inside each box at one end. If you were to stand these two boxes on their ends, one with the wooden block at the bottom and the other with it at the top, which could be knocked over easier by the horizontal force? If you want, make these boxes and have students experiment. Ask them how these ideas and actions relate to the rolling objects and soup cans. Have them think about the different ways in which these objects vary. Ask them, "Where is the center of gravity in each object that rolls?" Assuming that the rolling objects exhibit some form of symmetry, their center of gravity is in the middle of a line that represents the center of the circles that roll down the incline.

The speed with which these objects can roll depends on the way their weight is distributed relative to their center of gravity. The more the weight is closer to the center of gravity, the faster it will roll. But where is the weight distributed? With the hoops, the weight is along the circumference, away from the center. With the disks, the weight is uniformly distributed, and therefore closer to the center of gravity than in the hoops. With the spheres, it is a bit closer (imagine a sphere being a solid disk or cylinder with the outer corners of its circumference shaved off in a perfect curve). The technical concept involved is the *moment of inertia* that relates the diameter of the rolling object to the distribution of its mass.

In a truly fair test of objects, we would get a disk and a hoop with equal weight, diameter, and width. You can buy such a pair from Welch's Scientific Supply in Skokie, Illinois. The hoop is a heavy metal; the disk, wood. The disk resoundingly defeats the hoop. The soup cans are not quite equivalent because the vegetable soup does not begin as a hoop. However, it is a remarkable application of the concept.

This activity illustrates the eight phases. Although they signify eight somewhat different aspects of helping students to understand concepts and conduct an inquiry, they are highly interrelated. One flows into another; they are not rigid steps to follow slavishly. It is far better for you to think through yourself how to address creatively each of these eight ideas than it is to plod through each phase.

Diagnosing Existing Schemata

Misconceptions of varying depth and breadth that may be present in the schemata of your students can interfere with conceptual understanding. Fortunately, thirty students are not likely to have thirty different misconceptions for any given concept that you'll be addressing. The cognitive researchers are finding that usually no more than two or three are present. Discovering these misconceptions early is important so that you are aware of what must be confronted.

There are various methods of finding existing schemata and misconceptions, and all of them require students to express their thoughts, either in writing or orally (to the whole class or to a small group). Your task is to stimulate their awareness and subsequent expression of their conceptions. For example, you can use vocabulary or semantic mapping techniques: "What do you think of when I say *condensation?*" Write all their ideas on the board and then cluster things that go together.

The text or some other reading at this early stage may elicit thought and ideas. A page or a paragraph from the text may generate a reaction you can tap. Similarly, a short story may spark some powerful memories or associations that can be useful. Have you read "Silent Snow, Secret Snow," by Conrad Aiken?

You can ask the students to recall experiences with rain or with dew. "Have you walked in your bare feet on morning dew?" "Have you flown in an airplane and looked at the clouds?" "Did you ever go out in the rain in your bathing suit?" "Have you seen storm clouds roll in?" Any of these questions can be used as a writing assignment. You don't need an elaborate assignment, perhaps just some memories sketched on a 5-by-8-inch card. These thoughts, which can be discussed in small groups or with the class, can facilitate some *gentle* questioning about what is going on, what makes this happen, and so on. No heavy duty interrogation is used and no answers are given by the teacher.

Actually, throughout any activity you want to be aware of students' conceptions, as for instance, when you do something in the next phase that confronts their schemata.

Confronting Schemata

This is a crucial step for many reasons. You want to stage an event or demonstration or pose a problem or question that will grab the students both intellectually and emotionally. You are dealing with schemata, thinking processes, attitudes, motivation, interest—all mixed together. You want to create a kind of cognitive conflict or disequilibrium that cannot be simply dismissed. You want the students, because of their existing schemata, to be unable to assimilate readily what they are learning. If you have already identified a misconception concerning the phenomena or concept under study, you want this event or question to confront directly their misconception in a way that creates dissatisfaction.

Obviously phenomena can vary greatly in the extent to which they provoke awe, mystery, and puzzlement. Some can be quite exotic and novel, others simply unexpected, strange, and inconsistent with assumptions. Of course, what is new, counter-intuitive, or discrepant with one person's schema may be somewhat familiar to that of another. Furthermore, the explanation or concepts that underlie the phenomena should not be so complex or abstract that they are dismissed as incomprehensible. For misconceptions to be dislodged, alternative conceptions must allow some initial point of comprehension.

The question of the two soup cans is certainly a bit unusual. In the first place, who would think of rolling them down a hill? In the second, what do tomatoes and vegetables have to do with rolling? What schema of soup must be present to wrestle with this question? How do the students conceive of forces and factors that may affect rolling; what do they know about mass, gravity, friction, and inertia?

This kind of confrontation should cause uncertainty, doubt, perplexity, and ultimately, curiosity. Obviously curiosity can vary in intensity from mild to burning, but even a little can get students' attention. Intense curiosity drives sustained inquiry. It provokes scientists to spend lifetimes searching for answers to why our world *is*.

Exploring Phenomena

Scientists actually use the expression "messing around" to describe the next phase of inquiry. Sometimes they just need to verify what they have seen; they want to see it again and again, checking their observations. This exploration can be particularly helpful in establishing dissatisfaction with their misconceptions since an initial reaction to a discrepant event is to dismiss it as a "trick," a special case in which you fooled them, an exception to their "rule."

Sometimes they want to play with the phenomenon, to *get the feel of it*. This may be thought of as unguided or unstructured inquiry. It may be unsystematic, but it provides direct experience, or hands-on manipulation. In the soup cans example, allowing students simply to try out various things that roll gives them an experiential feel for what is occurring. Also during this time, if you encourage discussion about these phenomena, the students' conceptions will continue to be revealed.

For young children, manipulative skills are vitally important for their cognitive development. They are worthy of being a major objective of science, regardless of concepts. Imagine being blindfolded and running your fingers and hands through the following substances:

dirt	water	salt crystals
mud	liquid soap	sugar crystals
clay	finger paint	soap powder
fine sand	Silly Putty	baking soda
coarse sand	glue	wheat flour

Because you have experienced the feel of these substances, you can (and probably did) make some patterns out of this list. A crucial part of science for young students is experiencing the tactile sense and reflecting on these experiences to establish concepts of rough, smooth, creamy, sticky, and so forth. Consider letting students feel substances while blindfolded and describe the sensations in their own words. There could be some excellent comparisons and contrasts. You can probably envision the value of similar experiences with other sensory modalities.

Manipulative, hands-on science is not always messy, but it can be. The question is not, "Should I or shouldn't I bother?" but rather, "How can I do it in a way that minimizes the problems?" We have three suggestions for a messy activity such as this one. You can have part of the class do the activity (or part of it) at one time, giving you fewer children to supervise at once. If there is likely to be a mess, warn students the previous day (with notes to parents) to wear old clothes, and let them work on the floor with an old shower curtain to catch the debris. A shower curtain is easier to roll up and hose down (or throw away) than newspapers (which can get knocked about the room). Also, schedule messy activities toward the end of the day so that you don't have to clean them up very quickly before the next lesson.

Here is another delightfully messy activity that illustrates the exploration phase. Show the students a mystery substance. It looks like a fine white powder and feels a bit like flour. Add small amounts of water and mix until it looks like putty but doesn't behave or feel like putty at all. When you push your finger into it, it is hard and moves away from your finger. When you tap it with a pencil or spoon, it sounds hard.

The point here is not for the students to guess what the substance is. Think for a minute how valuable it is to do the actual feeling and pushing. To get the full impact of what is happening, they must do some exploration. Playing and messing around are absolutely essential to grasp the phenomenon intellectually. The impact of how differently this substance with water behaves from other known substances requires exploration. They simply cannot appreciate the phenomenon without squishing, dropping, thumping, poking, prodding, and so forth. Add a little more water and see how gooey it can be. It can drip like glue, but it doesn't actually stick. It easily slips off a surface without leaving a residue.

You can give each student a hunk of this substance or you can give them the powder and water and let them mix it themselves. You can also add a few drops of food coloring to the water first. With the water colored, they might notice that it does not combine with the powder in quite the way one might expect.

Exploration with this substance, called oobleck, arouses cognitive conflict and confronts schemata. Moreover it brings a wealth of raw data about students' conceptions of solids and liquids to you, the teacher. How do the experiences of the exploration relate to their schemata? Ask them, "What kinds of things happen when substances are mixed with water?" Think about this question yourself; we'll come back to oobleck later.

Generating Opinions

As soon as you initiate any inquiry, students are going to have opinions, which some will vocalize. Some opinions about phenomena and answers to questions will probably surface in the preceding phases. Note here that you want students to express their ideas and opinions, to generate creative ideas and explanations, to suggest factors and forces, to recall possibly related experiences, and so forth.

Eliciting opinions is an opportunity for you not only to diagnose conceptions but also to lay the groundwork for the appropriate scientific conception. You may think of this phase as activating schemata in hopes of getting relevant schemata on the table for consideration. For instance, it is important to realize that tomato soup in a can is thick, whereas vegetable soup is much more watery. Maybe not all children realize these facts. If someone suggests this relationship, perhaps a second set of cans could be opened and poured.

Ideas and opinions can be brainstormed in small groups, individually, or with the whole class, either orally or in writing. All ideas should be recorded—written on paper if individuals or small groups are generating ideas, which should then be shared with everyone and written on the board.

You should stimulate opinions through questions that provoke explanations of the specific phenomena at hand. You want the students to develop their own explanations, to speculate on possibilities, to use their own prior knowledge and imagination. This openness is central to maintaining their active involvement in the inquiry.

Here is an illustration: Help the class analyze their observations, inferences, and speculations about oobleck through a chart that compares and contrasts it with various known substances. They are already doing this process in their heads, perhaps randomly. Make it more formal and systematic. Ask them to suggest a number of different substances to which they'd like to compare oobleck. List these on the far left column of the blackboard or newsprint. Entitle four other columns: Similarities, Differences, Reasons, and Questions. These substances do not have to be powders to which water might be added. You might suggest Silly Putty and Elmer's glue. Have small groups of students take two or three substances to compare to oobleck, suggesting what should be entered into the chart.

For example, in comparing Silly Putty to oobleck, students would suggest that they both look kind of shiny and feel hard, yet they differ in color, stickiness, and the way they pull apart. The "reasons" category is quite difficult for most students. You want them to speculate creatively on what is going on. They may have come up with some pretty wild ideas earlier, during exploration. Although you certainly don't want to stifle their speculations at this point, you do want to channel them a bit through this comparative process. Thus, one group might suggest that oobleck is stickier than Silly Putty because it contains some glue.

For some students (especially younger ones), questions may be easier to suggest than reasons. You may want to use only that category or combine the two into questions and ideas. However, you should note the difference: Reasons are tentative hypotheses, whereas questions are things to try to find out. If students suggest the question "What will happen if we add water to Silly Putty?" they are not predicting any particular outcome. This is a good question, born of marvelous curiosity. Note that the next step might be to ask them to think about what might happen: "What are the possibilities?" One of your tasks is to help students move to this more thoughtful state of mind.

After groups have tried to use this chart with one or two substances, you can help students sharpen their thinking by requiring them to write their entries in complete sentences or questions for subsequent comparisons. Of course, they will resist this step mightily. It is too time consuming. However, it will provoke not only clarity of expression but also clarity of thought. One way to help them see the value in it is to have a time of formal sharing among the small groups in which they must read their entries without elaboration. Whether one small group or more than one has analyzed a particular substance relative to oobleck, all class members have an experiential base to draw on.

Other students should respond to the similarities, differences, and reasons suggested by a group. Such dialogue can serve to increase dissatisfaction with misconceptions when some students can readily see difficulties with others' explanations.

Conducting Systematic Inquiry

An important aspect of doing science is making the exploration more systematic, focusing your observations, looking for specific patterns that you think might be there. Often you want to test specific hypotheses, so you have to arrange the circumstances to determine their validity. This may mean designing an experiment, or it may mean carefully observing a somewhat different situation.

For instance, we selected several solid spheres of vastly different weights to roll. Later, we selected a dozen objects of several different types that rolled and all had about the same weight. In the first case, rolling spheres of different weights addressed the question "Does weight affect rate if the type of object is held constant?" In the second case, we were assuming that we should vary shape and hold weight constant. Why? Because we were investigating the question of why two soup cans of equal weight rolled at different rates. We assumed that somehow the different consistencies of the internal liquid has something to do with the different rate.

Now consider a naturalist studying wolves. For a fascinating look at this type of sciencing, see the movie *Never Cry Wolf*. There are numerous examples of how the scientist, living alone in the wilderness, systematically varied the locations he observed and how he followed several specific wolves from the same family throughout the different seasons. He started with an initial question, were the wolves decimating caribou herds? He moved from unstructured, open observation to hunches about various practices of wolves, especially their eating and hunting habits. His observations became increasingly systematic, designed to check out his hunches, confirming or disconfirming. Then he refined his hypotheses, discarding irrelevant information and invalid assumptions.

You, the teacher, have a vital role to play in moving the students into increasingly more systematic and sophisticated inquiry, both within a single activity and during the year across many activities. Although you definitely want them to acquire proficiency, you have to gauge how much to facilitate their inquiry with suggestions and structure. It does not make sense for them to have to discover what it took brilliant scientists years to figure out. Thus, they must do *guided inquiry*. That is, you have to provide a kind of guidance that encourages independent thought, which not only prevents the frustration of pursuing a myriad of blind alleys but also avoids a narrow and obvious path that will inexorably lead to the "right answer." This is artful teaching, indeed. It doesn't come from a book or a manual. It comes from working with a lot of children and knowing the particular children you're working with at the time.

For instance, some students may not discern the emerging pattern of solid spheres and disks and hollow spools, but this is a crucial aspect of the design of a structured experiment. Timing all the objects of the collection will produce a mass of data; a sophisticated thinker could discern a pattern from a table of times for these objects. Elementary school students would be overwhelmed.

These are formidable intellectual tasks for students: formulating hypotheses into questions that can be assessed, deciding which ideas to test, seeing how to vary one thing while holding another constant, deciding what situations to examine and what to look for, and the like. For instance, in an investigation of oobleck, students might decide to try out different substances mixed with water, perhaps flour, baking soda, and powdered milk. What question are they asking? They are not formulating some hypothesis; they are merely continuing an exploration. It may be worthwhile to explore such substances, but notice that it is not really structuring the inquiry. Some may be hoping that one of these is the mystery powder; others may just be satisfying their own curiosity because they never really noticed (or thought about) what happens when you mix these substances with water.

If you want the students to become more structured and systematic in their inquiry, they should be effective in the previous phase of generating opinions, ideas, and potentially relevant schemata. What happens when substances are mixed with water? What are all the different kinds of things that you have seen happen? Why? What is going on? A key substance to consider is sugar; a key concept to be grasped at a later point in the inquiry is dissolving, or more technically, solubility.

Understanding the phenomenon of oobleck can lead to the comprehension of solubility. Some substances are water soluble and others are not. The former will completely dissolve in small amounts; by increasing the quantity, the students will eventually reach a point where no more can be dissolved (a nice concept in itself—saturation point). In contrast, those substances not water soluble will simply not dissolve; they will be readily observed in the water, even in small amounts. Therefore, your guidance to ensure that both kinds of substances are used in the inquiry is crucial. Note that the students may or may not actually be testing an hypothesis (reasons that explicitly deal with dissolving).

Have the students experiment with five different substances: oobleck, sugar, salt, baking soda, and flour. Provide clear plastic glasses that will hold about 8 ounces of water. Make sure that all the water is at the same temperature and is not cold. Have small groups of three students each work with oobleck and two of the other substances. Place the glasses on sheets of paper that bear the name of the substance to be added.

The students should slowly sprinkle 1/4 teaspoon of one substance on top of the water of a glass and watch what happens. After 30 seconds, they should stir the water gently with a spoon. They should write down their observations while the water ceases its motion. They should repeat this process, adding a 1/4 teaspoon four more times, carefully noting what they observe on the five trials. They should wait a minute or two between trials to allow the water to settle. After the five trials, let all the solutions sit undisturbed for a while, perhaps during a recess period.

If all goes well, the sugar and baking soda will disappear (dissolve) on each of the five 1/4 teaspoons. The baking soda might begin to get a little cloudy on the fifth. The salt will disappear on the first 1/4 teaspoon but will be a bit cloudy. Thereafter, it will get increasingly cloudy, with salt granules drifting to the bottom when the motion from stirring slows and the solution becomes super-saturated.

The oobleck and flour remain clearly visible even on the first 1/4 teaspoon; the water is cloudy. Thereafter, the solutions become quite cloudy, with the substances settling to the bottom. Have the students report their findings to the entire class. Discuss any differences that may have occurred between groups with the same substance. You or they may repeat any "contested" findings. You may construct a simple summary chart on the blackboard for the five substances. Ask the students what patterns have emerged.

You and perhaps clever, older students may reasonably suggest that perhaps 1/4 teaspoons are too much to put in at once on the first trial for these two substances. In other words, perhaps they are water soluble and have low saturation points. One could repeat the trial for these three with tiny amounts of each substance. They will still be visible.

We have kept you in suspense too long; oobleck is cornstarch.

Debriefing Explanations and Concepts

Perhaps one of the most difficult aspects of teaching science is moving students from the exciting, highly experiential phases to the more reflective phases. All too often, students want a kind of Mr. Wizard science, a series of spectacular special effects with little thought about what is going on. It is essential that the inquiry be debriefed; students must carefully reflect back on what they have seen for it to have maximum impact on existing schemata. They must examine the validity of their interpretations and conclusions: "What have we found out and how does this new knowledge fit together with our sense of the world?"

As we have discussed, this reflection is not intellectually passive; creating meaning requires an active construction. In this phase (and the next two), *you must help students restructure their schemata.* The systematic inquiry of the previous phases lays the groundwork for schema change. Although some students may make dramatic shifts in schemata during the course of the previous phases, you must assume that most have not, that most require careful debriefing.

If you are clear in your own mind about the key concepts underlying the phenomena, a good set of questions will allow the students to engage in thoughtful reflection on what they have experienced. For instance, you might ask a series of questions about the summary chart of oobleck and other substances added to water.

In most activities in science there are "layers" of explanatory concepts. You can go into varying depths of explanations according to the students' background knowledge and development. In the case of the rolling objects, the opportunity exists for introducing such concepts as mass, gravity, inertia, and center of gravity. More advanced concepts such as acceleration and moment of inertia could be used with advanced students. You choose the level of sophistication. Note how there are several explanations, which differ in complexity and sophistication, about the soup cans and objects that rolled.

You must provide a clear explanation of the appropriate scientific conception that directly relates to the students' experiences with these specific phenomena *and* explicitly contradicts any misconceptions that have surfaced during the activity. You must help them solidify their understanding of the scientific conception or they may reinterpret what they've experienced in ways that are consistent with their misconceptions. You must repeatedly emphasize the key conceptual points among all the data and speculations generated.

Debriefing may be enriched by readings. The inquiry may give a textbook explanation of concepts and phenomena a powerful meaning that it would not have otherwise had. Thus, reading is not a supplementary phase but a meaningful part of debriefing. Students can discuss their understanding of concepts, do some related reading, and discuss the ideas again. Short passages might be read and discussed immediately in class; longer passages might be assigned as home reading to be discussed the next day. However, the debriefing of an inquiry just conducted must be done *immediately*. Delaying debriefing until the next day is a big mistake. Most students will forget significant aspects of what they did and thought.

Debriefing Cognitive Processes

One of the goals of this kind of science teaching is to develop better processes of inquiry. These processes are essentially cognitive, and students should reflect on them as well as on the concepts. Therefore, just as every activity should be debriefed for concepts, each should be debriefed to provoke *metacognition*. You should help the students think about their own thoughts and how their thinking progressed as they conducted the inquiry. There are several key places where their thinking may have shifted a bit; helping them become more aware of these shifts is important.

For instance, they should be aware that they shifted from exploratory to systematic inquiry at some point. This shift depended in large part on drawing some initial inferences, beginning to see some patterns and relationships, making some classifications and predictions, and so forth. To what extent were they aware of what they did and what they were thinking? Making these processes salient, even if you have to point out initially what you saw happening, will help the students clarify what was important; it was not just what they learned, but also how they learned it. Likewise, what were the key cognitive aspects that made the inquiry *systematic?* What was important in setting up the more structured aspects of observation or experimentation? How were the students checking hunches and testing hypotheses? What did they have to do?

Greater clarity and awareness of how they conducted the inquiry (or differences among groups) is vital if students are to grow in their ability to become independent of the teacher in designing more structured and systematic inquiry. In the example of rolling objects, you had to be somewhat directive in setting up the variables to be manipulated in the testing, but you want students to become increasingly able to make these decisions on their own. In general, there are two ways to effect this process in the phase of conducting the inquiry: (1) You can make relatively simple inquiries so that students can readily see what might be varied, or (2) you can model for them the process of deciding what to manipulate. Both these strategies should be used across various inquiries. Just remember that the goal is to foster independence. You must hit the right degree of challenge. Too simple a task or too much guidance can short-circuit their thinking.

Even young students can think about what they did and why they did it that way. Older students can think about their thinking as well. In inquiry that you have guided a bit more directly, you can ask the students why you did what you did. We want students to be increasingly thoughtful and aware of why they did the inquiry in a particular way and how decisions they made affected what they were able to conclude. Sometimes it may be possible to ask a metacognitive question of the students during other phases. However, you do not want to be intrusive, disrupting the flow of their work.

Although this kind of metacognitive debriefing enhances the students' capabilities, don't underestimate its value in affecting their attitudes toward inquiry and science. As students become more reflective, thoughtful, and able to conduct inquiry independently of the teacher, they gain in self-confidence and believe that they can understand science. Positive attitudes and beliefs will nurture two qualities that scientists believe are essential for doing science: intellectual curiosity and persistence.

Broadening Schemata

We note an eighth phase to show that inquiry really never ends; it spins into further inquiry. Just as there are layeres of depth to concepts and explanations, so there can be varying breadth in applications of concepts to related phenomena. Concepts can be investigated in other contexts, and variations on themes can be explored. For instance, oobleck led us into investigating various substances that were water soluble (and some that weren't). What about other solvents besides water? The concept of solubility extends in many different directions, such as paints that dissolve in turpentine but not in water.

In this phase, not only can you branch out but also you can circle back, using the concepts and explanations to explain the familiar. Why is there a lot of gunk on the bottom of the glass if I put in more powder than the box says before adding the water? Why does the salad dressing make blobs when I pour it into my grape juice?

This phase is especially important in helping students to apply the newly appreciated scientific conceptions to other specific phenomena than those directly investigated. These conceptions can be shown to have wide explanatory power and usefulness. In addition, you can continue to monitor their understanding of the scientific conceptions.

Any science curriculum requires some reading, obviously a good way to broaden schemata. Our contention is that the facts, concepts, and principles in books will have more meaning when preceded by substantial student-conducted inquiry. When the reading is motivated by engaged inquiry, it has a good chance of actually being completed and understood.

ACTIVITIES THAT ILLUSTRATE THE APPROACH

Recall the breadth of the science domains. We will not attempt to suggest activities that span this range. Obviously, investigation of some of these phenomena require sophisticated equipment and training. However, within each there are some acknowledged starting points that prepare young minds for the more complex concepts and principles of the domain. Your curriculum, texts, and materials will provide some guidance in major decisions of coverage. However, you will undoubtedly have some latitude in the smaller decisions about what can be emphasized, how much time to spend on a topic, and which activities to do.

We want to encourage you to incorporate as many activities that emphasize *both science concepts and scientific thinking* as you are able during the year. Some teachers have revamped their science curriculum to be entirely based on inquiry. That is, all science reading and writing revolves around ongoing student inquiry. These teachers started out where many other teachers feel quite comfortable: selecting one exciting activity to introduce each major topic of the curriculum.

They carefully thought through the critical concepts for students to understand and the likely misconceptions that students held. They considered the web of related concepts and ideas. They examined the text and supplementary materials. They used resource books (we will suggest some) that described events, demonstrations, or phenomena that would probably provoke puzzlement or contradict students' common conceptions. We have several other suggestions for how to incorporate inquiry activities into your classroom.

First, we don't believe that our approach requires elaborate equipment and expensive materials. You can start on a small scale with a limited budget. Most materials we will suggest can be found in supermarkets, in hardware stores, or in most homes. Even introductory chemistry concepts can be developed without expensive, exotic, or toxic chemicals. A wealth of chemistry occurs in foods and kitchens. Two extraordinary books have been written by Vicki Cobb that can help you understand this kind of inquiry: *Science Experiments You Can Eat* (1972) and *More Science Experiments You Can Eat* (1979).

Second, although we have emphasized the notion of confronting misconceptions through discrepant events, there is plenty of room in the curriculum for activities that motivate inquiry through curiosity. Cognitive conflict arouses, stimulates, and drives inquiry. However, motivation and intellectual engagement in the inquiry may be fostered in some students just by the topic alone. There are some activities that many students at certain age groups just simply enjoy doing, for instance, growing sprouts from various beans and comparing the size, shape, texture, and taste.

Be sure to obtain seeds for sprouting *that have not been chemically treated* (e.g., to retard mildew). Your best bet is to buy sprouting seeds from the health food store; mung beans, lentils, sesame, and alfalfa seeds are fairly common. Get quart jars with lids in which you can punch very small holes. You could also use cheesecloth to cover the jars. You should put about 2 tablespoons of the small seeds in a quart jar; for larger seeds, mung or lentils, put in a half cup of seeds. Soak the seeds in the uncapped jar for at least 12 hours by adding water that is three to four times the volume of the seeds. After soaking, put on the lid or cloth cover and drain off the water. Rinse and drain the seeds until the water appears to be clear. Put each jar on its side in a place where there is some light but not direct sunlight. The temperature should be cool. In a very gentle manner, repeat the rinsing and draining procedure each day.

Have the students keep a record of what happens in the jars, carefully noting changes in the seeds. These seeds are dormant; they will begin to germinate, developing growth-producing enzymes when exposed to water. However, older seeds may not be viable; the proportion of seeds that sprout may vary within a batch, depending on the ages of the seeds. Some seeds may take a week to sprout (e.g., beans), others only a few days. Students can compare these times. Some sprouts get tough if left too long; the seed package may have suggestions on sprouting times. As you may know, these sprouts can be eaten.

What are likely schemata your students have concerning these key concepts—dormant, germinate, viable, and enzyme? You might ask questions such as these: "Is a hibernating bear or a nocturnal bat dormant?" "Have you ever planted grass seed? What happened?" "What are germs?" "Can you think of some substances that change dramatically when water is added? Have you ever made Jello?"

These and similar questions can get students to express their conceptions of these words (concept labels). They can help you diagnose the state of their schemata. From among their responses, you must select ones that can help the students understand the phenomena—metaphors that are appropriate to both the scientific conception and to the students' age and development. Of course, you must note any misconceptions that emerge that must be confronted at some point in the activity.

Many books suggest activities and experiments for the classroom. Some of our favorite general books are listed at the end of this chapter. If you want to emphasize confronting schemata in older students (grades 5–8), you might enjoy *Invitations to Science Inquiry* (1987) by Tik Liem, a remarkable compendium of 400 science activities based on discrepant events.

A third idea for you to consider relates to the ages and stages of development of your students. There is a continuing debate concerning when and to what extent children are capable of certain kinds of thinking necessary for the more systematic forms of science inquiry. For contrast, consider the two extreme positions: (1) A child goes through specific developmental stages that cut across all areas, domains, and contexts; if he is incapable of a certain kind of thinking in one domain, he will not be able to do it in others until he has developed further intellectually; (2) a child develops various intellectual capabilities in different domains independent of others; with appropriate experiences in a domain, he may be capable of more sophisticated thought in it than in other domains.

You have probably guessed that we are somewhere between these two extremes. There is too much evidence of children demonstrating domain-specific knowledge and sophisticated thought (although significantly less able to do so in other domains) to believe in a general stage theory approach. However, there is also abundant support for the general idea that extensive manipulation of concrete objects and materials provides the experiential foundations for reflection, abstraction, and cognitive growth. Furthermore, it is obvious that the teacher has a key role to play in helping students develop abstractions and make connections among concepts.

Therefore, the science curriculum should encourage exploration, manipulation, and general messing around with a wide range of phenomena. However, these experiences must be debriefed, discussed, reflected on, and intellectually processed. Younger students can profit immeasurably from such experiences. For instance, they may spend years walking by and through leaves without ever carefully looking at them. There is so much among our flora that we pass by without reflection. Have the students collect many different leaves for the classroom. Ask them to compare, contrast, and categorize their collection.

These kinds of exploratory observations will pay off as the students get older. They will pave the way for not only formal reasoning and systematic scientific inquiry but also marvelous intellectual curiosity.

A final consideration is the distinction we made earlier between inquiries based on careful recording of observations and those that involve mathematical measurement. We want to affirm that both are equally valuable. Rather than highlighting this difference, think about these two questions: First, to what extent (or in what ways) do you want the children to use mathematics in the activity? In many activities, formal mathematical measurement can be optional (e.g., the paired trials of rolling objects but no timing by a stop watch). Although we favor incorporating mathematics in science activities whenever possible, the choice is yours.

Second, to what extent do you want to integrate mathematics and science? This question is broader in scope, going beyond a particular activity to the philosophy of your curriculum. You may want to blend the two fields intentionally so that students will see the powerful interrelations (especially the meaningfulness of applied mathematics). If so, you should consider the materials from the AIMS Project (Activities that Integrate Math and Science). Each monthly newsletter suggests three or four activities with excellent reproducible materials. The project also has an extensive set of materials that may be ordered for different grades. (For full information, see Resources list at the end of this chapter.)

Even if you are not interested in extensive integration of math and science, you should seize every opportunity for helping your students see how the two are mutually supportive. With adopted curricula in both areas, you do not have to feel that either will take a back seat to the other. Both have concepts and extensions, and there are ample differences that can be addressed. However, do not forget that at least some scientific inquiries require mathematics; and some concepts of mathematics can best be understood by students through their use in the real world. You have a natural situation for synergy; exploit it.

In the following activities, we will suggest ways to use mathematics and measurement wherever it seems natural to do so. We realize that your students may not have the appropriate background for some of these suggestions. Therefore, we'll try to allow for alternatives. Similarly, you may have to modify the activity to fit your students' level of development, the time of year, and so forth.

We will provide a straightforward description of how to conduct these inquiries, allowing a natural flow across our eight phases. You may decide to emphasize several phases as you help your students. Of course, it is important for you to become aware of and deal with students' misconceptions and naive schemata.

Activities Using Carbon Dioxide

Several fascinating activities involve creating or releasing carbon dioxide through a chemical reaction. At some point in the curriculum students will have to understand the difference between physical change and chemical change. These activities can illustrate the latter.

Arrange the class into small groups. Each group should have

- A clear plastic glass about two-thirds filled with water
- A clear plastic glass about one-third filled with clear vinegar
- A plastic teaspoon filled with baking soda
- Five or six raisins

Add the baking soda to the water and stir. Drop in the raisins and carefully observe what happens. Next, slowly pour the vinegar into the water glass. Observe what happens to the raisins.

Some of the raisins will "bounce"—rise to the top of the water, go down again, come up, and so on. This reaction may continue for 20 minutes. After about 5 minutes of careful observation of their raisins and those of other groups, the groups should write down their observations. It may be that for some groups, all the raisins bounced; for others, most raisins; and perhaps for some no raisins bounced.

This is another activity in which the charting of observations, reasons, and questions—which could be shared with the whole class—could facilitate inquiry. It is important that the students carefully observe and record all that they see and separate these observations from their inferences and explanations.

You can inspire more systematic thought and inquiry through a variety of questions if the students are having a hard time moving beyond their observations. For instance,

- Why don't all the raisins bounce at the same speed?
- Why are some not bouncing?
- Why are there bubbles on the raisins? Where did they come from?
- What are some differences among the raisins?

You want the students to consider how to get evidence to support their ideas or at least to further investigate the phenomena. Different groups might take on different aspects of the inquiry, or you could have all groups go through a process with your supervision. Consider the following:

- Investigate the raisins. Repeat the previous activity with different groups having raisins of different sizes or shapes. Also, raisins could be varied in dryness by leaving some in the hot sun or subjecting them to the hot air of a hair

THE NATURAL FORCES OF SCIENCE 157

dryer. Have the students time the rates of rising and falling with stop watches. Note the number of raisins that do not bounce.

- Investigate the solutions. Repeat the previous activity under different conditions: (1) Use smaller amounts of baking soda or vinegar; (2) leave out the baking soda; (3) put some blue food coloring in the vinegar; (4) add the vinegar quickly; and (5) change the order of adding the chemicals to the water—put the vinegar into the water first, then the raisins, then the baking soda. Make sure the students stand back on numbers 4 and 5. There will be a strong fizzing action.
- Investigate other objects. Repeat the activity with things other than raisins. This is a bit tricky. Small but heavy objects will not work. Mothballs and balls from roll-on deodorants work fine. They are more uniform in size, shape, and surface, so there will be less variability in their bouncing. Their bounces could also be timed.

These more systematic inquiries will lead to some observations and reasons that lead to the basis of the phenomena. Skillful questioning by you will again facilitate clarity of thought.

- What are the bubbles on the raisins?
- What is happening when the baking soda and vinegar are mixed?
- What causes the bubbles to "stick" to the raisins?
- Why don't the raisins catch any bubbles on the way down?

For a dramatic demonstration of the chemical reaction when vinegar and baking soda are mixed, try this experiment: Put some baking soda into a small balloon. Put a few ounces of vinegar into an empty, clear soda bottle. Carefully cap the bottle with the balloon, ensuring that no baking soda goes into the bottle. To do this, just tilt the balloon sideways onto the bottle. When the balloon has been fitted over the bottle's mouth, invert the balloon and tap it gently to get all the baking soda to fall into the bottle. Observe. The balloon fills up and may even shoot off. You can experiment with different quantities of vinegar and baking soda as well as different sizes of balloons and bottles. What was happening? Why did the balloon fill up?

A clue, of course, is the fizzing action from the previous activities. Students should examine the bottom of the bottle(s). When baking soda (sodium bicarbonate) and vinegar are mixed, a chemical reaction occurs. This is the key concept of the activity. The two substances break down and two new substances are formed: One is a gas, the other a powder that drifts to the bottom of the vinegar solution (actually a mixture of vinegar and water; you'll probably find no 100 percent vinegar in a store). As with any chemical reaction, the exact quantities of the substances will determine the amounts of the resulting substances. For instance, too much baking soda (or too little vinegar) will mean a small amount of gas and leftover baking soda.

Now what were the bubbles? They were the escaping carbon dioxide. As they bubbled up to the surface, some attached themselves to the raisins or other objects that were sufficiently bouyant to be raised. Once the gas was released at the surface of the water, the raisins fell again. This cycle continued until most of the gas was released and the chemical reaction ended. The raisin-lifting bubbles ceased.

What schema do your students have that would facilitate or inhibit their understanding of the concept of chemical reaction? How could they conceive of two substances interacting in such a way that two other substances are created? What misconceptions do they have about how substances interact or how they can change?

Several interesting activities will provoke students to apply their understanding of this chemical reaction. You can launch a cork (with streamers stuck to it with a thumbtack) from this reaction. Put the vinegar in the bottle as before, but this time put the baking soda into a piece of tissue paper (4 inches by 4 inches). Roll the tissue into a tube and twist off both ends to keep the baking soda from falling out. Drop this tube into the bottle and quickly insert the cork. As the tissue paper dissolves, the chemical reaction begins. The trapped gas will eventually cause sufficient pressure so that the cork will be blown off with a loud pop. You might want to try this outdoors.

These chemicals will make a rather nice (and safe) volcano. You can make a volcano mountain out of papier-mâché or clay. Make a mouth for the volcano with a test tube or narrow-necked bottle. Mix a solution of vinegar, water, red food coloring, and liquid soap; pour it into the mouth of the volcano. Prepare a tissue-paper tube of baking soda as before. Insert the tube and stand back.

Vinegar is not the only substance that will produce carbon dioxide. It does it quite well though. Sodium bicarbonate (baking soda) is a *base* (alkaline) and vinegar is an *acid* (it contains acetic acid). If students have not encountered these concepts earlier, you might want to address them directly. Also note the way acids and bases are used in the next set of activities.

There are other safe acid solutions with which you can produce carbon dioxide. For instance, put 1/2 teaspoon of baking soda into a glass of lemonade. Stir and drink quickly, while it's still bubbling. You have made a lemon fizz (because of the citric acid). Your students could experiment with other juices. Which ones will make fizz? They could chart (and drink), trying to figure out why some did and some didn't. (Just don't let each student have more than one glass; you don't want too much gas.)

Activities Using Indicators

Indicators are dyes that scientists use to determine the presence or absence of certain substances. We popularly use the expression "putting it to the litmus test," which derives from litmus paper, a small strip of paper that has been impregnated with litmus (a powder derived from certain lichens). In general, litmus paper turns red in the presence of an acid and blue in the presence of a base.

The chemical phenolphthalein is a marvelous indicator, turning red or pink in a base solution. If you don't have it in pure form, you can easily make some. Simply grind up a few Ex-lax tablets (plain, not chocolate); phenolphthalein is the main ingredient. Dissolve this powder in a little water. Here is a simple demonstration that should surprise the students.

Prepare three plastic glasses, each a third full: the first with the phenolphthalein solution, the second with 2 tablespoons of milk of magnesia in water, and the third with white vinegar. Pour the first into the second; depending on the concentrations, they will become pink or red when mixed. How can clear or whitish liquids become red? Now pour in the third glass. The red disappears and a whitish liquid remains. What happened?

When the phenolphthalein solution was mixed with the milk of magnesia, it turned red, indicating the presence of a base. The acidity of the vinegar neutralized the base (a suspension of magnesium hydroxide) in the solution, turning the indicator back to its colorless state.

As with other inquiries, we suggest that you introduce the basic procedures and let the students wrestle with what is going on. You could demonstrate this phenomenon yourself with the three large plastic tumblers. Discuss what the students think they saw. What did they expect would happen? Then let them try the experiment in small groups. Have large batches of the three solutions already prepared, labeled A, B, and C (or P, M, and V, which will help you keep them straight), from which you can give them *small* amounts. After they have verified the procedure for themselves, have them describe what they observed and then brainstorm what they think might have been happening. Have them write down reasons and questions. These should all be discussed with the entire class when completed. Your task is to help the students move to the next, more systematic step.

When all three chemicals are mixed (acid, alkaline, and indicator), the students can bounce the colors back and forth at will. With an indicator present, the color will change as one alters the proportions of acid and base. What the students have should now be clear or white; they should slowly add the alkaline (milk of magnesia) until the color changes to pink. Then they can slowly add the vinegar until the solution becomes clear or white again. If they add it slowly, they can just catch the dramatic blinking off of the pink as the solution becomes neutral. Help them to add chemicals slowly, in small quantities. Going back and forth in this manner will help them realize the *neutralizing* that is occurring.

As in all inquiries, you should carefully debrief the students for their thinking processes and the essential concepts involved. You should directly address their conceptions of acid, alkaline, indicator, and neutralizing. There are many common acids that we eat and drink daily, for example, lemon juice. Also, students have probably seen many commercials for *antacids* to relieve acid indigestion and heartburn. Milk of magnesia, Alka-Seltzer, and many others are common products for neutralizing stomach acids. How do they work? What do they do? In your debriefing for their process of thinking about these phenomena, did anyone make these connections? What metaphors or analogies came to mind while going back and forth between the colors?

You should explain that many acids and bases are very strong and dangerous to touch or taste. You could brainstorm or do a semantic map prior to this discussion. For instance, the students may know about battery acids.

There are also activities in which students can apply their understanding of indicators. For instance, you can make a good indicator from red cabbage. Simply grate the red cabbage and let the shreds boil in several cups of water for 5 minutes.

Remove the cabbage by draining and straining. Depending on the cabbage and the length of time it boiled, the water will vary in intensity from red to purple. Give each group of students three or four plastic glasses of this solution. Have the students add substances they believe to be acids and bases to separate glasses. Vinegar or lemon juice wil turn the indicator pink. Baking soda or milk of magnesia will turn it blue or blue-green.

Another intriguing indicator is poisonous and should be used very carefully. Iodine can detect the presence of starch. Students can apply their understanding of indicators to test for *starch* (another important concept) in a food by placing on it a few drops of iodine solution. If the reddish-brown color of the iodine changes to a bluish-black, starch is present. Some common starches students could test are popcorn, potatoes, bread, and tapioca (the root of the casava plant from Brazil, usually sold in dried pearls). You could compare these foods to slices of apples, onion, or other dried fruits and vegetables.

The Famous Egg Drop

Everyone knows that eggs are a source of wonder and delight to children. But did you know that Al Renner and his students at Cal Tech have made a science out of dropping eggs (Renner, 1977)? They throw eggs into the air, drop them off tall buildings, and even take them aloft on kites and planes (and let them go). Three Cal Tech students have dropped eggs from two miles in the air—and they did not break.

The question that these enterprising students and yours can investigate is this: How can you *package* an egg so it does not break when dropped from a great height? You can imagine a lot of experimentation and an incredible mess. Renner suggests creating practice eggs by piercing both ends with a needle or ice pick and blowing out the contents. Seal one hole with dripping candle wax. Fill the egg with water and then similarly seal the other hole. Water-filled eggs are virtually identical to fresh eggs, and they make less of a mess.

There are several different ways to pose this investigation to your students. We will start with the simplest. Divide the students into small groups and give each an identical package or container. It can be anything that you readily obtain in sufficient quantity: pint-size milk cartons, plastic or cardboard boxes, and so on. The task for each small group is to decide on some substance to put inside the container that will prevent the egg from breaking when dropped. You will hold an elimination competition, dropping their containers from increasing heights until all the eggs are broken. Students have tried Jello, bread, popcorn, styrofoam, puffed cereal, cotton balls, and sawdust with fascinating results.

What is the function of the substance? How will it prevent the egg from breaking? Ask the students these questions and discuss what is going to happen inside the container when it is dropped. Ask them to describe what happens to their bodies when they jump off something tall. What does falling mean? What are their conceptions of *gravity, acceleration,* and *energy?* Gravity causes the egg container to accelerate downward faster and faster, creating a substantial amount of energy (of the kinetic variety). When the container hits the ground, its speed immediately slows (decelerates) to zero. Where does the energy go? It must go somewhere. If most of it is not absorbed by the material inside the container, the eggshell will break from the force. Their task is to find a good shock absorber.

What schemata do they draw on to explain such phenomena? What misconceptions do they hold? What happens when a baby falls back onto his rear end? How about two football players colliding? Why do cars have shock absorbers and how do they work?

You should prepare some water-filled eggs and a suitable drop site. The groups have their containers and shock-absorbing substances. If you have given groups time (such as a weekend) to decide on a substance, they probably will have done some experimenting on their own. You may let them choose the starting height, if you want. It should depend a bit on the container you have selected for it may absorb some of the shock itself. If you cannot find a very high place in your school as a drop site, you could use a ladder and a minimal container, like a paper bag.

When filled with the substances and the eggs, the containers should be sealed in a manner that will allow easy reopening to see if the egg is intact. All containers should be dropped in the same manner. For instance, if the students are using milk cartons, all should be held by the "roof" end when dropped. Make sure that each group has labeled its container.

It is usually wise to have another responsible person assist you at the drop site— one to carefully do the dropping, making sure no one is underneath; the other, to make sure that the students remain outside the target area. Imagine dropping the containers off the roof of the school onto the playground. Two classes could compete, each divided into about eight groups. One teacher takes the sixteen containers up to the roof; the other draws a large circle in chalk on the playground below. Students must remain outside the circle. When a container is dropped, a member of that group retrieves it from the circle. When the circle is clear, another container is dropped. Containers are opened to see if their cargo has survived.

The debriefing of the activity is enhanced if a chart of groups and their substances is prepared in advance. At the drop site, the teacher need only enter heights at which the egg perished or survived. By reproducing this sheet before the drop, the teacher can have the students fill in their own copy of results when they return to class. All can compare the shock-absorbing qualities of different substances. Could something else have varied in the students' packaging? Ask the students to think about this question. Perhaps the groups positioned their eggs somewhat differently within the substance.

This activity can have many different extensions in which students apply their conceptual understanding and systematically think about the key factors. As we implied earlier, you could have one dropping session from a great height (like the roof) or slowly increase the height (using a ladder or windows on different floors). You could vary the containers holding the substance constant to see their effects. You could vary the size of the container (e.g., pint, quart, 2-quart milk cartons), allowing more substance.

Perhaps the most interesting variation is to allow great latitude in what can go inside the container. Rather than requiring a single substance, you can allow anything. Students can rig their own devices. Imagine the egg inside an air-filled balloon that was suspended in the water-filled carton.

A variation of this activity is one of the events in the Science Olympiad. The

Naked Egg Drop requires student groups to design a landing pad or catching device. Raw eggs are dropped from increasing heights to determine the winner.

The Science Olympiad (see Resources list) is a national organization designed to promote interest in science in schools. Individual elementary schools can conduct their own olympiad of science events by using guidelines provided by the organization. Their address is given at the end of this chapter.

CONCLUDING ISSUES

This chapter has suggested an approach to teaching science that emphasizes both scientific concepts and thinking. We want to encourage you to examine your science curriculum to find places in which you can incorporate the key ideas. Choose topics, concepts, or activities that you find personally interesting. Start with just a few. Do some background reading on the basic concepts and the layers of explanation.

As your students conduct inquiry and struggle with their schemata, you will have the difficult task of evaluating their work. Obviously, tests that rely on the recall of facts will not lead to the ideas we have been stressing. You will have to develop other means of assessing students' work.

One important vehicle is students' oral expression of ideas and conceptions. Whether presenting a report to the class, discussing an idea, or answering a question, a student's way of talking about her understanding is often quite revealing. Obviously, everything a student says does not have to be given a grade. Quite the contrary. You should try to establish an atmosphere of curiosity, openness, and expression of ideas without students' feeling that they are always being judged.

Written expression of ideas and thinking are particularly valuable. Students can respond to good questions that require more than factual recall; for example, essay questions can be used for tests or homework. Written reports of inquiries (individual or group projects) are similarly worthwhile for demonstrating conceptions. We have had good results from asking students to design follow-up inquiries that drew on the one just completed. Such designs, even if they are not carried out, reveal the quality of thought.

RESOURCES AND FURTHER READINGS

You will find more information about the topics covered in this chapter in the following works, some of which are also cited directly in the text.

Blackwelder, S. K. (1980). *Science for all seasons: Science experiences for young children.* Englewood Cliffs, NJ: Prentice-Hall.
Cain, S. E., and Evans, J. M. (1984). *Sciencing.* Columbus, OH: Charles Merill.
Cobb, V. (1972). *Science experiments you can eat.* New York: Lippincott.
DeBruin, J. (1986). *Creative, hands-on science experiences.* Carthage, IL: Good Apple.
Jacobsen, W. J., and Bergman, A. B. (1983). *Science activities for children.* Englewood Cliffs, NJ: Prentice-Hall.
Liem, T. (1987). *Invitations to science inquiry.* Lexington, MA: Ginn.

Renner, A. G. (1977). *How to build a better mousetrap car.* New York: Dodd, Mead.
Rowe, M. B. (1978). *Teaching science as continuous inquiry.* New York: McGraw-Hill.

You may also want to investigate the following resources:

AIMS Educational Foundation (Box 7766, Fresno, CA 93747). Ten-issue newsletter for
$22.50.
American Association for the Advancement of Science. (1975). *Program guide of* Science . . .
A process approach II. Nashua, NH: Delta Education.
Science Olympiad (854 Schoolhouse Lane, Dover, DE 19901).
Welch's Scientific Supply (7300 Linder Avenue, Skokie, IL 60076).

6

Social Studies—Dynamic
Human Interaction

INTRODUCTION

Of the major areas of the curriculum, we have saved the most complicated for last. Today there is no clear consensus among educators about what social studies in the elementary school ought to be. The confusion appears to stem from competing purposes, that is, emphasis on either *knowledge, thinking,* or *citizenship.* Even within each of these emphases, educators have strong differences of opinion about what it should include.

Educators who want emphasis on knowledge have disagreed on the particular knowledge that should be included. Should all the social sciences be addressed— geography, economics, political science, anthropology, sociology, and psychology— or just some of these? History held a prominent place in the curriculum for decades; how should history and the social sciences be related? Should elementary social studies address key concepts from these seven separate disciplines or interdisciplinary themes, ideas, and problems?

Those who would focus the curriculum on intellectual processes talk about inquiry, problem solving, decision making, values clarification, reflective inquiry, critical thinking, and so forth. Sorting out the differences and similarities among their approaches is a real challenge.

Concerns for citizenship have varied widely. Some educators have urged the inculcation of particular values; some, the development of informed and thoughtful participants in a democracy; others, political action on behalf of various issues. Still others interpret citizenship as being members of a global community.

You may want to read more about these differences. Examine the overview of these issues by: Barr, Barth, and Shermis (1977); Shaver (1978); and Voss (1986). Various texts reflect different emphases: see Banks and Clegg (1985); Ellis (1981); Fraenkel (1980); Jarolimek (1986); Maxim (1987); Nelson (1987); or Schuncke (1988).

We see these major purposes of knowledge, thinking, and citizenship to be more complementary than competitive. For students to understand the ideals and actualities of our democracy and become knowledgeable voters, informed community volunteers, or activists, they should be able to think clearly about issues and events, critically analyze information and statements, and so forth. They must be able to understand basic ideas and concepts that have explanatory power and to apply them to their lives. We suggest an analogous emphasis to that of the previous chapter on the natural sciences; students should construct essential understanding of the key concepts of social sciences and history by engaging in meaningful inquiry that also develops their cognitive processes. By emphasizing the interrelation of knowledge and thinking, you will be helping students become more effective citizens.

A Special Caveat

At this point we would issue a word of caution. You should be aware that in the past decade or so teachers have been urged to address a dazzling display of topics in social studies:

Ethnic studies	Global education
Women's studies	Law-related education
Future studies	Consumer education
Community studies	Environmental education
Urban studies	Career education

Although these would seem to be valuable, you need to realize that topical emphases in social studies regularly shift in response to current social issues. If the schools have been the lever that some people have used to change society, social studies have been their fulcrum. The preceding list offers topics not social science disciplines. Each could be the focus of a unit but should be addressed within a well-conceived curriculum that clearly builds on the knowledge of the disciplines.

For example, we recently had the opportunity to witness a sixth grade engaged in a unit on the law that purported to involve higher-order thinking. Activities had been developed by curriculum coordinators, with background reading taken from materials by the American Bar Association. To our dismay, the activities could be characterized largely as memorizing legal terms and definitional descriptions of various branches of the legal system. The readings might be charitably described as unclear. The perspective of the unit was extremely one-dimensional; only the superficial formal operations of the legal system were described. The concepts contained in a unit on the law should be taught within a broader framework of political science or a key concept such as government.

Social Studies and Children's Schemata

As in the natural sciences, the subject matter of social studies is all around us (and within us). It is what we are, what we have been, and why. In a sense, it is almost too close to home. Students are strongly influenced by what occurs and is spoken of in the home, neighborhood, and community; by their family history, ethnicity, and cultural traditions. From these life experiences come *schemata,* our ways of looking at the world and its people, our taken-for-granted social understandings. Some originate in our culture, some in our parents' kitchen, some on the playground. Like other schemata, they are an intimate part of us.

The content of social studies affords opportunities for the teacher to help students enrich their schemata of the world and its people, their own social world, and the broader culture around them. They can become increasingly aware of their own schemata and how they construct sociocultural meaning. As in the natural sciences, merely presenting students with new information is not enough.

If we found misconceptions in our students' minds about the phenomena of natural science, in social studies we find misinformation, misconceptions, misunderstandings, and biases and prejudices. We do not ascribe malicious intent; rather we simply note that beliefs and conceptions may be deeply and firmly rooted in feelings and not particularly grounded in accurate information. All humans have biases in areas of their lives. Some may prove singularly unamenable to change and impervious to new information.

Getting students' misconceptions to surface and be expressed is vitally important if you are to correct them. The strategies and activities of this chapter illustrate how this might be done. A major task for the teacher of social studies is to help students confront these ideas. They should be provoked to examine simplistic explanations about social phenomena to create more complex understanding. With that in mind, let's look at how the experts conceive of knowledge and inquiry in the seven disciplines.

THE DISCIPINES OF SOCIAL SCIENCE AND HISTORY

Knowledge

The concepts of elementary school social studies are derived from the knowledge structure of the seven disciplines, each of which has a somewhat different focus. Note the following general orientations, with key concepts appropriate for the elementary school:

- Geography: people interacting with their spatial environment, addressing location, physical features, population, environment, region, urban/suburban/rural distinctions
- Economics: people's use of material resources, considering concepts such as economic system, scarcity, production, goods and services, flow of trade, exchange, consumption, interdependence

- Political science: people dealing with power and authority, using ideas like political system, government, state, citizen
- Anthropology: people sharing common cultures, involving concepts such as custom, tradition, ethnocentrism, enculturation, acculturation
- Sociology: people organized as societies, considering ideas such as community, conformity, norm, stratification, sanction, institution
- Psychology (particularly social psychology): people interacting with each other in groups, using ideas like attitude, motivation, role, relationship
- History: human events over time (the broadest concern), drawing on the ideas of the social sciences as well as its own, such as change, civilization, nationalism, revolution

Inquiry

How do social scientists and historians construct knowledge, interpret facts, create concepts, and develop generalizations? Each of these disciplines has methods of inquiry that have been affected by two very different forces within Western civilization: the natural sciences and the arts. Many of those studying social phenomena have emulated physical scientists. They sought to establish "truth" through empirical inquiry and tried to formulate laws of social behavior, principles and theories that would explain and predict human phenomena. Many followed the path of instrumentation, measurement, formal hypothesis testing, experimental designs, and mathematical models. However, others in each discipline have rejected this approach as inappropriate.

The tradition of the arts has long sought to understand humans in an empathic way. Art, literature, music, theatre, dance, and language are concerned with expression, appreciation, communication, and understanding. These interests influenced some who studied social phenomena to adopt methods of inquiry that value seeing the world through the eyes of the other person. Understanding a group of people, a society, a tribe, a clique, or a class means realizing *how* they think about things, either by re-creating or by participating in their ways of seeing the world.

An important element in this debate is how we construct knowledge itself. To what extent can the person who creates the knowledge be separate from it? We can readily see that the physicist is not a part of the atoms he is smashing. Can we say the same thing about the historian studying U.S. involvement in Vietnam? What would you want to know about him: How old is he? Was he there? What was he doing between 1965 and 1972? Answers to these and other personal questions will greatly influence our beliefs about the history he produces because we believe that his inquiry—what he looks at, the facts he selects, and his interpretation of them— will be influenced by *his beliefs*. Our concern about the personal biases of the social scientist may be less pronounced if he is studying the size of a river or the height of a mountain. But if he is studying humans, we may rightly inquire about his frameworks (cultural, political, whatever).

When social scientists seek to emulate the natural sciences, they should realize that two key assumptions of natural science may not be present: identity in space and in time. A chemist can count on a gram of a pure element to behave identically to another gram of the same, similarly pure element. She can also assume that unless tampered with or having some kind of decay, the gram of pure element will be the same tomorrow as it is today. But can we make these assumptions about human and social phenomena? Are two 8-year-old girls from white, upper-middle class, Norwegian families interchangeable in our study? Not in the same sense as the grams are. Furthermore, we could not assume that either child would be exactly the same in some respects from one day to the next. A person changes with experience over time.

The inquirer must exercise extraordinary care, first, to be aware of his own inclinations, assumptions, and so forth, and second, to build into the inquiry procedures to balance these biases. Social science and history seem less amenable to the avowed objectivity of the natural sciences. They are more interpretive and, thus, more dependent on the existing schemata of the inquirer.

TEACHING FOR THINKING IN ELEMENTARY SCHOOL SOCIAL STUDIES

We now turn to three related but different approaches to the existing social studies curriculum that address the conceptual content and stimulate important cognitive processes:

- Critical thinking
- Convergent inquiry
- Divergent inquiry

Each of these builds on the cognitive processes of *schema* and *metacognition*. Critical thinking in social studies especially draws on the cognitive processes we've called *focus* and *pattern*. It involves carefully analyzing data and arguments and comparing them to what is known. Students must be able to distinguish between fact and opinions and realize how "facts" may be interpreted.

We realize that "critical thinking" has become a wonderful cliché, something that everyone wants for students. We have reserved this term for social studies to signify the difficulties we all have with sorting out ideas, concepts, attitudes, biases, and schemata. Although concerns with focus and pattern pervade the curriculum, the more interpretive nature of the social sciences requires some unusual effort on the teacher's part.

Let's look at a simple critical thinking activity.

Take an editorial or letter to the editor concerning an interesting topic, concept, or issue. Provide a copy for each student; make sure that each student has both a blue and a red pen. Ask the students to read the passage initially for its overall message. Without discussing the merits of the passage or if students agree, have them take it apart in the following manner. With the red pen, they underline any sentences in which the author is making some kind of value judgment, circling the key words that tip them off, such as *best, most, important, should, ought,* and so on. With the blue pen, they underline sentences in which the author believes he is presenting facts. Obviously, we cannot see into the mind of the author, but there undoubtedly will be sentences that are presented as factual statements. Of course, you and the students could use two different colors, as long as all agree on the color scheme.

It is important for students to do the actual underlining or highlighting, not just to think about it. They should actually make the commitment or judgment about these types of sentences. You could also have students work in small groups to discuss the passage and decide which sentences exemplify these two types of ideas. Some passages may contain compound or complex sentences with both kinds of expressions. You can help students use both colors to code each part appropriately.

You should debrief the passage, sentence by sentence, in the sequence in which it presents its ideas. The key points for the debriefing are for students to recognize when obvious opinions are being stated and to realize how a factual statement may have opinionated interpretations along with it. You will probably have some interesting debate when some students (or groups) have marked a sentence differently. Students may be able to recognize obvious exhortations and value judgments. They don't have to discuss whether or not they agree with the writer; you simply want them to realize that there may be different opinions. For some issues, some age groups, and some students, you may need time for sharing different opinions in order for students to realize that what they took for granted as factual may actually be an opinion that not all people share.

For instance, in an editorial on U.S. foreign policy, there may be a sentence stating, "The United States is the greatest nation on earth." We may believe that, you may believe that, all your students may take it as a fact, but they must realize that there are a whole lot of people that would disagree. The key word, *greatest,* reveals the value judgment. If this word were explained more fully, we might see that some underlying ideas can be considered factual, such as the United States has the most natural resources, the highest per capita food production, or the largest motion picture industry.

Statements that are presented as factual may be less obvious and require more processing. If someone asserted that the United States has the most natural resources, what does this seemingly factual statement mean? The issue is not do we or don't we, but what is the author really saying? What does she mean by "natural resources"? There is a certain amount of interpretive judgment by the author concerning what she is including and excluding. Is she talking about the oil that flows through the Alaska pipeline or the minds of our high school honor society students?

When discussing the interpretive judgments that go along with statements of fact, you don't have to come to final, definite conclusions about each sentence. Bring the key difficulties to the surface with an initial assessment of what the sentence means and go on. Since you are working through one sentence at a time, don't forget that there is an entire passage that has an overall meaning. Each sentence exists within this broader context. Once you have done a preliminary review of all the sentences, you should go back through them again for these interrelated meanings and the whole message.

We noted in Chapter 2 that inquiry, problem solving, and decision making are *extensions* of the cognitive processes involved in focus and pattern. In social studies, various authors have different definitions for these terms. For this discussion, we see inquiry very broadly as a process in which students wrestle with a variety of questions, problems, issues, and events that confront us. They may use key concepts from the social sciences and history to understand human phenomena.

Collaborative student inquiry offers valuable opportunities for small-group decision making and consensus building. These social psychological processes of thought, feeling, and action should be a key part of the dynamics of the classroom and of inquiry activities. Such interaction can help students develop the social skills necessary for participation in a democratic society.

It is useful to distinguish between convergent and divergent inquiry. In the former, you want the students' inquiry to converge on some concepts, ideas, conclusions, generalizations, or principles that you (and the curriculum) have in mind. The latter emphasizes the more creative and imaginative aspects of projection, allowing students to conduct an inquiry that may diverge into many unusual directions unanticipated by you or the curriculum. Although there is still structure to the inquiry, you encourage students to generate questions and seek answers in paths that the curriculum has not already charted (as in convergent inquiry).

Recall that in Chapter 2 we distinguished between extension and projection through two social studies inquiries: One asked students to investigate their community, its branches of government, operations, tax base, and so forth (see page 40). The other asked them to research the future, predicting from current trends, events, or circumstances (see page 45). Although students could go in a variety of directions in both inquiries, we see the community studies as convergent inquiry. The basic concepts concerning the community are circumscribed to a great extent. By giving students a focus or topic and a specific community, there is considerably less divergence possible than in the future activity (even if we narrowed the focus to the future of the family).

In divergent inquiry we are still trying to get the students to seek answers to intriguing questions. However, the emphasis is on encouraging students to spin off in directions of their own choosing and create meanings and ideas that were not prescribed by the curriculum. In the convergent inquiry on the community, although the students have some choices, their investigation focuses on the basic concepts and explanations that the teacher can emphasize or circumscribe. Divergent inquiry is more open-ended, allowing more room for students' productive and unanticipated tangents, discoveries, and creation.

Also in Chapter 2 we illustrated several very different types of "problem," one of which was what happened to Babylon. It has virtually disappeared from the face of the earth despite its incredible magnificence and magnitude (see page 42). There are a variety of historical records, accounts, and descriptions that could provide pieces of the puzzle. The city of Babylon had yielded to various conquering armies over the centuries. But it was not truly destroyed until the fourth century A.D., when the Roman Emperor Julian and Apostate, at war with the Persians, ordered the remnants of its mighty walls (once 187 feet thick) to be disintegrated, lest they afford any protection to the Persians. Thus, this activity could converge on the current historical understanding of Babylon's fate.

Quite a number of historical artifacts and oddities are available for divergent inquiries. For instance, what is Stonehenge? Why is it there? What was it used for? How about the gigantic stone heads of Easter Island? Who made them, how did they get there, and why?

Strangely, you could follow the convergent inquiry about the history of Babylon with a divergent one by noting the prophesy about Babylon in the Bible (Jeremiah 50): "Because of the wrath of the Lord it shall not be inhabited, but it shall be wholly desolate. . . . It shall be no more inhabited for ever." This historical document has been unquestionably dated to centuries before the occurrences that led to Babylon's demise. Note that Babylon is one of the few major ancient cities that was never rebuilt, although Alexander the Great tried. He was determined to make the site of ancient Babylon the capital of his worldwide empire. He issued 600,000 rations to his soldiers to rebuild the city. Immediately after making this declaration, he died and the project was abandoned. The prophecy of Jeremiah stands. How can we explain this?

Critical Thinking

Dozens of authors have written eloquently about critical thinking in social studies. Here is a recent compilation by Barry Beyer (1985) of specific intellectual operations.

- Distinguishing between verifiable facts and value claims
- Determining the reliability of a source
- Determining the factual accuracy of a statement
- Distinguishing relevant from irrelevant information, claims, or reasons
- Detecting biases
- Identifying unstated assumptions
- Identifying ambiguous or equivocal claims or arguments
- Recognizing logical inconsistencies or fallacies in a line of reasoning
- Distinguishing between warranted and unwarranted claims
- Determining the strength of an argument

You may have noted that we have discussed many of these operations earlier in various ways. Critical thinking does not belong solely to the social studies. These operations clearly are parts of what we've been calling *schema, focus,* and *pattern.* They definitely involve breaking down information and data in a variety of analytical ways, evaluating these pieces in terms of criteria and ideas in our own schemata, and creating patterns of meaning.

Thus, it is important to give students experiences with information, data, arguments, and the like in many different contexts and to help them acquire the intellectual habits of critical thinking. We can only go so far with isolated passages in which we check for emotionally charged words and phrases and similarly obvious cues. Students need to understand the criteria that historians, geographers, and other social scientists use in each of these operations. Judging reliability, relevance, accuracy, ambiguity, strength, and consistency requires work. They are best learned by immersion in a variety of specific contexts. Although there certainly is value in studying propaganda in its generic forms, such as advertising and slogans, there is greater intellectual power in grasping the social, cultural, and political context in which a particular propaganda effort existed.

Immerse yourself in the history of Germany between the world wars if you would understand why the misinformation machine of Herr Goebbels was so incredibly effective. Reading one of Hitler's speeches without this historical and social context makes the "facts" seem absurd. How could anyone fail to see the biases, distortions, and lies? Critical thinking is more than piercing the words and phrases; that's just the beginning. Creating meaningfulness is what social studies is all about. A frighteningly rich context may be seen in a 1936 film made by Nazi propagandists, *Triumph of the Will,* now available on video cassette.

Let's look at some additional activities that illustrate how you might do critical thinking in social studies. Let's assume that the students have been learning about several civilizations. It is common for texts to describe the Mayan, Aztec, and Incan civilizations, for example. But what does the concept of "civilization" mean? The students are learning a lot of facts about these three peoples, but how do they all fit together? One purpose for studying these peoples may be to understand the concept of civilization.

Work with the students to create a giant chart on the chalkboard that has four main headings:

Civilization

Features   Mayan   Aztec   Incan

Based on their readings, discussions, or prior knowledge, ask the students to brainstorm the key features of these civilizations. Your task is to help them eventually shape their ideas into somewhat abstract features of all civilizations. The pyramids in the Yucatan might suggest that a key feature is architecture. The ornaments of the king might suggest jewelry. You should create a list for the first column based on the students' ideas. They can work in small groups and look through the text. As in all brainstorming, you want to accept initial ideas and refine them later.

Before settling on a final list of features for the first column, students in small groups should discuss similarities and differences among these ideas. Groups should share their suggestions for refining the list of features. Notice that these features are concepts themselves. As such, they need a bit of processing to grasp their meaning. However, the next part of the activity will actually help develop the meanings of these concepts.

The major task of the activity is for student groups to fill in the "cells" of this big matrix. For each feature, they must find the relevant data for each of the three civilizations. They should review whatever resources they have on the Mayans to fill in as many cells (features) as possible, then try another people. In other words, have them work with columns, rather than going across rows (checking for jewelry in each). Looking for various features of one civilization at a time will help students see how different features fit together.

After students have done as much filling in as they can, have a time of sharing for each cell as you go down a column. Discuss differences of opinion about the "facts" and try to reach consensus. Have students support their assertions. When you have filled in a civilization's features, ask students to think about any other factors that might explain or help them understand why these people did any of these things. This question may allow some interesting ideas to surface that the features did not pick up (e.g., geographical considerations). Seemingly isolated facts often can be woven together and understood through this process.

The chart is an analytical device with the features as key conceptual categories. Next, have the students look across the rows for each separate feature. They can compare and contrast the three civlizations through these concepts. This process also sharpens their understanding of the concept behind each feature. Occasionally, there will be empty cells, where no pertinent information was uncovered. You can always use this gap as an impetus for inquiry, if you desire. Also, you may find a "discrepant" entry. Two cells are quite similar and the third remarkably different. That should provoke thought.

In a final debriefing, after all the features have been discussed, you should return to the original question of what is civilization? You and the students may decide that some of the features are interesting but do not constitute a key aspect. This idea can be further investigated by asking the students to use the same categories of features with the civilization of the United States in the 1980s. Fill in a fourth column for these features, then compare and contrast the four civilizations.

Obviously this kind of matrix can be used with a wide variety of concepts. It is a variation of semantic mapping. Almost anything can be put into columns and rows.

Critical thinking activities may also involve careful observation and inference, analyzing information to draw warranted conclusions. An important way to understand the social scientists' criteria for determining accuracy, relevancy, and so on is to engage in the inquiry itself. You can use small-scale, mini-inquiries as critical thinking activities to develop the students' capabilities. Such activities would be quite focused and convergent. Here is a simple one that can be very instructive for students.

Select two brief excerpts from video tapes or video-taped TV programs that students will have to observe, analyze, and compare. For instance, for a fourth-grade class beginning a study of deserts, we have used about 5 minutes from *The Black Stallion Returns* (set in North Africa) and 5 minutes from a documentary on the Kalahari desert. Both excerpts are primarily visual, with little dialogue or voice-over. Both show key aspects of the people who lived in the desert, two quite different cultures.

The students should view the two video pieces back to back with no discussion. Divide the students into small groups and give them a handout with a list of questions to be answered through group consensus. They should fill in a chart that has a column of questions and two columns for answers addressing the two cultures. They must complete the blank cells. Here are some possible questions:

1. What are the main features of the desert in which they live?
2. What is the name of these people?

3. Where in the world are these deserts located?

4. What shelter do these people use?

5. What is their work?

6. What are the most important things in their lives?

7. Describe some differences between these two peoples?

8. Describe some similarities between these two peoples?

9. What are some things that you have that they could really use?

10. What question would you like to ask them?

Notice that these questions vary considerably. Question 2 is fairly factual and depends on careful listening. Questions 4 and 5 require interpreting observations in terms of the concepts of shelter and work. Question 1 allows the students to decide on what features they noticed or considered "main." Similarly, questions 7 and 8 allow for selective reflection. Question 3 is quite inferential; a wide variety of data might be used to infer location. Question 6 goes a bit beyond inference and interpretation to use evaluative criteria for importance. Although all these questions require students to draw on their schemata, 9 and 10 rather explicitly ask them to relate their lives to these peoples.

Notice that we did not simply have students answer these questions after viewing the clips; that would be placing a premium on memory. Instead, we showed the two tapes, then showed the questions. After they have made preliminary answers, we did show each tape again and let them rethink their responses.

In debriefing an activity like this, make sure the groups discuss the differences in their responses, especially to the more interpretive questions. You can always show the tapes a third time to help settle arguments or clarify specific points. The chart organizes key ideas for comparative analysis of the two cultures. Debriefing may bring out some interesting assumptions and misconceptions that students make (especially the ethnocentric variety).

For instance, for question 9, one group of students stated that both these desert peoples could use air conditioning. This led to an excellent discussion about electricity and appliances that our culture depends on but these two do not. A number of students had taken for granted the presence of electricity in the lives of these desert peoples. If the teacher had merely lectured, she would not have known the way the students actually conceived of this crucial aspect of desert life. Furthermore, the students would not have realized that they were taking something for granted. They learned something about their own thinking.

There are several key points about this strategy for critical thinking. You can take advantage of the proliferation of video tapes, but you don't need to show them for hours. Students obviously like this medium, but you need only find the "right" few minutes to provide a provocative stimulus to their reflection. Guided questioning is usually necessary to focus their attention on key analytical points. However, you should vary the types of questions.

Of course, you don't need to have two cultures for students to get experience in these specific operations. In fact, younger students should have just one. Students can look for cultural artifacts, customs, dress, and so on. It is also valuable occasionally to have no sound whatsoever, just visual observation.

The medium of video tape for analysis and comparison offers virtually endless possibilities. Archival films for a great many events of the twentieth century are readily available. Such "documents" should be subjected to the same rigorous analysis for bias, ambiguity, and the like as any written document. We can pay our students a great service by helping them to analyze film and video critically. Perhaps sadly, their ideas and their worlds are more shaped by these media than the printed word.

One valuable and simple way to help them see the interpretive slants of film and video is to show them excerpts from various historical dramas, such as two different portrayals of an event or famous person. Select the excerpts to show clearly that the director or actors are interpreting rather than simply portraying facts. This often comes as a revelation to students.

Teaching for Student Inquiry

In the previous chapter, we looked at an approach to encouraging student inquiry into the natural phenomena of the sciences. In this section, we will illustrate how this approach is modified somewhat for inquiry into social phenomena. We see seven appropriate phases of teaching students to conduct an inquiry:

- Diagnosing existing schemata
- Confronting schemata
- Generating opinions
- Conducting systematic inquiry
- Debriefing explanations and concepts
- Debriefing cognitive processes
- Broadening schemata

In science inquiry teaching, we suggested an additional phase, exploring phenomena, after confronting schemata. It will probably be rare for you to give hands-on, manipulative exploration with social phenomenon that precedes formal inquiry and data collection. With natural phenomena, this "messing around" stage allows the students to play with your provocative stimuli. In social studies, the stages of confronting schemata and generating opinions are enhanced to maximize the expression of personal beliefs, attitudes, and schemata.

We have made a distinction between convergent and divergent types of student inquiry, which vary in the kind and amount of structure established by the teacher. In inquiry that is more convergent, the teacher

- Plans the key hypotheses to be investigated and the concepts to be learned
- Arranges the essential data for the students to assess and analyze
- Plans the basic interpretations, findings, conclusions, or generalizations to be made

In inquiry that is more divergent, the teacher allows and encourages the students to assume more responsibility for

- Pursuing a variety of unplanned hypotheses, concepts, ideas, and issues
- Locating, assembling, or collecting their own data
- Making their own interpretations and understandings

These two types of inquiry are less a dichotomy than two ends of a continuum. We hope that students can become increasingly able to conduct their own inquiries with less structure from the teacher. If the social studies they encounter in school is to be transferred into life, they must become capable of independent inquiry, thought, and action in a rather unstructured and complex world. In the sections that follow, we will describe the phases of teaching for inquiry, both convergent and divergent.

DIAGNOSING EXISTING SCHEMATA. Obviously, you will draw on your own prior knowledge of these students, their community, and our society and culture to help you decide what inquiries are worth doing. You probably will not have an inquiry each day. Ask yourself, what of the many aspects of the social studies curriculum should be arranged for substantial inquiry? What schemata are in dire need of confrontation? What misconceptions and conceptual gaps might be addressed through discrepant information, stereotype attack, and so forth?

Because of the closeness of social studies ideas to the affective aspects of schemata, it is important for you to give considerable thought to how students' prior experiences (in their lives and vicariously through the media) relate to the concepts of the curriculum. Young children in the primary grades are incredibly accepting of anything coming from adults or television as factual, often not distinguishing between reality and fantasy, fact and fiction. Older students will likewise accept a TV "docu-drama" as historical fact.

Rather than bombarding students with presentations of "truth" or telling them they are wrong, you should allow their actual ideas and sentiments to surface. (Recall the electricity in the desert.) You must create a climate in which they can express their opinions, share their ideas, and describe their beliefs and attitudes. If for each science phenomenon or concept we can expect one or two misconceptions, for each in social studies we can probably triple that number. The complexity of social phenomena leads to a complexity of misunderstandings. We feel it is vital to bring the students schemata and attitudes out on the table, or else you will not be able to address effectively what needs to be addressed.

No one is going to share openly their schemata or attitudes if they feel they will be laughed at, demeaned, or insulted. No one likes to be corrected or told they are wrong. Students are all too aware of the power of the teacher and the dynamics of the school and classroom. If you believe that it is worthwhile to understand your students' schemata, the climate you create for students' expression of ideas and opinions must be accepting and nonjudgmental, devoid of sarcasm and innuendo. This means holding back until you have created the right opportunity for students to realize a different way to think or know.

Often when you don't point out the "rightness" of an idea, other students in the class will say it for you. Longer "wait time" allows other students the opportunity to offer opinions. If one does provide exactly the idea that you would have, it may be more palatable to the students (peer expression or pressure), but it also maintains the students' discussion, interaction, and thinking. So often a statement by the teacher is taken as a signal that God has spoken. That is the final word; we need not talk nor think any more.

During the year you must stay alert to opportunities. You must listen to students, not only in social studies class but all the time, for cues to schemata that might be profitably confronted. A combination of your knowledge of the students and your assessment of the curriculum may suggest good areas to address. For instance, one teacher we know was aware that the curriculum called for her to teach about the westward expansion of the United States. She heard her students talking about their vacation plans, which included some trips to the West Coast by automobile. She realized that the students had no conception of what the wagon trains of settlers had experienced. Their schema for "going west" included bridges, superhighways, fast-food restaurants, motels, and so forth.

She did a simple confrontation based on that diagnosis. She asked the class members to describe their previous vacations, especially auto trips to the western states. Then she gave them road maps of the interstate highway system and asked them in small groups to plan a route from Tennessee to various West Coast cities. After they had done so, she added the zinger: "The Mississippi River has had major flooding and all bridges have been destroyed. You still want to get to your destinations; how can you do it by car?" After students had wrestled with that question for a while, she injected some more constraints: Superhighways became closed by construction projects, terrorists have been attacking travelers on certain routes, and blizzards have closed off certain highways through the Rockies.

After a session of wrestling with these difficulties, even if only in their imagination, students were more willing to examine various information about the actual experiences of the wagon trains. The teacher presented a wide variety of media, stories, songs, films, and maps about these pioneers.

CONFRONTING SCHEMATA. What will provoke the expression of ideas, schemata, and attitudes? We have found that, as in science, you need some "grabbers." Students can be stimulated by the puzzling, the mysterious, the discrepant: situations that run counter to expectations, problems with no simple resolution, and questions without obvious answers. Events, passages, artifacts, film clips, and a host of other items can be vehicles for motivating inquiry. When the students cannot remain complacent in their current schemata, when they are unsettled and knocked a bit off-balance, they become more likely to express their schemata and sentiments and to desire additional information.

There are various general techniques for provoking students in this way. Sometimes it is sufficient to ask them to wrestle with something strange and unfamiliar: an artifact from the distant past or another culture like a piece of sculpture or a tool: "How would you describe this piece? What is it? Who made it? What was it used for? What can you infer about these people?" Sherlock Holmes was able to take bits and pieces of evidence and construct a pattern that explained an event. Students can be induced to do just that.

Several artifacts from the same civilization could be analyzed both individually and for relationships among them. Works of art and jewelry, as well as devices for cooking and clothes making, can offer fascinating insights into peoples lives. These need not be from ancient civilizations or exotic cultures. Just get a collection of tools common to nineteenth-century farms or households. Students will be surprised at how much difficulty they have in determining how these implements were used.

In addition to artifacts, our world holds a fair number of unusual or unexplained events. Just pick up any of the dozens of *Ripley's Believe It or Not* books or a compendium of amazing and incredible facts. Consider Stonehenge and the Easter Island statues. Also, there are certainly enough customs that students would consider bizarre in a good cultural anthropology book in your public library to stimulate their thinking.

An alternative approach asks you to find conflicting opinions on the same topic. This might include different points of view on a controversial issue (from today or yesteryear). Our country and others have had no shortage of differing opinions (sometimes violent) on all manner of international, national, state, and perhaps local governmental policies. The easiest way to locate some of these is in a good library with a willing staff. Old newspapers are another excellent source. For instance, historians often compile primary documents that contradict each other to illustrate the complexity of the issue under study (e.g., Who fired the first shot on Lexington Green, the British or the colonists? Eyewitness accounts contradict each other).

Another technique for provocation is to confront students with material that goes directly against obvious assumptions, stereotypes, and popular beliefs. For instance, have them read writings of colonists sympathetic to the Crown during the American Revolution. It has been estimated that only a third of the colonists wanted independence from England, a third wanted to remain a British colony, and the other third was indifferent. If you can't find a good primary source, perhaps a historical novel such as *Oliver Wiswell* by Kenneth Roberts (1981) would suffice. It is a fictional autobiography of a Tory that is quite critical of the treatment of loyalists by those we call patriots.

Milton Meltzer (1982, 1984, 1987) has compiled a series of books that tell the history of a different group of people in America. Using primary documents, letters, diaries, and journals (that children can understand readily), he allows the people of that time to describe their lives in their own terms. Another collection of fascinating primary documents is *The Private Side of American History,* edited by Gary Nash (1975). An excellent resource for interpreting historical documents such as these (and also enjoyable reading) is *After the Fact: The Art of Historical Detection* by Davidson and Lytle (1982). Refer to the Resources at the end of the chapter.

There is an aspect of confronting schemata and attitudes that you need to consider carefully: the students' *willingness* to consider new information or to disconfirm their assumptions and beliefs. We know that when students, as humans, encounter data and ideas, they immediately engage in the cognitive processes we've labeled schema, focus, and pattern. The patterns of meaningfulness that they construct relate directly to existing schemata. When their schemata are confronted with discrepant information, puzzling questions, or discordant ideas, they may just reject the whole set of data as too overwhelming. Social psychologists discovered long ago that dire warnings are often discounted more than moderate ones.

Even if they are willing to try to reconcile the new data with their existing schemata, they will first try to *make the new fit the old*. We humans prefer to distort the discrepant so that it will conform to what is believed. For an extreme case, consider the bigot with an invincible stereotype of some group of people. Personal experiences with individual members of this target group don't change the bias; they become "exceptions."

In a similar vein, when students have become enticed into inquiry by puzzling, discrepant, or provocative information, they do not inquire with clean slates. The initial presentation by the teacher may have startled them, jarred their schemata. However, if inquiry begins with a question, students probably will have formed a tentative answer. The way in which their schemata directed their focus for analysis and influenced how things were pulled together into a meaningful pattern (even a partial one) will strongly affect any hypothesis of inquiry.

Thus two related factors are present when students begin your activities: the complexity of the existing schemata and the students' openness to changing it. The more open and willing they are to disconfirm existing beliefs and biases, the more readily they will change schemata in the direction of the knowledge structure of the discipline involved. However, the more time and energy that has been invested in constructing the existing schemata, as well as the more important their function in a person's life, the less likely these are to change at all.

Here are a couple of unusual activities that provoke students' schemata. As we said earlier, old newspapers can be a rich source of the weird and the wonderful. See how far back your library's archives go. Most have newspapers on microfilm. Find a microfilm reader that also allows you to make photocopies.

For instance, locate the personal advertisement section of an old newspaper. You may be surprised by what you see, especially if you go back to the nineteenth century. Here are some entries. Have students read them and react.

CHICAGO TRIBUNE, January 7, 1869:

Matrimonial—A widower without encumbrance and of good business qualifications and 40 years of age, with a capital of about $30,000, would like to become acquainted with some lady not over 40 years of age with the same amount of capital. Object matrimony. Address W.Y., Tribune Office.

Personal—A young lady of 20 summers wishes to correspond with gentleman of means. View, matrimony. Age preferred, 25 to 45 years. Correspondence confidential. Address Miss N.J.C., Tribune Office.

Personal—The advertiser (a young gentleman of means) is desirous of forming the acquaintance of some lady (widow preferred) not over 35 years of age who, feeling lonely, like myself and needing someone to befriend and love her may address in the most strict confidence, SINCERITY, Tribune Office.

NEW YORK HERALD, December 19, 1900:

COMIC Artist would like to meet experienced and original paragrapher, Box 88, Court St., Brooklyn.

GENTLEMAN (36) refined, lonely desires acquaintance educated lady, employed during day; object, social companionship; no triflers; references, Matrimony. Address L.R., 217 Herald Downtown.

PRETTY, honorable girl, very wealthy, desires early marriage. N.H., Box 157, Canastoga, N.Y.

BEAUTY, blue waist, accompanied, who noticed two gentlemen. Pabst's Saturday 8 o'clock. ADMIRER 444 Herald.

REFINED, deserving lady wants immediate loan of $75. Room, pleasant home in return. NO TRIFLERS. Herald Downtown.

What do these data mean? What do they tell you about the culture, customs, and social life?

You may also confront some assumptions students hold by having them read newspaper stories from the past. Even headlines can be remarkably discrepant to present assumptions and beliefs. For instance, you can find newspaper stories and headlines from October 1941 predicting an attack by the Japanese on the United States. To what extent was the destruction of Pearl Harbor a surprise? Or how did the entire Japanese fleet get close enough to Hawaii in December 1941 to launch their attack? Why was most of the U.S. Pacific fleet anchored and unprotected? Why weren't we prepared and watching for attack?

Of course, books also can be primary sources. Earlier, we mentioned the difficulties of the wagon trains as they traveled to the West Coast. An excellent book that can be used to confront stereotypes of women in a formative period of American history is *Women's Diaries of the Westward Journey* by Lillian Schlissel (1982). A strong conceptual overview by the author is followed by four edited diaries that describe in very moving narratives what the transcontinental trip by wagon was really like. The personal strength of the women in the face of extraordinary hardships is unmistakable, even through the matter-of-fact, daily accounts. (See Resources list.)

GENERATING OPINIONS. Since students can't physically "mess around" with the phenomena in social studies, we must encourage them to express and explore thoroughly their ideas, opinions, beliefs, and attitudes concerning the confronting stimuli.

There certainly are many techniques you could use, among them small-group discussion. This approach can give more "air time" to each individual student (if properly done) than whole-class discussion is likely to offer. Another technique is to have each individual write down her initial ideas, reactions, or hunches on a 3-by-5-inch card before going into the small group. The written ideas become something that can be shared. They also elicit a commitment of sorts to one's own schemata. However, we would not require the small groups to reach consensus; they can report to the whole class a range of ideas.

There are several critical tasks you must help students accomplish during this phase of generating opinions:

- Defining the problem and formulating good questions
- Realizing patterns and suggesting hypotheses
- Defining terms and concepts

Defining terms and concepts clearly and thoughtfully is of particular importance when generating opinions about controversial issues. It is far better to elicit schemata early than to let attitudes and feelings remain latent, disrupting understanding, unbeknownst to you. In so doing, explaining and clarifying what each student means is crucial. Misconceptions from semantic differences, unspoken assumptions, and impulsive statements are commonplace in discussions of controversial issues. Techniques of critical thinking are valuable in this part of the inquiry. For instance, consider students reading passages, stories, and articles or viewing films or television news about any of these international conflicts: Iraq/Iran, U.S.S.R./Afghanistan, Israel/Arab nations.

Most students will have some opinions on each of these conflicts, even if it's only a sense of who is the "good guy" and who is the "bad guy." These conflicts do not appear to involve the United States directly. What about the United States and Libya? Or U.S. domestic issues? How will students' schemata influence their openness to one another in discussions, their willingness to examine data, or their ability to draw conclusions?

Students have plenty of naive schemata, misconceptions, and opinions concerning the other two "superpowers," the Soviet Union and Peoples Republic of China. It is probably impossible to understand today's geopolitics without a sense of history. For instance, is the Union of Soviet Socialist Republics the same entity as Russia? We tend to use these two terms interchangeably. What conceptions do students have about the people of the Soviet Union?

The Soviet Union includes about one-sixth of the entire land of the planet. It contains an astonishing mixture of different cultures and people. A good activity to confront schemata and generate opinions is to collect a series of pictures of the various Eurasian people of the Soviet Union and array them for students without telling them who they are or where they are located. *National Geographic Magazine,* February 1976, included an excellent article, with pictures and a foldout map, of the various ethno-linguistic groups of the Soviet Union. Ask students to describe orally or in writing who they believe each to be, where they are from, what they are like, and so on. Then ask students working in small groups to categorize these different people (pictures). What categories do they create?

After they share and discuss their categories, you may show them some key ethno-linguistic distinctions: the Slavic people (e.g., Russians, Byelorussians, Ukranians), the Baltic people (Latvian and Lithuanian), and the Uralic or Finnic people (Finnish and Estonian). These various European people may be quite familiar to students, but there are others much less so. Various people of the Caucasus Mountain region (students may have heard the term *Caucasian*) are very different in customs from the Europeans (e.g., Georgians). There are also people from Iranian ethnic groups (Afghans, Baluchi, Tajik, Kurdish). There are many different Turkic people, some of which are Moslems (including the Azerbaijanians, Tatar, Turkmen, Uzbek, Kirgiz, and Kazakh), others of whom appear more Asian (e.g., the Siberian Yakuts and the Tuvan). Finally, there are people whom we tend to see more readily as Asians—the Mongolians Buryat and the Siberian Chukchi (who look much like Eskimos).

If these distinctions seem too complex for the age group of your students, use two or three (e.g., Slavic, Turkic, and Mongolian) that will make the key point: The Soviet Union and Russia are not the same entity. The Soviet Union is one of the most multicultural nations in the world.

The Soviet Union of today is a union of fifteen republics, the largest of which is the Russian Soviet Federated Socialist Republic. The term *soviet* refers to elected legislative assemblies. Most of these republics were conquered by Russia between 1530 and 1890, a period of enormous expansion, under the tsars (emperors). To this day, a great many citizens of these republics retain a strong sense of regional and ethnic identity.

In planning for student inquiry, such as the preceding, you must confront your own opinions. How will they influence the data that you provide? What is your own understanding of the Communist Party of the Soviet Union? What are your opinions about communism? About the incursion of Soviet troops into Afghanistan? One way to handle data collection with such controversies might be for you to encourage students to collect their own data, and then you search for supplementary data that provide some differences (perhaps contradictory, perhaps additional considerations).

Fortunately, a good curriculum can provide a framework for this phase of inquiry. Hypotheses, concepts, and terms can be clarified by the knowledge context in which students are working. Good texts offer main ideas, generalizations, and theories that can help form questions for inquiry. However, relying too heavily on the text can cut off thinking and miss key schemata.

CONDUCTING SYSTEMATIC INQUIRY. Once schemata have been confronted, opinions generated, questions formulated, terms defined, and tentative hypotheses stated, it is time to attack the data. You can certainly provide data for the students, all at once or in stages. Or you can facilitate their own data collection. Consider that the systematic nature of the inquiry requires the following five aspects:

- Brainstorming and accessing data sources
- Collecting and assembling the "raw" data
- Evaluating, arranging, and compiling the data
- Analyzing in terms of key concepts
- Drawing conclusions

These five may seem redundant, but each has a key idea or two for you to bear in mind. Students should spend some time thinking about where they could obtain information relevant to their questions. This is the key "access" notion. It is valuable to consider all the possibilities, not just the simplest. This step can really profit from a groups' ingenuity and experience. Of course, you can help, but you should allow the students the opportunity to struggle.

Another key point of this step is trying to get a range of perspectives and sources. Ask students to consider the limitations or potential biases of different sources. Editorial policies of newsmagazines and newspapers can be inferred by comparisons of articles on the same current event or topic.

Next, unless you have provided the data, students have to make some important decisions about what parts of the data they have found they will actually collect. What will they record, copy, extract, and so on? For any given source, they will be pulling out pieces, and they may not know which to pull. What criteria do they use? For instance, imagine a class studying the history of their local community. The students have a question about different groups of people who settled there. The library has ample census data that goes back many decades. What data should they gather? What should they record?

To a certain extent, the isuse here is this: What do they really want to find out? Is their question too broadly stated? Have key concepts been sufficiently defined? Although these are important considerations, we would urge a different approach. Allow the students to experience an *interaction* of questions and data sources. Don't be afraid to let them refine their questions if they encounter exciting data that may illuminate somewhat different aspects of the inquiry than they originally anticipated.

There are several reasons for allowing refinement. First, it helps students' thinking processes to maintain an open and inquisitive stance. Second, it helps them see the need for clarifying and carefully thinking through questions and concepts. Third, they might just find something a whole lot more rewarding than they might have otherwise. It is called serendipity.

Intimately related to collecting and assembling data are the acts of evaluating, arranging, and compiling. As in good critical thinking, data and their sources must be evaluated for their authenticity, biases, ambiguity, and so forth. Students should organize their data to see what goes with what and where they have gaps. Arranging data into initial patterns may show areas of incompleteness and can also be extremely helpful in preparing for analysis.

How students analyze data and draw conclusions will depend on the categories used in compiling the data as well as their hypotheses. Key concepts from the hypotheses are like sifting screens that select "facts" for students to consider. However, data should not only support or contradict hypotheses like an on-off switch. They should also be arranged in categories that can enrich their understanding, in general, and offer alternative explanations, in particular.

Let's return to the inquiry about the various groups of people that settled in the community. Let's assume that the students collect data on the number of people by ethnic group reported in the categories that the census uses. What will they have? What assumptions are built into these categories and this type of data?

Each category is essentially a concept that has multiple meanings. In one sense it is an abstract notion, in another a convenient definition for the census takers. Although these overlap, they may not be quite the same. We are not asking the students to split hairs. We are asking them to use their critical thinking skills to make sure that they understand what is contained in these data. Accepting someone else's analytical categories is fine if you really do understand what they mean. In a topic where students will have extensive (and perhaps ill-conceived schemata), careful attention to the ways data are compiled is crucial.

You should ask the students to research the meanings of any categories they plan to use. Tell them to check with sources to ensure they can explain all relevant distinctions among these categories. Key points to check: (1) Are they mutually exclusive? (2) How is it determined into which category each datum will be placed?

Here is another concern that you should ask students to check: Have the criteria for inclusion in any of these categories been changed over time? These shifts frequently occur when sets of data have been collected over a long period of time. Unless students are looking at very raw data or collecting it themselves, and thereby creating their own categories, they must become knowledgeable about how these data were collected and compiled; they must look carefully at what is included or excluded from each category. They must train themselves to ask these questions.

Another general analytical technique is to work on the given categories some more, either collapsing them or pulling them apart. Students can combine categories that they can justify putting together. Breaking apart the categories is trickier because it means working with smaller pieces of data than the total numbers in each category. Of course, working with basic data allows the creation of the students' own categories. However, their sources may provide some subgroups within categories or some cross-tabulations by other factors.

To a certain extent, students must grapple with the meaning of concepts throughout an inquiry. A good inquiry is not just a straight-ahead path. It has twists and turns in which students explore meanings, examine their assumptions, and think. You must be alert to each opportunity to stimulate their thinking with timely and provocative questions. What you don't catch during the inquiry process, you can always address in the debriefing.

DEBRIEFING EXPLANATIONS AND CONCEPTS. At some point the formal inquiry ends and you should lead students in a discussion of the major ideas. They should clarify what they have specifically learned in this inquiry. Presumably they have enriched their understanding of the key concepts, made some new connections with existing schemata, or changed their schemata. Well, some students have; others may still be struggling to put it all together. You want to help them all solidify connections among ideas and to previous schemata. You need to stimulate a debriefing discussion with several good open-ended questions that get students thinking and talking about what they have learned from this activity. Finally, you have to provide a clear, concise explanation of the key concepts that you want to emphasize.

A major function of debriefing is to encourage those students who have synthesized in new and exciting ways to share their new conceptions with the others. Often new conceptions or explanations will be well received by students. When a schema change really clicks for a student, he can sometimes express the new idea in a rich and powerful way that other students with the same prior schema will understand. They can invoke metaphors and analogies that would not occur to us. They can make references and allusions to popular songs, TV shows, and movies. They can illustrate the ideas with events on the playground. Some will even draw parallels to video games in the arcade. These connections may sound fairly dreadful to you, but these are the substance of their lives. On the other hand, be aware of potential misconceptions they express or nuances that are not quite appropriate, and be prepared to clarify and make key distinctions among conceptions.

Another technique that we have found valuable is asking students individually to write their ideas down. We do not mean a full-blown essay or paper; just a paragraph, three or four sentences: "What did you get out of this? What does it mean to you? How are you now thinking about these ideas?" If students are keeping a journal or you have periods of free writing, encourage this kind of writing. Its purpose is not formally to record or report their conclusions but rather to express how they are now thinking. It is more personal, showing their schemata about these ideas.

For many students, the act of putting down their ideas in this way helps them to pull their thoughts together. It is crucial that writing is not presented at all like a test. It should never be graded. It is an opportunity to collect thoughts. You can write back encouraging notes but not correcting comments. It can be a valuable diagnostic tool for you, if it is an honest expression of how a student is thinking. Any pressure from you for correctness will result in a parroting of someone else's conclusions.

DEBRIEFING COGNITIVE PROCESSES. At each phase in the inquiry, you are helping the students think about what they are doing. You can help them think about their choices and processes, if it does not interrupt the flow of their work. After the formal inquiry is complete, you should help them think back to how they conducted the inquiry. Reflect on the key decisions, the important clarifications, the shifts in thinking along the way: "Would you have reached different conclusions if you had made this assumption instead of that one?" Trace back how data were assembled, what had to be done to understand them, and so forth.

Ask the students to draw comparisons between this inquiry and others they have made: "How were the processes similar? What was different? What have you learned about doing these things?" These questions should stimulate metacognition, getting the students to become more aware of how they attack an issue, a piece of data. The content of social studies is close to who they are and how they see life. Helping them to become increasingly aware not only of what they think but also of how they think can be extremely valuable throughout their lives.

BROADENING SCHEMATA. There are two main things you can do in this final phase of teaching for inquiry. First, you can help students make connections between the concepts and conclusions of this inquiry and others in the curriculum. Often the specific ideas of an inquiry will relate to key principles, generalizations, or theories of the curriculum. You will have to help students make these connections through questioning. If the hypotheses of their inquiry were rooted in such larger ideas, this task will be easier. In fact, these connections may emerge in earlier phases.

Second, students should think through new areas or situations in which the ideas of this inquiry may be applied. Is this concept related to any other situations you can imagine? Does it explain something else you have encountered? This moment may offer opportunities for additional inquiry. Encourage students to suggest areas that these concepts might help illuminate. You may be pleasantly surprised at the insights they have and the directions they suggest. These opportunities may allow a shift from convergent inquiry that you have structured for them to more divergent inquiry in which they assume more responsibility. They are more likely to take initiative for their own inquiry when it is on a topic of their own choosing.

The following is a lengthy illustration of a convergent inquiry that the teacher structures to a great extent. It can lead into more divergent inquiry by students.

Most students and adults in the United States have some basic familiarity with the native American tribes. Every locale has its "original" people. What happened to them? What is their place in our local community's history? Let's take one part of the country and address these questions from the perspectives of geography, anthropology, and politics. We believe that many disjointed facts from your own schooling may be pulled together in a powerful way.

Present students with these two lists. What are they describing?

Group A	Group B
• Massachuset	• Huron
• Powhattan	• Erie
• Narraganset	• Seneca
• Montauk	• Cayuga
• Penobscot	• Mohawk

Without the kind of introduction we gave you, students may be tempted to suggest that these are bodies of water, Indian chiefs, islands, or even street names. They are some of the Indian tribes of the northeastern woodlands. Present the lists with these initial questions: Where did each tribe live, and why are they divided into two groups?

Have the students work in groups of three to try to locate where these tribes lived. Give them a blank map, outlining major geographical features, such as the one in Figure 6.1. Have them orient themselves to key landmarks (bodies of water, current states, etc.). They should later use this map when writing in pencil where each tribe may have lived.

Students should use a variety of reference materials, especially maps and atlases. Later in this activity, they may need to use dictionaries, encyclopedias, or texts. Even though we are researching tribes that lived 300 or 400 years ago, there are some important clues to their habitats. Maps and atlases reveal counties, towns, lakes, and rivers named after these tribes. Of course, clues like these might be misleading, as we shall shortly see. Even if students are not terribly familiar with these reference materials, this activity provides a good incentive for learning how to locate information.

Students should be able to give approximate locations for these ten tribes with only a bit of digging. The difference between Group A and Group B appears to

Figure 6.1

center on location: One group of tribes is located along the eastern seaboard, the other inland, around the lakes. Most social studies books discuss the differences in culture, customs, housing, and so forth that stem from this geographic difference. And yet, the story is a bit more complex. Ask students to try to find the following tribes, also belonging to these two groups.

Group A	*Group B*
• Ottawa	• Oneida
• Nanticoke	• Susquehanna
• Wappinger	• Onondaga
• Pequot	• Tuscarora
• Abenaki	• Wenro
• Lenni Lenape	• Tobacco
• Mohegan	• Neutral
• Passamaquoddy	• Nottaway

Some of these Indian tribes may be familiar and their locations possible to approximate. Students will find others quite difficult without a good reference book on North American Indians. The map in Figure 6.2 indicates approximate locations; you can share it with the students after they search. It will help their understanding if they color-code the two groups; we have put a box around the names of the tribes of Group A.

How does the geographic pattern fare with these additional tribes? The tribes of Group A are not entirely along the East Coast; the Ottawa are clearly not. The tribes of Group B do cluster around the inland lakes (with the exception of the Tuscarora and Nottaway, who are on the coast). At some point in their searching, students may ask, "Who are the Neutral? That isn't an Indian name." Ah, yes! It is not. That is what the Europeans called a tribe, whose own name for themselves was the Attiwendaronk. Conversely, the Europeans called the Lenni Lenape, the Delawares, and they called the Tionontati the Tobacco. Also the French called the Wendat, the Huron, meaning "ruffian" or "unkempt."

This issue of tribal names is confusing since tribes called themselves by one name, other tribes referred to them by another, and Europeans often gave them yet

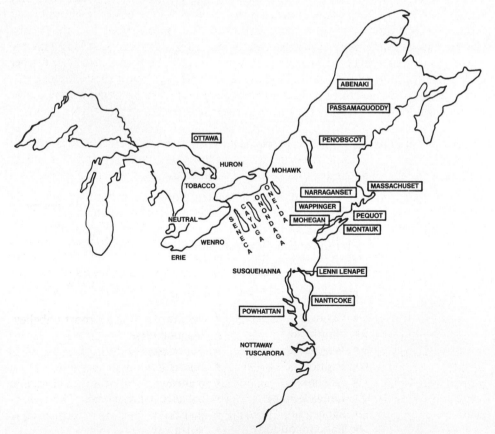

Figure 6.2

a different name. Books sometimes confuse the matter further by using various spellings; these tribes had no written language. For instance, the Mohegans in the area now called Connecticut were neighbors of the Mahicans; various books refer to either of these as Mohicans.

In addition to giving careful consideration to the name of a tribe, a key question to this inquiry is what is a tribe? It is best to let the inquiry go to a point such as we are at now before confronting the students' schema of tribe. Ask the students, "What is a tribe? How do we know if some group should be called a tribe? Is it numbers? Is it common loyalties? Is it living together?" For instance, Powhattan was a chief who united previously separate bands of Indians that came to call themselves by the name of their great leader. There were several other important instances of groups of Indians "coming together," as we shall soon see.

As you get students to generate opinions about these data, some may suggest that the tribes along the East Coast were the first to have contact with the Europeans. This is an interesting hypothesis. Ask them to consider their hypothesis carefully: "What does 'contact' mean? What Europeans do you mean? Who? When? What do you know about the Europeans who came to the Americas?"

Next, add some additional data about Europeans or have the students collect it themselves. From which European countries did people come? Where did they locate and what did they come to the Americas to do? An important distinction that should emerge is between *settlers* and *traders*. In a very general sense, the English, Dutch, and Swedish were more interested in settling and farming, whereas the French were more involved in trading and trapping. (The Spaniards lived further south than the area of the tribes the students are investigating.) These three groups of Europeans settled along the East Coast, whereas the French ranged more across the northern areas (modern-day Canada) and the Mississippi River valley, much further west.

Here is another concept that may emerge from the students; if it doesn't, you can interject it: Are some of these tribes extinct? The answer is yes; from Group A, the Massachuset, Wappinger, and Pequot; from Group B, the Susquehanna, Tobacco, and Neutral.

Clever children, thinking critically, may immediately ask, "What do you mean by the term *extinct?*" You should ask this question of them at some point. What schema do they have for this term? Do a semantic mapping. We will bet dinosaurs pop up. Does *extinct* mean no longer any living persons of that tribe? Do we mean "full-blooded" member of the tribe? How would we know the answers to either of these questions? Or do we mean no longer a grouping of people who might think of themselves as a tribe.

One of the tricky aspects of investigating these peoples is the almost unbelievable disruption of their lives and cultures that occurred after the Europeans came to the continent. From a variety of causes (which we'll discuss shortly), some tribes were totally annihilated; others were decimated and their remnants assimilated into other tribes. Some of these tribes can be found on reservations, others in cities and towns. Many migrated far from their original, ancestral homelands. What happened? As students will see, sometimes social studies is like peeling an onion, layer by layer.

Here is another important aspect of this question of tribes, which students may stumble on earlier from looking at reference materials or from their own recollections: There are two "tribes" whose names are well known that we have not yet mentioned. Can you think of who is missing? Ask the students. They are the Niuqnogla and the Siouqori (we've spelled them backwards to give you a chance to think). Who are these people?

Most history books for elementary schools unwittingly have created confusion about these two groups of Indians. The terms *Algonquin* and *Iroquois* have been used to describe both tribes and language families. There was a specific tribe that the Europeans called the Algonquin who lived north of the Huron. You can add this tribe to your map. They and each of the other tribes in Group A belong to a cultural and language family we call Algonquin (or Algonkian). Historians and anthropologists hypothesize that they shared a common set of migrating ancestors from prehistory. All the tribes in Group A spoke a dialect of Algonquin.

Similarly, the tribes of Group B are from the Iroquoian cultural and language family. They too shared a common set of ancestors. What makes this story complicated is the fact that the Europeans referred to five particular tribes as "the Iroquois" even though in a sense all the tribes in Group B are Iroquois. In fact the word *iroquois* is an Algonkian word meaning "real adders."

Ask students what "common cultural and language background" means. What might be its significance? Ask the students to think about their ideas (or the text's) concerning the towns, log palisades, and communal houses of the Iroquois in comparison to the villages and wigwams of the Algonquin. The differences in culture that may have been attributed to geography (inland lakes versus East Coast) must be reconsidered in light of different historical and cultural backgrounds.

The English settlers did have more initial contact with the Algonquin tribes than with the Iroquois. Our American English includes more words from the Algonquin languages than any of the other languages of the native Americans. Some of these are *moose, woodchuck, skunk, chipmunk, raccoon, opossum, squash, hominy, moccasin,* and *toboggan.*

Students might hypothesize that common ancestors and similar dialects might mean family ties, friendships, and alliances. They would be only partly correct. Although these language families shared cultural customs, religious beliefs and practices, housing construction, and so forth, they were rather continually at war. The Algonquin tribes fought with one another; Iroquois tribes warred against one another; Algonquins and Iroquois fought continually.

A major exception to the warfare within the Iroquois tribes was to play a key role in the history of what came to be the United States. Just prior to the Europeans' arrival, the five Iroquois tribes around the Finger Lakes in what is now upstate New York joined together into the Iroquois Confederacy, the Cayuga, Onandaga, Oneida, Seneca, and Mohawk. The Five Nations agreed to be governed by a common council of representatives from the five tribes. Hiawatha was a key figure in this group. A good question for students is "What constitutes a 'nation' or a 'confederacy'?" These five tribes were later joined by the Tuscarora (who migrated north away from the coast) to become the Six Nations of the Iroquois Confederacy. Many books simply refer to these tribes as "the Iroquois." Although there were a few confederacies within the Algonquin, like the Powhattan and the Abenaki, their importance in history was not as significant as the Iroquois Confederacy.

The Iroquois Confederacy remained in bitter warfare against not only the Algonquin tribes but also the Huron, an Iroquois nation of four smaller tribes. The entrance of the Europeans changed whatever balance of power existed among these peoples. One incident was to have singular meaning. The French explorer Champlain was actively trading with the Huron. In 1610, he went on a raid with them against a Mohawk village in the confederacy. Champlain and his men used their muskets against the Mohawks. The French went on to enjoy good trading with the Huron and several Algonquin tribes for years. However, that incident sparked the enmity of the Iroquois Confederacy toward the French thereafter. More important, the confederacy allied themselves with the English in what we call the French and Indian War.

Ask the students to examine the map of the tribes to see how the location of the Iroquois Confederacy might have influenced events. Their location played a dual role. First, they bitterly opposed French expansion in the new world, preventing French trading outposts and forts south of the Great Lakes. Second, they provided one side of a vise that trapped the Algonquin tribes of the East Coast. As the English defeated Swedish and Dutch interests in the coastal areas, they fought the Algonquin tribes. The diseases of the Europeans as well as their weapons picked off the squabbling, unaligned Algonquins, one by one. Alliances among the Algonquins and retaliations against the encroaching English settlers came too late. To where could the Algonquins of the East Coat migrate? Westward migration was blocked by their mortal enemies of centuries, the Iroquois. Some fled northward to join the Abenaki confederacy. By 1680, several were annihilated (e.g., the Pequot and Massachuset); others had migrated and been assimilated into other Algonquin tribes.

The Iroquois Confederacy strengthened their hold on the Great Lakes area by an awful destruction of their longtime foe, the Huron. Secretly camping out in the winter snow, the Mohawks led a surprise attack at the break of spring in 1648. The Hurons were overwhelmed and savagely destroyed. In the coming months the warriors of the confederacy swept around and down the peninsula between Lakes Ontario and Erie and Lake Huron, destroying the Tobacco and Neutral as well. Remnants of these three tribes that escaped the slaughter fled westward and were later known as the Wyandot.

During the French and Indian War of 1754 to 1763, the centuries-old warfare of English versus French and Iroquois versus Algonquin continued with predictable alliances. In general, the Iroquois assisted the British; Algonquin tribes helped the French. The defeat of the French sealed the fate of the Algonquin tribes in the Northeast. A popular Spencer Tracy film, *Northwest Passage,* immortalizes Roger's Rangers as they employed the great stealth of the native Americans to slip into Abenaki territory and destroy the last major Algonquin stronghold in the East. Remnants of these Algonquin tribes migrated west to become assimilated into the Ottawa.

But the story is not quite over. The Iroquois sided with their old allies, the British, two decades later during the American Revolution. History records some dreadful massacres of colonists by Iroquois at the instigation of the British. When that war was won, a major order of business for the colonies was making the frontier safe for further settlement and taking retribution upon the Iroquois. Once again, the Europeans, now Americans, were assisted not only by superior weapons but also by their germs. Smallpox killed more Indians than did bullets.

In drawing conclusions about what happened to these tribes, students will come up with the role played by migration and assimilation into other tribes, as well as death from diseases and warfare with other Indians, English colonists prior to the Revolutionary War, and Americans after the war. However, along the way they will have generated insights into concepts like tribe, nation, alliance, confederacy, and so forth. This is clearly convergent inquiry, with the teacher providing the key data and provoking their questioning along specific lines. However, after debriefing students to solidify these ideas, you can greatly broaden their schemata by *divergent inquiry* in a number of different directions.

Students could inquire into the fate of other Indian tribes in the Americas. How did geographical factors and tribal alliances affect relations with the white men? What roles were played by disease and weapons? The plains Indians "inherited" the horse from the sixteenth-century Spanish invasion of Mexico. Did having horses, which the woodland Indians did not, make a difference in their fate? What geographic factors might have been involved (the Florida swamps, the vast rolling plains, the enormous mountain ranges, etc.)? These questions are good points of departure for inquiry.

Another divergent inquiry activity is to investigate the patterns of settlement of immigrants from different European countries in the United States. Both the frontiers and the cities are histories of one influx after another of particular ethnic groups. Who were these new Americans? Where did they originate? Why did they come to the new world? Where did they go? Why there? Students could select various parts of the country to investigate the ebb and flow of diverse groups. Or they could select one country and track the emigration of its people to the states and territories of the Americas. Whether one would emphasize the melting pot or goulash with distinct vegetables, this ethno-history is worth understanding.

CONCLUDING ISSUES

One chapter cannot do justice to all the possibilities in social studies. For more depth, you will have to consult other books devoted entirely to social studies. For example, there are many excellent resources for specific methods and techniques for

- Using globes and maps
- Getting the most out of the media
- Demonstrating data-collection procedures (e.g., for interviews, oral histories, surveys, case studies)
- Using computers

Of course, whatever you consult, you will undoubtedly modify and adapt ideas to fit your students.

You will also be responsible for evaluating your students as they conduct an inquiry, discuss conceptions, struggle with new schemata, and so forth. The familiar tests of factual recall, using short answers and multiple choices, are obviously not up to this task. Here are some suggestions:

For you to assess how children are conceiving an idea, they must express their conceptions and demonstrate their thinking. Of primary importance is establishing a classroom climate that encourages oral expression of ideas and thinking. Norms of reflection, analysis, discussion, dialogue, and the like can provide the teacher with relevant ongoing data.

In addition to norms of oral expression, written expression of ideas and thinking (for older students) is crucial. Students can respond to good questions that require them to describe their understanding as homework. In a test, this means using primarily essay or short-essay questions.

You can assess individual or group projects or inquiries with written or oral reports. This group work can still have individual accountability from follow-up assignments for each student, such as short papers asking them to reflect on a key aspect of the group inquiry. Also, each student could design another inquiry on a similar question that would not be conducted.

Evaluation of the complexities of thinking, like teaching for thinking, may be more involved than narrower concerns. However, it is well worth the effort.

RESOURCES AND FURTHER READING

You will find further information about the topics covered in this chapter in the following works, some of which are also cited in the text.

Beyer, Barry K. (1979). *Teaching thinking in the social studies.* Columbus, OH: Charles Merrill.

Davidson, J. W., and Lytle M. H. (1982). *After the fact: The art of historical detection.* New York: Knopf.

Linton, C. D., ed. (1984). *American headlines year by year.* Nashville, TN: Thomas Nelson.

Martin, B. A. (1977). *Social studies activities for the gifted.* Buffalo, NY: D.O.K. Publishers.

Meltzer, M., ed. (1987). *The American Revolutionaries: A history in their own words, 1750–1800.* New York: Crowell.

———(1984). *The black Americans: A history in their own words.* New York: Crowell.

———(1982). *The Jewish Americans: A history in their own words, 1650–1950.* New York: Crowell.

Nash, G., ed. (1975). *The private side of American history, Vol. I: To 1877.* Orlando, FL: Harcourt Brace Jovanovich.

Schlissel, L. (1982). *Women's diaries of the westward journey.* New York: Schocken.

Singleton, L. R. (1986). *Tips for social studies teachers.* Boulder, CO: Social Studies Education Consortium.

Conclusion

The present focus on teaching for thinking is not merely a fad, but rather it is the culmination of several forces that have been working for decades. Neither is it the end of a pendulum's swing that will oscillate back to some other concern such as the affective. In fact, we have argued that it would be a serious mistake to divorce the cognitive from the affective. Students' feelings, attitudes, emotions, and the like are intertwined with their schemata.

We have tried to build a case for considering the relationship between how students think and what they think about. Cognitive processes should be developed within specific knowledge contexts. Teachers should carefully examine their curricula in terms of the six major aspects of thinking we have suggested: schema, focus, pattern, extension, projection, and metacognition. What concepts should be specially addressed? What prior knowledge and misconceptions might students have? What areas would be fruitful for more inductive activities? For inquiry? For small-group projects? What kinds of questions does the text include? What questions can I pose that will initiate the kind of thinking I want them to do? And so forth.

We stressed the knowledge structures of various disciplines as important contexts for meaningfulness. Our four subject area chapters described strategies for developing cognitive processes within each of these. In addition, the science and social studies curricula frequently offer extraordinary opportunities for developing the thinking involved in reading, writing, and mathematics.

Can you imagine a school curriculum with only two subjects: the sciences and the social studies? You would do each with your students for half the day. Mathematical ideas and processes would be carefully woven into the natural phenomena of science. For instance, the measurement and recording of physical phenomena would be used not just to reinforce mathematical ideas but also to introduce them in compelling contexts. Similarly, what students read and write about would be intimately related to the human interactions of the social studies. The stories, legends, and poems of a people would be blended with their history, location, and culture.

Of course, mathematical ideas can flourish within social studies as well. Witness the prevalence of charts, graphs, and tables to deal with demographics. Also, students' reading and writing can be developed within the sciences. There is great need for expressing one's ideas and understanding expository texts in any area.

One area of school life that we did not directly address is the instructional use of microcomputers. It would seem worthwhile to have this *tool* pervasively available for students. One obvious use is for word processing as an aid to writing. We did mention the value of the Logo language in developing a computational form of geometry. There are also a number of excellent simulations in science and social studies as well as software that promote some good thinking and problem solving. In fact, we have substantial experience doing each of these with children from kindergarten through eighth grade.

We urge a bit of caution. There is no substitute for human interaction in teaching and learning. Microcomputers are excellent tools to assist the thinking processes. So are pencils. We know that there are many times when we must ask the children to put their pencils down and think first. They may need extensive dialogue with one another. The crucial development of language requires oral communication and lots of it. When *appropriately* used, the microcomputer can assist thinking. It should supplement the important strategies we have discussed.

The perspective of this book and its particular emphases represent only one way to break up this enormously complex field. In fact, there is no one best way to describe, analyze, or discuss cognition and instruction. One value of the emphasis on knowledge contexts is that it encourages us to look at thinking in more integrated, comprehensive, and coherent parts. The field is continuing to evolve in what we feel is a good direction. Who can predict how we will be thinking of all this in 2001?

References

Adams, J. L. (1979). *Conceptual blockbusting.* New York: W. W. Norton.

American Association for the Advancement of Science. (1975). *Program guide of Science . . . A process approach II.* Nashua, NH: Delta Education.

Anderson, C. W., and Smith, E. L. (1987). Teaching science. In V. Richardson-Koehler (ed.), *Educators' handbook.* White Plains, NY: Longman.

Anderson, R. C. (1977). The notion of schemata and the educational enterprise. In R. C. Anderson, R. J. Spiro, and W. F. Montague (eds.), *Schooling and the acquisition of knowledge.* Hillsdale, NJ: Erlbaum.

Anderson, R. C., Hiebert, E., Scott, J., and Wilkinson, I. (1985). *Becoming a nation of readers.* Ubana: University of Illinois, Center for the Study of Reading.

Banks, J., and Clegg, A. (1985). *Teaching strategies for the social studies: Inquiry, valuing, and decision-making* (3rd ed.). White Plains, NY: Longman.

Barr, R. D., Barth, J. L., and Shermis, S. S. (1977). *Defining the social studies.* Washington, DC: National Council for the Social Studies.

Beyer, B. K. (1985). Critical thinking: What is it? *Social Education* 4, 270–76.

Blachowicz, C. (1986). Making connections: Alternatives to the vocabulary notebook. *Journal of Reading* 29, 643–50.

Bransford, J., Sherwood, R., Vye, N., and Rieser, J. (1986). Teaching thinking and problem solving: Research foundations. *American Psychologist* 41, 10, 1078–89.

Brown, A. L. (1978). Knowing when, where, and how to remember: A problem of metacognition. In R. Glaser (ed.), *Advances in instructional psychology* (I). Hillsdale, NJ: Erlbaum.

—— (1982). Learning how to learn from reading. In J. A. Langer and M. T. Smith-Burke (eds.), *Reader meets author/bridging the gap: A psycholinguistic and sociolinguistic perspective.* Newark, DE: International Reading Association.

Carey, S. (1986). Cognitive science and science education. *American Psychologist* 41, 10, 1123–30.

Carpenter, T. P. (1985). How children solve simple word problems. *Education and Urban Society* 17, 4, 417–25.

Carpenter, T. P., Moser, J. M., and Romberg, T. A. (eds.). (1982). *Addition and subtraction: A cognitive perspective.* Hillsdale, NJ: Erlbaum.

Charles, R., Lester, F., and O'Daffer, P. (1987). *How to evalute progress on problem solving.* Reston, VA: National Council of Teachers of Mathematics.

Cobb, V. (1972). *Science experiments you can eat.* New York: Lippincott.

—— (1979). *More science experiments you can eat.* New York: Lippincott.

Costa, A. L. (1984). Mediating the metacognitive. *Educational Leadership* 42, 3, 57–67.

Davidson, J. W., and Lytle, M. H. (1982). *After the fact: The art of historical detection.* New York: Knopf.

DeBono, E. (1970). *Lateral thinking.* New York: Harper & Row.

Donaldson, M. (1979). *Children's minds.* New York: W.W. Norton.

Driver, R., Guesne, E., and Tiberghien, A. (eds.). (1985). *Children's ideas in science.* Philadelphia: Open University Press.

Durkin, D. (1978–79). What classroom observations reveal about reading comprehension instruction. *Reading Research Quarterly* 12, 481–533.

Durr, W. K., Pescosolido, J., and Poetter, W. M. (1978). *Encore basal manual.* Boston: Houghton Mifflin.

Eaton, J. F., Anderson, C. W., and Smith, E. L. (1984). Students' misconceptions interfere with science learning: Case studies of fifth grade students. *Elementary School Journal* 64, 365–79.

Ellis, A. K. (1981). *Teaching and learning elementary social studies.* Boston: Allyn & Bacon.

Encore Basal Reader. (1978). Boston: Houghton Mifflin.

Feuerstein, R. (1979). *The dynamic assessment of retarded performance: The learning potential assessment device, theory, instruments, and technique.* Baltimore: University Park Press.

Fraenkel, J. R. (1980). *Helping students think and value: Strategies for teaching the social studies* (2nd ed.). Englewood Cliffs, NJ: Prentice-Hall.

Forrest-Pressley, D. L., Mackinnon, G. E., and Waller, T. G. (eds.). (1985). *Metacognition, cognition, and human behavior,* 1 and 2. New York: Academic Press. Especially Gavelek, J. R., and Raphael, T. E. *Metacognition, instruction, and the role of questioning activities.* (Vol. 1).

Gardner, H. (1983). *Frames of mind: The theory of multiple intelligence.* New York: Basic Books.

Gardner, M. (1961). *The second scientific American book of mathematical puzzles and diversions.* New York: Simon & Schuster.

Ginsburg, H. P. (ed.). (1983). *The development of mathematical thinking.* New York: Academic Press.

Glaser, R. (1984). Education and thinking: The role of knowledge. *American Psychologist* 39, 2, 93–104.

Gordon, W. (1961). *Synectics.* New York: Harper & Row.

Graves, D. H. (1983). *Writing: Teachers and children at work.* Portsmouth, NH: Heinemann Educational Books.

Guilford, J. P. (1977). *Way beyond IQ.* Buffalo, NY: Creative Education Foundation.

Hillerich, R. (1986). The incomplete basal program. *Early Years* 17, 28–30.

Humes, A. (1983). Research on the composing. *Review of Educational Research* 53, 2, 201–16.

Jarolimek, J. (1986). *Social studies in elementary education* (7th ed.). New York: Macmillan.

Johnson, D. W., and Johnson, R. T. (1987). *Learning together and alone: Cooperation, competition and individualization.* Englewood Cliffs, NJ: Prentice-Hall.

Johnson, D. W., Johnson, R. T., and Holubec, E. J. (1986). *Circles of learning: Cooperation in the classroom* (rev. ed.). Edina, MN: Interaction Book Co.

Joyce, B., and Weil, M. (1985). *Models of teaching.* Englewood Cliffs, NJ: Prentice-Hall.

Kamii, C. (1982). Encouraging thinking in mathematics. *Phi Delta Kappan,* December, 247–51.

Langer, J. A. (1982). The reading process. In A. Berger and H. A. Robinson (eds.), *Secondary school reading: What research reveals for classroom practice.* Urbana, IL: National conference on Research in English and ERIC Clearinghouse on Reading and Communication Skills.

Liem, T. (1987). *Invitations to science inquiry.* Lexington, MA: Ginn Press.

Linn, M. C. (1986). Science. In R. F. Dillon and R. J. Sternberg (eds.), *Cognition and instruction.* Orlando, FL: Academic Press.

Maxim, G. W. (1987). *Social studies and the elementary school child* (3rd ed.). Columbus, OH: Charles Merrill.

Meltzer, M. (ed.). (1982). *The Jewish Americans: A history in their own words, 1650–1950.* New York: Crowell.

———. (ed.). (1984). *The black Americans: A history in their own words.* New York: Crowell.

———. (ed.). (1987). *The American revolutionaries: A history in their own words, 1750–1800.* New York: Crowell.

M.E.R.I.T., Chapter 2 Project. (1986). *Developing metacognitive skills.* Philadelphia: School District of Philadelphia.

Nash, G. (ed.). (1975). *The private side of American history, Vol. I: To 1877.* Orlando, FL: Harcourt Brace Jovanovich.

Nelson, M. R. (1987). *Children and social studies.* Orlando, FL: Harcourt Brace Jovanovich.

Nesher, P. (1986). Learning mathematics: A cognitive perspective. *American Psychologist* 41, 10, 1114–22.

Neisser, U. (1976). *Cognition and reality.* San Francisco: W.H. Freeman.

Ogle, D. (1986). K-W-L: A teaching model that develops active reading of expository text. *The Reading Teacher* 6, 564–70.

Palincsar, A. (1984). The quest for meaning from expository text: A teacher guided journey. In G. Duffy, L. Roehler, and J. Mason (eds.), *Comprehension instruction: Perspectives and suggestions.* White Plains, NY: Longman.

Parnes, S. (1972). *Creativity: Unlocking human potential.* East Aurora, NY: D.O.K. Publishers.

Perkins, D. N., and Salomon, G. (1987). Transfer and teaching thinking. In D. N. Perkins, J. C. Lockhead, and J. C. Bishop (eds.), *Thinking: The Second International Conference.* Hillsdale, NJ: Erlbaum.

Peterson, P. L., and Swing, S. R. (1983). Problems in classroom implementation of cognitive strategy instruction. In M. Pressley and J. L. Levin (eds.), *Cognitive strategy research: Educational implications.* New York: Springer-Verlag.

Posner, G. J., Strike, K. A., Hewson, P. W., and Gertzog, W. A. (1982). Accommodation of a scientific conception: Toward a theory of conceptual change. *Science Education* 66, 211–27.

Reeve, R. A., and Brown, A. L. (1984). *Metacognition reconsidered: Implications for intervention research.* Urbana: University of Illinois, Center for Study of Reading, Technical Report #328.

Renner, A. G. (1977). *How to build a better mousetrap car: And other experimental science fun.* New York: Dodd, Mead.

Resnick, L., and Ford, W. W. (1981). *The psychology of mathematics instruction.* Hillsdale, NJ: Erlbaum.

Roberts, K. (1981). *Oliver Wiswell.* New York: Fawcett.

Rumelhart, D. E. (1981). Schemata: the building blocks of cognition. In J. T. Guthrie (ed.), *Comprehension and teaching: Research reviews.* Newark, DE: International Reading Association.

Schlissel, L. (1982). *Women's diaries of the westward journey.* New York: Schocken.

Schoenfeld, A. H. (1983). Metacognitive and epistemological issues in mathematical understanding. In E. A. Silver (ed.), *Teaching and learning mathematical problem solving.* Hillsdale, NJ: Erlbaum.

———. (1985). Psychology and mathematical method: A capsule history and a modern view. *Education and Urban Society* 17, 4, 387–403.

Schuncke, G. M. (1988). *Elementary social studies: Knowing, doing, caring.* New York: Macmillan.

Shaver, J. P. (1978). Implications from research: What should be taught in social studies. In V. Richardson-Koehler (ed.), *Educators' handbook: A research perspective.* White Plains, NY: Longman.

Silver, E. A. (ed.). (1983). *Teaching and learning mathematical problem solving.* Hillsdale, NJ: Erlbaum.

Spiro, R. J., Bruce, B. C., and Brewer, W. F. (eds.). (1980). *Theoretical issues in reading comprehension.* Hillsdale, NJ: Erlbaum.

Stauffer, R. (1969). *Reading as a thinking process.* New York: Harper & Row.

Sternberg, R. J. (1986). *Intelligence applied: Understanding and increasing your intellectual skills.* San Diego: Harcourt Brace Jovanovich.

Sternberg, R. J., and Detterman, D. K. (eds.). (1986). *What is intelligence?* Norwood, NJ: Ablex.

Tierney, R. J., and Pearson, P. D. (1981). "Learning to learn from text: A framework for improving classroom practice," *Reading Education Report,* 30. Urbana, IL: Center for the Study of Reading.

Voss, J. F. (1986). Social studies. In R. F. Dillon and R. J. Sternberg (eds.), *Cognition and instruction.* Orlando, FL: Academic Press.

Index